Choosing a Mother Tongue

MULTILINGUAL MATTERS
Series Editors: John Edwards, *St. Francis Xavier University, Canada* and *Dalhousie University, Canada* and Leigh Oakes, *Queen Mary, University of London, UK.*

Multilingual Matters series publishes books on bilingualism, bilingual education, immersion education, second language learning, language policy, multiculturalism. The editor is particularly interested in 'macro' level studies of language policies, language maintenance, language shift, language revival and language planning. Books in the series discuss the relationship between language in a broad sense and larger cultural issues, particularly identity related ones.

All books in this series are externally peer-reviewed.

Full details of all the books in this series and of all our other publications can be found on http://www.multilingual-matters.com, or by writing to Multilingual Matters, St Nicholas House, 31–34 High Street, Bristol BS1 2AW, UK.

MULTILINGUAL MATTERS: 169

Choosing a Mother Tongue

The Politics of Language and Identity in Ukraine

Corinne A. Seals

MULTILINGUAL MATTERS
Bristol • Blue Ridge Summit

For the Hromada and in memory of Misha

DOI https://doi.org/10.21832/SEALS4993
Library of Congress Cataloging in Publication Data
A catalog record for this book is available from the Library of Congress.
Names: Seals, Corinne, author.
Title: Choosing a Mother Tongue: The Politics of Language and Identity in Ukraine / Corinne Seals.
Description: Blue Ridge Summit: Multilingual Matters, 2019. | Series: Multilingual Matters: 169 | Includes bibliographical references and index. | Summary: "This book investigates narrative accounts of the current Ukrainian war, providing a detailed analysis of how national and linguistic identity are discursively renegotiated during a time of mass conflict. It examines connections between language, culture and politics after the Russian-Ukrainian war"— Provided by publisher.
Identifiers: LCCN 2019022072 (print) | LCCN 2019981219 (ebook) | ISBN 9781788924993 (hardback) | ISBN 9781788925006 (pdf) | ISBN 9781788925020 (kindle edition) | ISBN 9781788925013 (epub)
Subjects: LCSH: Ukrainian language—Political aspects. | Language revival—Ukraine. | Language maintenance—Ukraine. | Ukrainians—Ethnic identity. | Ukraine Conflict, 2014—Personal narratives.
Classification: LCC P119.32.U38 S43 2019 (print) | LCC P119.32.U38 (ebook) | DDC 306.44/09477—dc23
LC record available at https://lccn.loc.gov/2019022072
LC ebook record available at https://lccn.loc.gov/2019981219

British Library Cataloguing in Publication Data
A catalogue entry for this book is available from the British Library.

ISBN-13: 978-1-78892-499-3 (hbk)
ISBN-13: 978-1-78892-567-9 (pbk)

Multilingual Matters
UK: St Nicholas House, 31–34 High Street, Bristol BS1 2AW, UK.
USA: NBN, Blue Ridge Summit, PA, USA.

Website: www.multilingual-matters.com
Twitter: Multi_Ling_Mat
Facebook: https://www.facebook.com/multilingualmatters
Blog: www.channelviewpublications.wordpress.com

Copyright © 2020 Corinne A. Seals.

All rights reserved. No part of this work may be reproduced in any form or by any means without permission in writing from the publisher.

The policy of Multilingual Matters/Channel View Publications is to use papers that are natural, renewable and recyclable products, made from wood grown in sustainable forests. In the manufacturing process of our books, and to further support our policy, preference is given to printers that have FSC and PEFC Chain of Custody certification. The FSC and/or PEFC logos will appear on those books where full certification has been granted to the printer concerned.

Typeset by Nova Techset Private Limited, Bengaluru and Chennai, India.

Contents

	Acknowledgments	ix
1	Historical Language Ideologies and Sociopolitical Conflict in Ukraine	1
	A Recent Sociopolitical Language Event	2
	A Short Linguistic History of Modern Ukraine and Modern Ukrainian	3
	Linguistic Purism	6
	Surzhyk	8
	Ukrainian Language Politics	9
	Dialogic Language Ideologies	13
	Positioning in Discourse	15
	Outline of the Book	16
2	Language and Identity After the Orange Revolution	19
	Post-Structuralist and Social Constructionist Views of Identity	19
	Narratives in Discourse	22
	Imagined Communities and Imagined Identities	22
	Imagined Identity in Ukraine and the Orange Revolution	24
	Language Ideologies Following the Orange Revolution	28
	Olesya: Language is Part of the National Consciousness	30
	Yana and Alyona: It Depends Where You Are	35
	Further Remarks	38
3	Othering and Positioning During a Time of War	41
	Reigniting Discussions of National Identity	41
	The Current Study	43
	Naming Ideologies by Naming Events	46
	When Friends Become Enemies	48
	Ukrainians but not Ukrainians	57
	One Nation, One People	59
	Being Ukrainian is Speaking Ukrainian	62
	Focusing on the Individual	67
	Further Remarks	72

4	Who's Responsible? The Politics of Language	74
	Metonymy and Russian Responsibility	74
	The Government but Not Necessarily the People	79
	The General Population as Responsible	86
	All as Responsible	89
	Further Remarks	95
5	Renegotiating Identity and 'Changing Your Mother Tongue'	97
	Embodied Language	98
	Dialogic Echoes	99
	A Previous History	100
	A Recent Event	111
	Views from the Diaspora	121
	Further Remarks	127
6	Investment and Loyalty in the Ukrainian Diaspora	130
	Diaspora and Transnational Research	131
	A Model for Immigrant Identity, Investment and Integration	134
	Renegotiating Identity in the Diaspora	135
	The Host Society's Perception	139
	Distance from the War	141
	Language Ideologies and Integration	149
	Negotiation Between and Within Diaspora Communities	154
	Looking from the Outside In	162
	Redefining Investments in the Diaspora	164
	Further Remarks	165
7	'It Doesn't Matter What You Speak': Challenges to Dominant Language Ideologies by Ukrainian Young Adults	167
	Underlying Acceptance Amid Complexity of Ideologies	168
	Speak What You Know	175
	Dispelling Myths – Western Ukraine	178
	The Language I Speak Doesn't Change Who I Am	181
	Further Remarks	184
8	Conclusion	186
	Discursive Themes	188
	Reconsidering the Local and the Global	189
	Changing Your Mother Tongue	190
	Concluding Thoughts	191
	Appendices	192
	Appendix A: Transcription Conventions	192
	Appendix B: Participants in New Zealand	192

Appendix C: Participants in Canada and the United States	193
Appendix D: Participants in Ukraine	193
Appendix E: Klara's Joke as Told Originally in Ukrainian and Russian	194
References	196
Index	209

Acknowledgments

I would first like to acknowledge the support of the wider Ukrainian community, both in Ukraine and in diaspora communities around the world. Through shared stories over varenyky making and pysanka painting, you have spoken life into this book. Thank you also to my family, spread near and far, who continued to push me forward when I became tired or disheartened at times when negative world events again loomed large. A huge thank you also to Multilingual Matters and Anna Roderick in particular for often refocusing me on the task at hand, though always doing so in a supportive way. Thank you as well to Victoria University of Wellington's Research Committee for supporting the many hundreds of hours of work that went into narrative collection, analysis, transcription and book creation. Finally, thank you to my amazing team of research assistants, including Natalia Beliaeva, Keely Kidner, Kaitlyn Smith, Evan Hazenberg and Sydney Kingstone, all of who brought fascinating insights and admirable dedication to every part of this research. Дякую.

1 Historical Language Ideologies and Sociopolitical Conflict in Ukraine

Underlying all of the social and linguistic theories of identity and language is a very real understanding that we study these connections because of their importance to people everywhere. This reminder was brought to the cognitive surface in the most beautiful way when I sat down in April 2015 to talk with Ilona, a Ukrainian woman in her 30s living in the United States. The primary focus of our conversation was about her thoughts on language, education and politics in Ukraine and abroad. Towards the end of the interview, I asked Ilona if she felt that the Ukrainian language was related to her personal identity. She responded:[1,2]

> When I practice a conversation with my daughter in the future, I do it in Ukrainian, and it's just- when I think of myself in the future or just in general, the self-image of me in Ukrainian, it's different than if I were to think of it in any other language. It just feels like home, feels natural as opposed to either Russian or English… It's home. The language, Ukrainian language, is home. It's childhood. It's the sun… The person that I want to be, the person that does everything right and does everything the way I want to be, is the ideal person I strive to be, she speaks Ukrainian.

In this, Ilona was able to articulate what many people experience internally without necessarily having the opportunity or ability to express discursively: the connection between language and identity. In particular, Ilona's description captures multiple areas of language and identity research that will be explored in this book, including *imagined identities, investment, positioning* and *dialogism*, among others.

Ilona's interview was one of 38 interviews that I conducted with Ukrainians between 2014 and 2016. All interviews were conducted in the language(s) that the participants chose to use during the interviews (most participants used English the majority of the time). All excerpts are accurately transcribed in both language choice and grammatical form. As will be discussed later in Chapter 3, the participants were all in their 20s or 30s. They all grew up in Ukraine, but from there they diverge. Some of the participants now live in the United States, some in Canada, some in New Zealand and some still live in Ukraine. They have a wide range of linguistic, socioeconomic, religious and educational backgrounds. They have invested in many different life decisions, and their current linguistic practices reflect their past, present and anticipated futures. One thing that they all share, however, is experience and ongoing familiarity with the discourses connecting language, culture and politics in Ukraine.

The perceived connection between language, culture and politics is, of course, not unique to Ukraine. However, what is unique in the current investigation into this is that these 38 interviews were conducted during the Ukrainian War between Ukraine and Russia, occurring on the Eastern Ukrainian border and on the Crimean Peninsula. As a result, historically embedded Discourses[3] of language, culture and politics, as well as newer Discourses of national loyalty rose to the forefront of many Ukrainian community conversations. These rising Discourses of national identity have markedly increased, as compared with regional identity, since the events of Maidan beginning in November 2013 (Shulga, 2015). Protests in Ukraine prior to Maidan were mostly socioeconomic in nature, but following Maidan they have remained primarily ideological and political in nature, and the vast majority have been for a single unified Ukraine (Tsentr Doslidzhennya Suspil'stva, 2014 April, 2014 September). Additionally, national identification was found to be most prominent in Ukrainians 18–30 years old (Shulga, 2015: 237), further adding significance to discursive explorations found in the current book. This discussion is continued in greater depth in Chapter 3.

Furthermore, as a member of the New Zealand Ukrainian community, and as a Ukrainian-American with Ukrainian heritage on my mother's side, I became very familiar with the prevalence of ideological conversations taking place. Metadiscursive negotiations of language and self had again found center stage for Ukrainians, both in home and host countries. This book is a result of attempting to capture some of the dialogues taking place, and to investigate how dialogism and positioning can assist in better understanding individuals' discursive negotiations of self.

A Recent Sociopolitical Language Event

In May of 2012, not long proceeding the start of the Ukrainian War, the Ukrainian Rada (Ukraine's Parliament) erupted into a brawl, with physical and verbal abuse occurring across and between dozens of parliamentary representatives. The source of the conflict was not surprising for those familiar with Ukraine's linguistic history (cf. Maiboroda *et al.*, 2008; Masenko, 2004), though it was shocking enough to others that the clash was broadcast through news outlets internationally (Herszenhorn, 2012; Onyshkiv, 2012; RT Staff, 2012; The Guardian Staff, 2012; The Telegraph Staff, 2012).

The cause was none other than a language bill. Frequently referred to in public discourse as the 'Russian Language Bill', this legislation stated that any administrative region of Ukraine with 10% or more of its population being made up of an acknowledged national minority must recognize the language of that minority officially as a 'regional language', thus giving institutional access to resources in this language within the respective administrative region (Elder, 2012; Hersenzenhorn, 2012).

An initial issue with such a policy is the presupposition that everyone within a minority group speaks the same language, in addition to the fact that this discussion surrounded those national minorities recognized as such. However, the discussion of this measure in the Rada did not reach such details, as the explosive concern surrounded the very real fact that this law would effectively give regional language status to Russian in many Ukrainian administrative regions, especially in the East and South, where Russian-speaking populations are the majority (Csernicskó, 2015). To clarify why it was (and often still is) seen as contentious to give regional language status to a language used in practice as the majority language in some regions of Ukraine, the discussion must first be given historical grounding.

A Short Linguistic History of Modern Ukraine and Modern Ukrainian[4]

Ukraine achieved its current state of independence in 1991. Prior to that time, the area now known as Ukraine spent decades existing as a territory subsumed within the expansive Soviet empire. In fact, some scholars, such as Andrew Wilson (2009) have called Ukraine's independence 'unexpected', in that there has historically been such vast diversity throughout this region that many scholars thought that Ukraine was not viable as an independent nation. However, other scholars, such as Zenon Kohut (2004, 2011) have argued the opposite – that Ukraine's shifting politics, history and shifting identity have led to Ukraine's independence as a logical conclusion. Given Ukraine's ever-shifting and variously interpreted history, understanding the Soviet era language policies is an important first step in recognizing how these experiences have impacted on existing language ideologies and linguistic policies.

In 1990, just after the fall of the Soviet Union and just before Ukraine's declaration of independence, Kirkwood (1990) published an in-depth overview of the Soviet language planning process and policies that had been in place since the official founding of the Soviet Union in 1922. For example, Kirkwood discussed how Soviet policy was based on the idea that it was essential to require the standardization of language, even pronunciation, such that everyone was required to aim for the Russian language, specifically the Moscow dialect, as their primary language (Kirkwood, 1990: 3). The most important institution for implementing these policies became the educational system (Kirkwood, 1990: 4).

Interestingly, as Kreindler (1990) argues, all languages were originally promoted publically as equal under Lenin during the early planning of what would become Soviet Union policies (Kreindler, 1990: 48). Perhaps surprisingly, this trend then continued when Stalin took control in 1922 and shifted to the process of Nativization until 1938. Stalin's Nativization began restricting linguistic practices, mandating that all people could use their local languages for daily, community-based communication practices, but Russian was to be the political language and was mandatory in schools by the time children entered the third grade. Stalin, a Georgian himself, then further restricted Soviet language policy by ending Nativization and making Russian a compulsory language for all people in the Soviet Union in 1938, in effect opening the way for the beginning of Russification (Smith, 1998).

Many minority languages were soon relegated to 'non-viable' status by Khrushchev in the 1950s, thus officially beginning the Russification language policy (Kreindler, 1990: 49). At this time, 'giving up one's language and shifting to Russian was now deemed "progressive", "mature", according to the laws of natural development' (Kreindler, 1990: 56), an ideology that has continued to impact the Ukrainian language even today (Kulyk, 2011). Therefore, it became difficult for the minority citizens of the Soviet Union to successfully argue otherwise. As Ukrainians were a minority in the context of the entire Soviet empire, languages other than Russian spoken in the Ukrainian region (including Ukrainian) were also deemed minority languages. Therefore, Western Ukrainians, who did (and still do) have widespread Ukrainian language use were targeted for Russification and Sovietization (Shevelov, 1989). Furthermore, these language policies were also connected to religious identity, as many Eastern Europeans, including Ukrainians, were Orthodox (Hroch, 1999: 319), which was also a group deemed to be critical for Russification (Pavlenko, 2006), further showing the wide reach of Russification policies.

By the end of the Soviet Union, Ukraine had the largest Russian-speaking group outside of Russia (Pavlenko, 2008: 16). This is why even today Russian is widespread throughout Ukraine and is a language of high status in Eastern Ukraine (Pavlenko, 2008: 12). As a result of Russification, the Russian language is the largest minority language in Ukraine, but as a result of Ukrainisation policies since 1991 (cf. Seals, 2014), Russian is also a contested language in parts of Ukraine (Marten, 2010; Masenko, 2009; Masenko & Horobets, 2015; Masenko & Orel, 2014; Osnach, 2015; Pavlenko, 2010, 2011). This divide has also been shown to connect with increasingly common non-accommodating bilingualism in Ukraine (Bilaniuk, 2010), which can be understood in terms of people tending to 'adopt positive linguistic distinctiveness strategies – that is, to diverge –...when they see language as an important social dimension of their group' (Liebkind, 1999: 147). However, there is still contention over accommodating and non-accommodating bilingualism, with many ideologies involved, such as participants in the current study repeatedly stating: 'Ukrainian speakers always accommodate to Russian speakers, but never the reverse, so why should they anymore?' (explored further in Chapter 6).

Feelings about the Ukrainian language have arguably increased since Ukrainian was declared the only official state language of Ukraine in 1991. Since then, there has been a widespread increase in the use of Ukrainian in the country (Bilaniuk & Melnyk, 2008). However, there is still a large variation of usage in regions, with the South-Eastern oblasts (administrative regions of the former Soviet Union) being instructed in it as little as 2% of the time, and the Western oblasts instructing in it as much as 99.9% of the time (Bilaniuk & Melnyk, 2008: 79) (see Danylenko, 2015 for an overview of the sociopolitical and regional history of the development of the Ukrainian language and varieties).

Historically, Central and Western Ukraine have been Ukrainian language dominant, while Eastern and Southern Ukraine have been Russian language dominant (Del'Gaudio, 2011; Masenko, 2009). When asked about language of preference for print and screen media, 75% of people in Western Ukrainian said Ukrainian, 65.3% of people in the East said Russian, and 58.4% of people in the South said Russian (Besters-Dilger, 2009). Currently, in the West, Ukrainian is the language of use for most people across all forms of communication. However, in the East, bilingualism and diglossia have been giving way to an increasing preference for Russian (Masenko, 2009).

It has also become increasingly important to recognize the presence of native bilingualism in Ukraine. In 2001, the Ukrainian Census showed that 67.5% of people said Ukrainian was their mother tongue, 29.6% said Russian was, and 2.9% said 'other' (bilingualism was not an option). However, in a survey conducted a few years later by Masenko, 55.5% of respondents said Ukrainian was their mother tongue, 32.0% said Russian, 11.1% said they were natively bilingual in Ukrainian and Russian, and 1.4% said 'other' (Masenko, 2009). Furthermore, similar results were found by Khmel'ko who also conducted a largescale survey following the Ukrainian Census in 2001, with 54.4% of adults saying Ukrainian, 30.4% saying Russian, 12.4% saying both Ukrainian and Russian, and 2.8% saying 'other' (Khmel'ko, 2004: 4).

When looking specifically at the Ukrainian language, the current codified variety of the Ukrainian language that is considered the standardized form came about in the early 20th century, ironically as a result of the Ukrainian Communist Party being 'horrified' by the increasing presence of Ukrainian in the country (Dingley, 1990: 178). As a result, modern day

Ukrainian has more Russian similarities than Halician ones, the latter of which were used by Western Ukrainians for centuries and can still be found preserved in some diaspora communities around the world (cf. Seals, 2014 for a discussion of heritage Ukrainian; cf. Del' Gaudio, 2018 for a comprehensive overview of Ukrainian dialectology). While the standardized variety of Ukrainian is much closer to Russian than it used to be, it still remains approximately 38% different in lexicon (Bilaniuk & Melnyk, 2008: 70).

To provide further linguistic background, the Ukrainian language comes from the same historical Slavic language family as the Russian language, and they share the Cyrillic alphabet (with a few notable exceptions, including the Ukrainian vowels *ï* and *i*). Phonologically, the two languages also share much in common, though some rules (such as those governing palatalization and vowel reduction) are markedly different, which can sometimes lead to a difference in meaning (cf. Seals, 2010; Seals & Coto-Solano, forthcoming). There are also some morphological differences, especially involving tenses, but as noted above – the largest differences are found between the Ukrainian and Russian lexicons, with approximately one third of Ukrainian lexicon being different and much of this difference being influenced by Polish (via shared historical territories in Halicia) (cf. Bilaniuk & Melnyk, 2008; Del'Gaudio, 2011, 2012, 2015, 2018; Seals, 2014). Finally, it should be noted that the variety of Russian spoken in Ukraine has also experienced regional variation, as it has been influenced by Ukrainian and is not the same grammatically, phonologically, or lexically as standardized forms of Russian found in Russia today (cf. Del'Gaudio, 2011).

Linguistic Purism

Language ideologies can also still be found in Discourses of linguistic purism in Ukraine, reflecting linguistic debates held in the country for over 100 years. The term *language ideologies* is used synonymously with the term *linguistic ideologies* in this book, and draws upon a linguistic anthropology tradition, referring to 'conceptualizations about languages, speakers and discursive practices. Like other kinds of ideologies, language ideologies are pervaded with political and moral interests and are shaped in a cultural setting' (Irvine, 2012, np.). This understanding of language ideologies originates from Silverstein's (1979) conception of it as 'any sets of beliefs about language articulated by the users as a rationalization or justification of perceived language structure and use' (Silverstein, 1979: 193).

Importantly, the term *language ideologies*, as discussed in this book, aligns with the above definitions but is different from the definition presented by Rumsey, which sees language ideologies as 'shared bodies of commonsense notions about the nature of language in the world'

(1990: 346). Rumsey's definition presupposes that people from a particular cultural background share ideologies, which minimizes the variation that exists within and between communities of all sorts, as well as the conflicting ideologies that can exist within a given individual. Rather, the concept of language ideologies as used in this book includes the unlimited variety of ideologies to do with language varieties (including their linguistic and social aspects) that can exist together (and at times against each other) at any given time.

Language ideologies in Ukraine reflect the country's complex history of being subsumed into different national bodies, most recently by the Soviet Union until Ukraine's independence in 1991. The process of Russification that Ukrainians experienced (as described above) led to internalized ideologies regarding the value of the Russian and Ukrainian languages, ideologies which still exist today. Many Ukrainians still internalize beliefs that Ukrainian is lower in quality than Russian, thus contributing to its reduced status in many areas of the country and showing the influence of Russification still today (Bilaniuk, 2003; Kulyk, 2011). For example, many Ukrainian speakers impose required 'quality' conditions on the widespread usage of Ukrainian but don't put the same conditions on Russian (Kulyk, 2011). Not only does this speak to the assumed superiority of the Russian language in such instances, but it also hinders the ability to raise the status of the Ukrainian language. More recently, Russian has even been the dominant language of print media in Ukraine, with Besters-Dilger reporting in 2009 that an estimated 65.6% of newspapers printed in Ukraine were in Russian and at least 75% total newspapers existing in Ukraine were in Russian (including those imported from Russia to Ukraine) (Bersters-Dilger, 2009).

These ideologies of linguistic inferiority have also led to discourses around linguistic purity, with many Ukrainians referring to 'pure' Ukrainian as being preferred. This question of the 'purity' of the Ukrainian language is of much interest to many Ukrainians, as is evidenced in a volume by Karavans'kyiy (1994), which examines what the Ukrainian language was like before assimilationist measures made it more like it is today. Yermolenko (2000) also created a grammar book, which is for training oneself in the linguistic forms of Ukrainian most associated with high cultural capital, further showing the ideologies associated with particular varieties of Ukrainian in Ukraine. This Discourse around 'purity' is even found at the academic level. A survey conducted by the Faculty of Sociology at Kyiv National University in 2007 found that younger people (18–29) were using less 'pure' Ukrainian with their parents and families than the older generations were (Vyshniak, 2009). Younger generations were tending to use more mixed language with Russian, which Vyshniak (2009) argues is a failure of Ukrainian state language policy, and which he argued means that there is a need to actively work against the historical tendency to displace the Ukrainian language in the public sphere.

Surzhyk

Perhaps most notable in language ideologies relating to linguistic purism (cf. Jaffe, 2007; Kroskrity, 1993, 1998) in Ukraine is discourse around the mixed variety called *surzhyk* (Russian and Ukrainian mixed language variety), which in fact developed as a result of this linguistic purism (Bilaniuk, 2005, 2010; Krouglov, 1999). Surzhyk is often attributed to people who had bilingual abilities of varying degrees but who did not feel completely proficient in one language or the other (especially in the case of Ukrainian usage), resulting in the use of surzhyk.

However, after extensively investigating the linguistic structure of surzhyk, Del'Gaudio (2012) and Demchenko (2012) argue that surzhyk is in fact a variety of the Ukrainian language that systematically incorporates regional features plus the addition of Russian elements. Likewise, Del'Gaudio (2015) presents an underlying structure that he has identified for all surzhyk varieties, and this underlying structure is the native dialect for the majority of his informants who are 40–70 years old and living in urban Central-East and Northern Ukraine. Likewise, Taranenko (2013) found that the underlying structure of surzhyk is relatively stable in Dnipropetrovsk, Kyiv, Poltava, Zhytomyr, Chernizhny, Kharkiv and other areas, therein showing that surzhyk is actually grammaticalized and not the random variety that those opposed to it argue it is.

However, surzhyk is highly stigmatized in Ukraine, and is viewed as 'not real Ukrainian' by much of the population, despite the fact that it has regular, widespread usage (cf. Bilaniuk, 2005). This popular view of surzhyk is arguably a result of *symbolic domination*, which occurs when minority language speakers 'accept the centralized state's often negative evaluation of their language[;] they denigrate the very language they call their own, while accepting the authority of a dominant, state-supported language that they often do not speak very well' (Gal, 1998: 114). That is not to say that people do not speak varieties of the Ukrainian language near to the standard; however, many people also frequently make use of surzhyk, especially in more informal contexts. In fact, Bilaniuk (2005) notably recorded a case in which people were subconsciously using surzhyk while talking about how they thought they themselves never used it. Additionally, as recorded by Del'Gaudio (2010), the use of surzhyk depends more on the interlocutor than on the content of sentences, marking it as having interactional purpose.

Furthermore, while tracing the historical development of surzhyk and its current linguistic forms found throughout the country, Del'Gaudio (2015) argues that by understanding more about Ukrainian ideologies of linguistic purism, we can understand more about the influence these ideologies have on Ukrainians' 'linguistic consciousness' of language variation and change. It is in fact this rising consciousness of and alignment with purist ideologies that has led to younger (20–35) Ukrainian respondents in Del'Guadio's (2015) research using more standardized forms of Ukrainian and/or Russian as opposed to surzhyk. This active movement away from the grammaticalized surzhyk further shows the effect of internalizing prominent language ideologies. Surzhyk, thus, is an excellent example of symbolic domination resulting from the very prevalent purist language ideologies that exist in Ukraine. Young people's movement towards standardized varieties also makes sense according to Braha's (2011) theory that the use of a particular language or variety is noticed more by people who themselves are more conscious of their own sociolinguistic ideologies – as are the current young adults of Ukraine (discussed more in subsequent chapters).

Ukrainian Language Politics

Given the contentious, and oftentimes violent, history of linguistic repression in Ukraine's history, it is not surprising then that Ukrainian language ideologies exist with such force today. As stated by Bondarenko (2008), there is an interconnectedness of current Ukrainian culture and mentality with the historical development of the Ukrainian nation. Furthermore, much research has been done across the years showing the ongoing political contention associated with language choice and use in Ukraine, which has been publically considered a major identity marker in discourses found about and within the country, tied to politics and to region (Bilaniuk, 2005; Csernicskó, 2017; Hillis, 2015; Himka, 2015; Kohut, 2011). The language situation has become so contentious that following the first events of Maidan, many people reported their feeling that Ukrainians who spoke Russian were 'traitors' in their eyes (Csernicskó, 2017: 123).

Many Ukrainian scholars have documented how this language debate has been utilized by both Ukrainian and Russian politicians to retain Ukrainians' interest and investment in their campaigns and/or to manipulate public sentiment. As has been well documented, the Ukrainian people are consistently manipulated by the language issue because politicians keep reigniting questions around language recognition (Csernicskó, 2017; Masenko & Horobets, 2015). This issue regularly appears at the forefront of Ukrainian media during election times. In a 2009 interview, Ukrainian sociolinguist Larysa Masenko talked about how during the 2007 parliamentary elections, there was a billboard campaign that appeared in Crimea and read, 'Water. Roads. Language' («Вода. Дороги. Язык») showing the centrality of the language issue once again to Ukrainian politics (Kovalçhuk, 2009). The issue was also used during the 2010 and 2012 elections to maintain political tensions (Csernicskó, 2017). Furthermore, as argued by Osnach (2015), the current war in Eastern Ukraine was sparked off by the language debate, which was taken advantage of by Russian politicians to mobilize pro-Russian supporters and was used by

Russia as an excuse for invading Ukraine (Csernicskó, 2017; Osnach, 2015). This discourse was picked up by Russian sympathizers living in Ukraine and has continued to exist in public discourse, manipulating public sentiment (Osnach, 2015).

This drawing upon language ideologies for political gain is not new to Ukrainian politics either. As documented by Kulyk (2007), Leonid Kuchma (President of Ukraine 1994–2005) played both sides of the language debate, sometimes supporting the Russian language and sometimes the Ukrainian language, contributing to citizens' lack of trust in Ukrainian politicians. Furthermore, Kulyk discusses how Kuchma said that Ukrainian should be the only official language of Ukraine but then didn't even learn Ukrainian himself until he was in office, showing the type of lip service by Ukrainian politicians of which Ukrainians have grown weary. Likewise, Besters-Dilger (2011) documented how Leonid Kravchuk played both sides of the language debate during his presidency (1991–1994). His slogan was 'there is no nation without a language,' but then he consistently warned against 'too much Ukrainisation' (Besters-Dilger, 2011: 355–356).

As can be seen in the following maps, the trends in languages spoken (more Ukrainian or more Russian) are mirrored in how people voted in the 2010 presidential election (as they were in elections prior as well), again showing how language and politics often co-occur. Similar to the 2004 election, the 2010 election was notable, as the two leading candidates represented very ideologically divided groups. Yulia Tymoshenko was the candidate to whom was attributed more mainland European-aligned policies and ideals, as well as supporting Ukrainian state language policies. Viktor Yanukovych was the candidate to whom was attributed more Russian-aligned policies and ideals, as well as supporting Russian language usage in Ukraine. Similar to the 2004 elections, Yanukovych's winning result led to claims of voter fraud and political interference, which in 2004 led to the famous Orange Revolution from November 22, 2004 until January 23, 2005. The Orange Revolution, co-led by Yulia Tymoshenko, is an event often credited with 'awakening Ukrainian national identity' (discussed further in Chapter 2 and Chapter 5).

Figures 1.1 and 1.2 show the strong connection between language use and linguistic ideologies in Ukraine, with the first map displaying residents' reported dominant language in 2008, and the second map showing how people voted in the 2010 election. As can be seen, the figures almost mirror each other, again showing the strong connections between language and politics in Ukraine.

Politics have continued to be extremely complicated in Ukraine, with the start of the Ukrainian War adding even further to the unknown regarding political outcomes. As shown in Figure 1.3 the results of the

Historical Language Ideologies and Sociopolitical Conflict in Ukraine 11

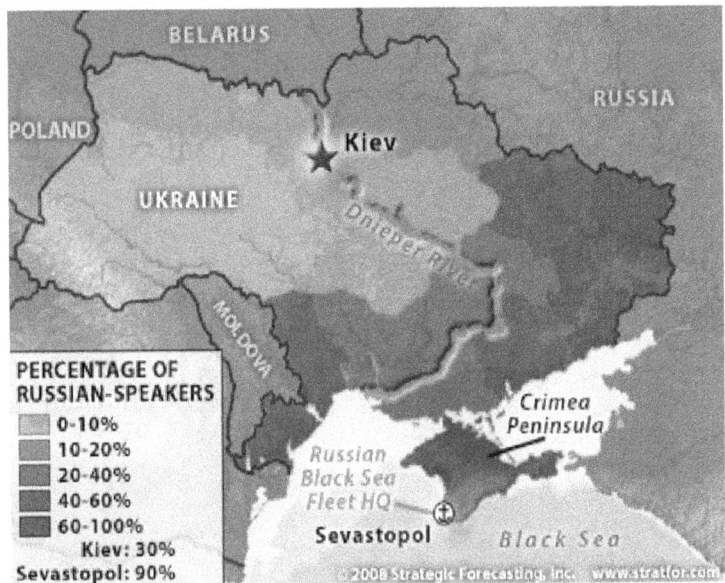

Figure 1.1 Map of Russian-language-dominant speakers in Ukraine in 2008[5] (Permission courtesy of Stratfor Worldview, a geopolitical intelligence platform)

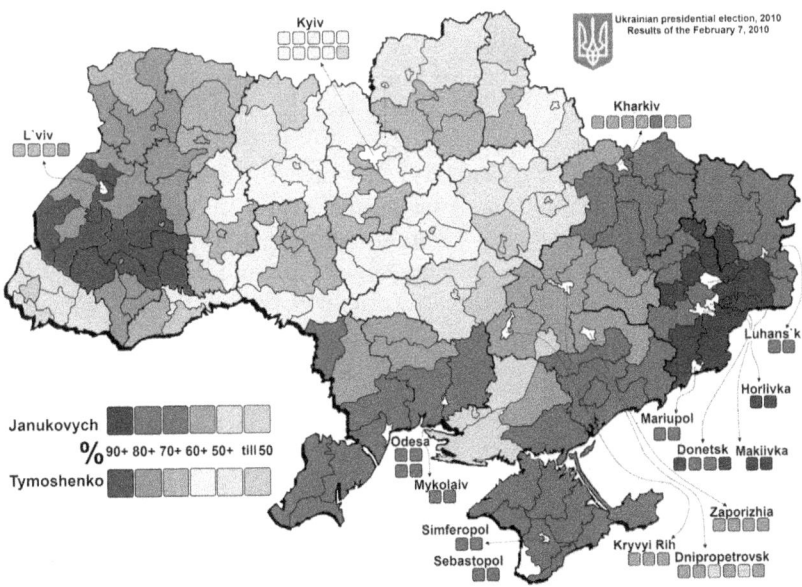

Figure 1.2 Map of 2010 Ukrainian presidential election results[6]

12 Choosing a Mother Tongue

Figure 1.3 Map of 2014 presidential election results[7]

2014 Ukrainian presidential elections were a direct reflection of the events of EuroMaiden and political and social upheaval at the start of the Ukrainian War (discussed further in Chapter 3). Yanukovych had just been ousted from the position of President of Ukraine, and pro-Ukrainian businessman Petro Poroshenko achieved a landslide victory in the first round of elections (over 50% of the vote), meaning that according to Ukrainian legislation, the traditional second round of elections did not occur.[8]

However, as shown in Figure 1.4, which illustrates the results of Ukraine's 2019 first round of presidential elections, there is somewhat of a hybrid effect of traditional Ukrainian politics (as seen in the 2004 and 2010 elections) and current continued societal disruption as a result of the Ukrainian War. At the beginning of April 2019, the greatest percentage of votes was held by political newcomer Volodymyr Zelensky. This result caused quite the upheaval, as Zelensky is a Ukrainian screenwriter and comedian with no political experience, most famously known for portraying a teacher turned president in his successful Ukrainian television comedy show. Incumbent President of Ukraine, Petro Poroshenko, received only slightly more than half of the votes received by Zelensky, coming in second place, which was widely regarded as a message sent to the president by a dissatisfied Ukrainian public. Interestingly, as shown in the map below, Zelensky's supporters were mostly found spread across the center of Ukraine, while pro-European Poroshenko and pro-European Tymoshenko split voters in the West. Pro-Russian Yuriy Boyko took the

Figure 1.4 Map of 2019 presidential election primary results[9] (Permission courtesy of dekóder, a German news platform)

Ukrainian East and South. It should also be noted that the Ukrainian diaspora overwhelmingly voted in favor of President Poroshenko (Goncharova, 2019), aligning with much of the diaspora population's vision for a Ukraine further distanced from Russia (cf. interviews in Chapters 5 and 6).

Following the second round of presidential elections (i.e. the run-off election between the top two candidates) on April 21, 2019, it was announced that Zelensky won over 70% of the popular vote, while Poroshenko received less than 30%.

Dialogic Language Ideologies

Now that a brief history of recent Ukrainian sociopolitics has been covered, the linguistic theoretical underpinnings of the current book will be discussed. Key to this discussion is the concept of *dialogism*, as the question of language in Ukraine dialogically echoes a history of linguistic repression and conflict. This in turn understandably reignites fears in the form of language ideologies, such as those that led to the Ukrainian Rada brawl in 2012.

To understand the concept of *dialogism*, it is important to introduce the suite of concepts with which it is frequently attributed. Most famously introduced and discussed by Soviet literary scholar Mikhail Bakhtin in the early-mid 20th century (and later translated into English in the mid-late 20th century), the concepts of *heteroglossia, polyphony* and *dialogism* were used to interpret and understand the interactions that take place between characters in a novel, as well as between the novel and the reader. These concepts have proved useful across a variety of disciplines, including linguistics. As Bakhtin discusses them, *heteroglossia* refers to the many words and thoughts of others, including quotations and attributed and appropriated expressions, which become comingled together in our understanding of the world (Bakhtin, 1984, 1992). *Polyphony* extends the notion of heteroglossia, arguing that all words, language and communication are multi-voiced, carrying traces of prior words, texts, voices, styles, etc., and are thus not original to the current speaker (Bakhtin, 1986). Finally, *dialogism* builds upon these concepts by saying that any text (verbal, visual, written, semiotic, or otherwise) is part of a connected network of texts. Each text, including each communicative event, presupposes and draws upon earlier texts, and anticipates potential future responses and reactions (Bakhtin, 1986, 1992; Todorov, 1984).

The concept of dialogism was also further expanded by Kristeva (1980) when she coined the term *intertextuality* in discussing Bakhtin's ideas. For Kristeva, it is not just words that are dialogic; it is in fact any aspect of language that is part of the network of past and present. For example, even the way in which a word is pronounced or a sentence is structured links the speaker and hearer to their own mental library of texts, therein influencing how they interpret what they hear and how they respond, as well as how they think another may respond based upon past experiences with interaction. Furthermore, intertextuality is tied to ideas of culture, such that prior, shared culturally embedded texts must be accessible to both the speaker and the hearer in order for a message to be fully interpreted. For example, if a reference is made to 'the yellow brick road', both the speaker and hearer must have access to *The Wizard of Oz* as a prior text in order for this to be intertextually accessible and thus dialogically resonate as intended by the speaker.

The need for intertextual links is important to understand when looking to interaction. For example, even in the event that two utterances by different speakers appear to be identical (such as Bakhtin's examples of '"Beautiful weather!" – "Beautiful weather!"' (Bakhtin, 1986: 125)), these utterances are not truly identical in the dialogic understanding of language. This is due to the fact that prior interactional encounters had by each speaker mold the underlying assumptions which inform the meaning of the statement. Additionally, the interactions which result will also depend upon the interlocutor and thus will determine how the utterance is understood and what type of uptake occurs (cf. Bakhtin, 1986, 1992; Day, 2002).

Therefore, within language ideologies, we find dialogic expressions of the differing intertextual links which are informing the individual's view of the world. For example, those within the Ukrainian Rada who reacted with outrage towards the proposed language bill in 2012 were drawing upon prior texts of historical Ukrainian sociolinguistic repression, as well as anticipating future reactions against their own protests. Likewise, those who reacted in favor of the language bill were responding to their own dominant intertextual links to narratives of historical and contemporary minority language suppression, as well as to anticipated reactions from the opposing political side. Therefore, both sides were responding in ways which to them seemed most reasonable, given their respective dialogic *positionings*.

Positioning in Discourse

Positioning theory (Davies & Harré, 1990; Harré & van Langenhove, 1991; van Langenhove & Harré, 1999) also contributes to our understanding of what occurs when we examine discourses of language ideologies dialogically. Positioning is a reflexive process in sociolinguistic identity negotiation. The theory of positioning focuses on how individuals discursively identify and re-identify themselves and others in relation to the events, topics and other conversational participants involved in the moment-to-moment discursive events taking place. This identification of self and other is done 'by drawing on available categories, reevaluating them, and establishing relationships between them' (Liebscher & Dailey-O'Cain, 2013: 26). People can also be said to be *indexing* these categories, whereupon they draw on ideologies associated with what it means to belong to a certain social category and speak a certain way. As explained by Bucholtz and Hall (2005: 594):

> In identity formation, indexicality relies heavily on ideological structures, for associations between language and identity are rooted in cultural beliefs and values – that is, ideologies – about the sorts of speakers who (can or should) produce particular sorts of language.

These ideological categories can frequently be attributed to 'membership categorization', whereby certain actions or characteristics are attributed, or indexed, to a certain 'category' of people, and by enacting these attributes, a person is positioned as being a member of this category (which is not to say that the person being positioned this way would also self-position as such) (Benwell & Stokoe, 2006). Therefore, it is possible for someone to index a category to self-position in a particular way, but others still have their own other-positioning to do of this person, such that they may either align their other-positioning with the original self-positioning, or they may reject the initial self-positioning in favor of a different positioning.

The process of drawing upon these existing categories in and of itself is a dialogic process, as the individual sorts through existing texts, influenced by wider societal ideologies and Discourses, to determine what will be seen as relevant categories from which to draw (Liebscher & Dailey-O'Cain, 2013; Maheux-Pelletier & Golato, 2008; Sacks, 1992). Harré and van Langenhove (1991) envisioned the concept of positioning to be a dynamic alternative to Goffman's (1981) notion of the 'interactional role' within a *participation framework*. Rather, as described above, self- and other-positions can shift moment-to-moment and are highly context dependent. As stated by Liebscher and Dailey-O'Cain (2013: 26), 'Positioning is a natural and unavoidable process of interaction.' Furthermore, if the individual indexes ideologies or membership categories for which the interlocutors do not have intertextual access, that initial indexing may not be understood, and a different indexing and positioning will take place. Social identity positioning in interaction has proven very useful in understanding more about people and how they take part (or resist taking part) in different levels and aspects of the societies and communities that surround them (e.g. Kang, 2013; Menard-Warwick, 2007; Mykoliuk, 2009; Seals, 2013, 2017a). This area of inquiry has also provided much insight into how people make sense of the world around them and how they negotiate that sense-making with others.

Positioning, therefore, is a constant give-and-take between interlocutors, and is affected dialogically by their own prior experiences and texts, present ideologies and goals, and anticipated futures. As such, studying discourse gives us a window into this give-and-take that is occurring, as people *language* their cognitive processes, talking out their thoughts as a means by which to, quite literally, give them voice and sort through them (Swain, 2006), drawing upon Vygotsky's (1987[1934]) *mediation*. When discursively expressing internally held ideologies and experiences, such as those found in the interviews in the current book, identity is naturally connected and negotiated to and through discourse. Thus, *identity* is a third focus of this book, and Chapter 2 will begin with a review of relevant identity literature.

Outline of the Book

The book continues with Chapter 2, which is focused on language and identity after the Orange Revolution in Ukraine – a major political movement in 2004 that many Ukrainians point to as the first time during which they considered what it means to *be* Ukrainian. The pilot research conducted in 2009 for the current book is also described, and the participants of that research are introduced. Their interviews are analyzed in the context of post-Orange Revolution but pre-EuroMaidan and pre-Ukrainian War. Furthermore, the theoretical framework for the book is further introduced.

Chapters 3 and 4 then directly consider discourses related to the Ukrainian war. Chapter 3 introduces the 38 participants of the main study, who were interviewed throughout 2014 and 2015. Their discursive positioning is analyzed, along with the ways in which they discursively construct allies and enemies. Chapter 4 continues looking at narratives of the war but looks more closely at specific linguistic strategies used by the participants, including metonymy, personification, repetition, dialogism, positioning and more. This chapter also considers how responsibility for the war is discursively assigned, and how reflexive positioning is negotiated.

Chapter 5 then introduces an exciting and unexpected finding, from which this book takes its name. This is the Discourse of 'changing your mother tongue' that occurred throughout the participants' narratives. This chapter explores what participants mean by this idea and how they see it being achieved. Furthermore, participants' accounts are discursively analyzed to uncover intertextual threads to past discourses as well as the presence of dialogic double-voicing. Both participants within Ukraine and those within diaspora communities are included, and their discourses are compared and contrasted to find both points of similarity and areas of divergence.

A focus on diaspora communities continues in Chapter 6. This chapter introduces the Model of Immigrant Identity, Investment and Integration, and shows how narratives from those in the diaspora can be analyzed through this model to uncover the dialogism, intertextuality and investment reflected in each account. Furthermore, this model is used to examine participants' moment-to-moment shifting identities, including the aspects of identity struggle they face during a time of war in the home country.

Finally, Chapter 7 begins by presenting a counter-narrative found within some of the participants' narratives – that of 'it does not matter what language you speak'. This counter-discourse is analyzed to uncover threads of double-voicing, as well as intertextual responses to the dominant 'real Ukrainians speak Ukrainian' Discourse. The significance of this counter-discourse is discussed. Chapter 8 then presents a summary of findings across the chapters. This final chapter ends with a discussion of the research and theoretical implications arising from the findings of the book as a whole, and the book concludes with final thoughts.

Notes

(1) The current quote is presented in a more easily accessible format with false starts, repetitions and pauses removed, so that the focus remains on the content of what Ilona said. Interview excerpts presented throughout the rest of the book are linguistically transcribed for discourse analysis, focusing on both what was said and how it was said.
(2) All excerpts are transcribed in the language(s) that the participant(s) used during the interviews. Any grammatical errors have been retained for accuracy of transcription.
(3) The use of capitalized *Discourse* is different from everyday spoken or written text (small 'd' *discourse*) and is defined by Gee (1996) as 'ways of being in the world, or forms of life which integrate words, acts, values, beliefs, attitudes, and social identities, as well as gestures, glances, body positions, and clothes... so as to take on a particular social role that others will recognize' (Gee, 1996: 127).
(4) Ukraine's complex language history goes back much further than what is presented here, including the role of countries/kingdoms such as Poland, Lithuania, Kievan

Rus', the Ottoman Empire, etc. However, the current book is primarily linguistically, not historically, grounded and thus presents only as much modern history as is needed to understand the context of the research presented herein. For a more complete history of Ukraine, please see Kappeler *et al.* (2003), Subtelny (2000) and Wilson (2009).
(5) Created by Stratfor Worldview in 2008.
(6) Created by Vasyl' Babych and available via Creative Commons licensing.
(7) Map created by Nick.mon and available via Creative Commons licensing.
(8) All candidates for president in Ukraine may run in the first election. If no single candidate takes over 50% of the total votes, there is a second election during which time only the two people who received the most votes in the first election run.
(9) Created by dekóder and retrieved from https://www.dekoder.org/de/article/debattenschau-praesidentschaftswahl-ukraine-selenskyj

2 Language and Identity After the Orange Revolution[1]

Post-Structuralist and Social Constructionist Views of Identity

A significant portion of current research on language and identity is situated within post-structuralism or social constructionism (e.g. Bucholtz & Hall, 2005; Chen, 2013; Giroir, 2014; Kinginger, 2004; Menard-Warwick, 2006, 2007, 2009; Mendoza-Denton, 2008; Norton, 2000, 2013; Norton & Morgan, 2013; Potowski, 2007; Zimman, 2014). Simply put, post-structuralism comes from social constructionism, but to understand both, it is necessary to discuss each in turn.[2]

Beginning with social constructionism, this theoretical framework takes the position that reality and knowledge are socially constituted. That is, reality and knowledge always exist within historical, cultural, political and economic contexts. Therefore, all meaning is relative to its cultural and historical context of interpretation. Because of this, there is no absolute truth; all 'truths' are relative to the contexts in which they exist. Whether or not a 'truth' is believed is dependent upon the contexts in which these truths are constructed and interpreted. As a result, identity categories are likewise contextually dependent and change over time. For example, what it means to be a woman (or an academic, or young, or educated, etc.) in one place and time is not the same as in another place and time. With all this in mind, then, social constructionists are interested in how people create and view identity constructs.

Post-structuralism begins by drawing upon social constructionism but then takes a more critical stance. In post-structuralism, it is understood that people use language to co-construct an understanding of reality. This is different from merely reflecting upon a pre-existing reality, as post-structuralism views reality as co-constructed in each moment. Furthermore, the meaning of words within this co-constructed reality depends on context and is established through the creation and noticing of difference (Derrida, 2001; Stoegner & Wodak, 2015). Further dependent upon context (including a consideration of power relations) is how individuals are positioned in different subject positions within interactions. Expected positions can then be performed (Butler, 1999) through interaction, or alternate positions can be taken up. Furthermore, post-structuralism focuses on how the roles of power (of societies and individuals) and resistance (cf. Foucault, 1977a) are crucial to understanding how identities are formed, constrained, performed and negotiated. As explained by Norton (2013: 45), 'It is through language that a person negotiates a sense of self within and across different sites and different points in time, and it is through language that that person gains access to – or is denied access to – powerful social networks that give learners the opportunity to speak'.

Further, post-structuralist ideas of identity draw upon several key concepts in the social sciences, including subjectivity, positioning, performativity and intersectionality. Subjectivity is connected to agency, in that they both consider how much power an individual has, how much this power is constrained, and what can be done within those constraints. Norton (2013: 4) explains the connection between identity and subjectivity as such: 'A person's identity must always be understood in relational terms: one is often subject of a set of relationships (i.e. in a position of power) or subject to a set of relationships (i.e. in a position of reduced power)'. The notion of subjectivity then further relates to the notion of positioning (Davies & Harré, 1990; see Chapter 1). The way you position yourself and others is constantly negotiated, re-negotiated, shifting, context dependent and dynamic. Menard-Warwick (2009) draws upon the concept of positioning when explaining how this works in identity negotiation: 'In all interactions, speakers claim identities for themselves and assign similar or contrasting identities to their interlocutors, a process referred to as the negotiation of identities. Claiming identities for oneself is often referred to as 'reflexive positioning', while assigning identities to others is termed 'interactive positioning' (Menard-Warwick, 2009: 38).

In addition to considering the roles of subjectivity and positioning, a post-structuralist view of identity also considers how identity is performed. Drawing upon Butler's (1999) ideas that all identities are performed, post-structuralism takes the perspective that no identity category (including gender, ethnicity, age, nationality, etc.) exists on its own as an absolute; rather, you *do* them and thus make them into being. This includes ways of 'doing' and ways of 'being' that occur within larger societal contexts and draw upon the Discourses (Gee, 1996) of those larger contexts. A person may highlight a particular aspect of their identity as more salient at times by performing it to a greater extent, but all aspects of identity are always present.

Because all aspects of identity are always present, this also means that each of these aspects influences every other aspect, which is how we understand *intersectionality* (Crenshaw, 1993). Given that you are never just one aspect of your identity, each part affects the whole, and therefore every person experiences life differently. For example, while women may have gender in common, experiences of Latinx women are not the same as experiences of African American women, nor are the experiences of lesbian Latinx women the same as experiences of straight Latinx women, and so on, as we incorporate all possible identities and contextual factors, leading to the conclusion that no two people experience life in the same way. Therefore, identity categories are not seen as '"variables" but rather as sets of relationships that are socially and historically constructed within particular relations of power' (Norton, 2013: 11).

While the ideas underlying both social constructionism and post-structuralism are similar, post-structuralist ideas of identity focus more on the power relations involved in enabling and constraining the co-construction of reality. For this reason, post-structuralist ideas of identity have become very popular in studies of critical education and critical literacy. One of the most well known of these is arguably Bonny Norton's (2000, 2013) work with immigrant women in Canada. In her work with Eva, Mai, Katarina, Martina, Felicia and others, Norton analyzed the women's narratives told through interviews and journals. She found overwhelming support through this narrative analysis for ideas that have become central tenets for many in applied linguistics and applied sociolinguistics, notably the ideas of investment, imagined identities, and identity as a site of struggle, all of which factor into the current book.

Investment as a concept focuses on an individual's relationship to society, but also examines associated contexts, environments, social barriers, power relations and identities (Darvin & Norton, 2016; Norton, 2013; Norton Peirce, 1995). Investment is different from the cognitive concept of motivation because an individual can be motivated but not invested (i.e. motivated to learn a language but not invested in the classroom environment of which they are currently a part). People invest with the expectation that they will acquire symbolic or material resources as a result of doing so. Additionally, the concept of imagined identities draws upon Anderson's (1991) concept of imagined community, and is explored further in depth below. Finally, identity has been conceptualized by Norton (2000) as a site of struggle (Norton, 2000: 127). That is, identity includes how people see themselves, but also how others position them, the Discourses and ideologies that surround them, and the institutional and personal factors and contexts that can enable or hinder them: 'structure and agency, operating across time and space, can accord or refuse… the power to speak' (Darvin & Norton, 2016: 36).

Further drawing upon Norton's work, Menard-Warwick (2009) conducted an ethnography at a community language center in California, in the United States. She worked with adult learners of English who had immigrated to California from multiple Spanish speaking countries in Central and South America. Menard-Warwick focused primarily on the social construction of gendered identities in her book, though her overall procedure and findings resonate strongly with the current book. Like Norton, Menard-Warwick found that her participants used narratives to negotiate a moment-to-moment construction of selves. Also, the aspects of their pasts that they chose to retell highlight their own social construction of themselves and their socioculturally situated historical trajectories. Through a discourse analysis of the participants' narratives, Menard-Warwick was able to find what intertextual links resonated the most for participants between their pasts, presents, and imagined future selves, and how they dialogically constructed their realities.

Narratives in Discourse

The first common thread that connects Norton and Menard-Warwick's work with the current book is the use of narrative discourse to discover how people construct their social realities. There is a long-standing tradition of working with narratives in identity research in particular (e.g. Block, 2015; Georgakopoulou, 1997, 2007; Georgakopoulou & De Fina, 2012; Giroir, 2014; Menard-Warwick, 2009, 2013; Pavlenko, 2001). Norton (2013) explains that '[n]arratives can be defined as texts that connect events over time – while reflecting on and making sense of these events' (Norton, 2013: 49). Therefore, narratives allow participants to discursively draw connecting threads across time and space. In so doing, they reflexively position themselves in these narratives, reflecting upon their positions and negotiating them as they go. At times, participants may be omniscient narrators, while at other times they may become active characters in their own stories (Toolan, 2001).

It is, however, important to remember that narratives are always reconstructions of actual events (Menard-Warwick, 2013; Schiffrin, 1996, 1997). That is, participants are retelling events through their own perspectives and biases. As part of this, they also select what is to be told and what is to be passed by, therein reconstructing their own sense of reality (Ochs & Capps, 2001). However, it is exactly this reconstruction of reality that proves to be so valuable. By examining *how* things are said in addition to *what* is said, we can better understand people's identity negotiations, ideologies, positionings and responses to things that were said before or things that are still to come (Eakin, 1999; Menard-Warwick, 2009, 2013; Ochs & Capps, 2001; Pavlenko, 2001; Peterson & Langellier, 2006; Schiffrin, 1996, 1997; Wortham, 2001). Therefore, narratives prove to be an ideal resource for investigating topics such as those presented in the current book.[3]

Imagined Communities and Imagined Identities

A second common thread connecting Norton and Menard-Warwick's above-mentioned studies with the current book is the role of imagined identity for the participants, including the role of national identity. The idea of language indexing national identity has been explored by a number of social science scholars (Anderson, 1991; Blommaert & Verschueren, 1998; Rosa & Burdick, 2017; Wodak & Boukala, 2015), as has the idea of language indexing ethnicity (Bucholtz, 2011; Dolgova Jacobsen, 2008; Lo & Reyes, 2009; Makihara, 2007; Shankar, 2008). Fishman first discussed the idea of a shared national identity by focusing on a group's shared pursuit of goals in 'enhanc[ing] the position of the nationality in a world in which social change is markedly rapid and conflictive' (Fishman, 2006 [1972]: 118). Anderson (1991 [1983]) expanded the concept of national identity to include what he calls 'imagined communities', which include people who self-identify as belonging to the same group. Namely 'it is an imagined political community – and imagined as both inherently limited and sovereign' (Anderson, 1991 [1983]: 6). In general, national identity is a powerful construct encompassing ideologies of shared languages, cultural practices and often ethnicity. As such, individuals of a shared national identity may effectively eliminate borders if coming together as an imagined community (Roberts, 2004), or they may create borders that are ideologically defended through language (Dolgova Jacobsen, 2008; Sharma, 2005; Zhang, 2005). Furthermore, imagined communities exist in the mind – it is only because people *believe* they share commonalities that they *act* on such presupposed commonalities. In fact, as Friedman (2016) found when working in Ukrainian classrooms, individuals can even position themselves on the periphery of an imagined community, while still aligning with discourses found within that community.

De Cillia *et al.* (1999) also conducted an in-depth examination of how nationhood is discursively constructed, drawing upon Anderson's (1991 [1983]) notion of imagined communities in so doing. They connect their critical discourse analysis (cf. Fairclough & Wodak, 1997) of the discursive construction of nationhood to underlying historical events associated with them that contribute to collective memory. They do this through the use of their discourse-historical approach (van Leeuwen & Wodak, 1999; Wodak, 1996, 2001; Wodak *et al.*, 1990), which 'inter alia tries to uncover discursive strategies of dissimilation (aiming at the construction of national differences) and discursive strategies of assimilation (aiming at the construction of intranational sameness,' further interpreted through narratives (De Cillia *et al.*, 1999: 151–152). In sum, the construction of discursive difference and sameness (Hall, 1996; Martin, 1995) (what Bucholtz (1999) refers to through practice as 'positive and negative identity practices') is at the root of the creation of imagined communities (Benhabib, 1996; De Cillia *et al.*, 1999). Furthermore, De Cillia *et al.* (1999) crucially draw attention to the fact that even when discussing the discursive construction of 'nationhood', there is no singular national identity. Rather, what national identity looks like and how it is conceived of is multiple and depends upon the ideologies, experiences and social networks (Milroy, 2008; Milroy & Milroy, 1985) of the individuals asked.

Imagined Identity in Ukraine and the Orange Revolution

The Orange Revolution was a set of mass scale protests that took place in Ukraine following the 2004 presidential elections. As mentioned in Chapter 1, the 2004 election was very heated ideologically, with two candidates running for president who represented opposite ideological ends: Viktor Yushschenko represented a more European-oriented Ukraine (and was represented by the color orange during campaigning), and Viktor Yanukovych represented a more Russian-oriented Ukraine (and was represented by the color blue). The protests that erupted during this time were a result of reports from election monitors that Yanukovych's initially reported win in November 2004 had been the result of electoral fraud (D'Anieri, 2005; Magaloni, 2010). Widespread protests ensued. Historians have attributed the protests to long-brewing dissatisfaction among the Ukrainian public with current political and economic situations, with the 2004 elections being viewed as the final linchpin to set mass protests in action (Wilson, 2009).

Following exit polls that showed Yushchenko as having received more votes, therein displaying contradictions with the numbers announced at a national level, Yushchenko and his campaign team publicly called for protests of the election results (Copsey, 2005; Kuzio, 2005; Wilson, 2009). Ukrainians answered Yushchenko's call, and mass scale protests erupted in a number of cities across Ukraine. The largest protest occurred in the Maidan Nezalezhnosti (Independence Square) in Kyiv, and is often referred to by Ukrainian scholars as 'the 2004 Maidan'. Over 500,000 Ukrainians took part in the Kyiv Maidan protest, leading to a visual sea of orange in the Square. While pro-Yushchenko protests took place in Kyiv and in many of the Western regional centers of Ukraine, pro-Yanukovych protests took place in many regional centers of Eastern and Southern Ukraine. Following the protests and a number of resulting national separatist actions, the Supreme Court of Ukraine annulled the results of the election, stating that too much voter fraud had taken place to establish who the winner should be (D'Anieri, 2005; Kuzio, 2005; Magaloni, 2010; Wilson, 2009). A new run-off election was held on December 26, 2004 under the close watch of election monitors. Yushchenko won by over five percent, and he was officially declared President of Ukraine by the Election Commission on January 10, 2005. His inauguration was held in Maidan Nezalezhnosti on January 23, 2005, attended by thousands of supporters in orange, marking the official end of the Orange Revolution (Wilson, 2009).

The Orange Revolution has been pointed to by a number of Ukrainian scholars as one of the first times in modern history that Ukrainians were asked to consider their imagined identities and the future in which they wanted to invest – more European-aligned or more Russian-aligned (Copsey, 2005; Kuzio, 2005). This is important to understand, as this national meaning-making Discourse has been dialogically called upon again and again in the wake of the recent Ukrainian war. An example of this can be seen in the following conversational excerpt from October 2014 with Kyrylo, a Ukrainian-identifying university student and political activist in his early 20s from Eastern Ukraine, now living in the United States:[4]

Kyrylo: xx uh- and uh, it's totally Russian region and people speak only Russian language?

Corinne: [mm hmm]

Kyrylo: [the:y] can understand Ukrainian,
but what happened in two thousand four my mom,
didn't like Russian she decided that she's Ukrainian,
and start to integrate to,
Ukrainian language so,
she ((laughing)) is ((laughing)) working ((laughing)) on it
like how to transfer all her family to Ukrainian language

In this excerpt, Kyrylo's main focus was on answering a question I had asked him earlier about people changing the language they speak (the focus of Chapter 5). However, in answering this question, Kyrylo makes an intertextual reference to the Orange Revolution, dialogically connecting it to the events of the present. When he states that his mother 'didn't like Russian' and 'decided that she's Ukrainian', he specifies that this happened in 2004, which is the year the Orange Revolution began. In intertextually linking to the events of 2004, Kyrylo is dialogically pulling forward the voices and events of the Orange Revolution as a background explanation for his mother's otherwise seemingly sudden decision to change her language. Furthermore, Kyrylo is positioning both himself and me as people familiar with the Orange Revolution and as understanding of his mother's decision, by not feeling that he needs to provide further explanation or justification. In this short excerpt, Kyrylo also dialogically links to Discourses of nationality being tied to language by saying that switching to the Ukrainian language is connected to her conscious decision 'that she's Ukrainian' and not Russian (cf. Braha, 2011). This statement of being 'not Russian' also draws upon ideological Discourses found in some areas of Ukraine that a person cannot be Ukrainian and speak Russian (see Chapter 3 and Chapter 5). Finally, Kyrylo also gives voice to his mother's investment in imagined futures for her family as Ukrainian, by stating that she is trying to 'transfer all her family to Ukrainian language'.

The intertextual references to Discourses of national identity and language that Kyrylo makes in the above excerpt were something that I was already familiar with. Even growing up in the United States, as I did, I had heard similar statements made by family and friends my entire life. In fact, one of my strongest memories of language ideologies had to do with repeatedly being told while growing up to not tell any Russian speakers that I have a Ukrainian background, for fear that such a revelation would immediately cause them to position me as an enemy. This, of course, is an ideology that I have long since learned to take with a grain of salt. However, this ideology, and ones similar to it, have been reflected in the many conversations that I have had with Ukrainians over the years. An example of this can be found in the joke told in 2015 by Klara, a Ukrainian-identifying woman in her 30s from Central Ukraine now living in the Kyiv capital region:[5]

Klara: ((English)) Okay.
    Okay, I will tell it in Ukrainian.
    So… Erm…
    ((Ukrainian)) A girl, Christine, from Karpaty ((West Ukraine)) went to Moscow,
    found a job there,
    and met a good guy named Mikola.
    She was very happy,
    they fell in love,
    they were friends,
    then they had a daughter.
    But then Oksana ((she changes the name of the girl)) kept asking her beloved,
    'Let's go to my parents,
    I miss them so much,
    let us go to our place,
    I'll show you everything,
    no one will hurt you,
    everyone will love you because you are such a fine guy!
    Everyone will like you very much.
    I miss my parents a lot, let's go.'
    For a long time he was saying 'No.
    You know, I'm afraid.
    There are Ukrainians there.

They will beat me' –
'Oh, who will touch you?
You'll come to our village and everything will be just fine.'
At last,
in their fifth year together,
Oksana persuaded Mikola and they went to her parents'.
They came there-
came near Karpaty,
she was so happy to see everyone,
to talk to everyone,
but she couldn't even talk to the girls to their hearts' content because wherever she went he followed her.
And she thought that she had to send him somewhere with the guys,
so that he wouldn't be afraid to talk to them alone and so that she could chat to the girls.
And she says,
'Well, here is a bottle of horilka ((Ukrainian vodka)),
here is a piece of salo ((Ukrainian traditional food)),
go to the village,
come into the house and say "Christ is born!"'
Because this was at Christmas time.
'Well, and so you will make friends.'
As soon as the girls got together,
as soon as they started discussing their girly matters,
no later than in ten minutes,
Mikola runs in,
all in a complete mess,
his coat torn, his hat lost,
he runs in,
his eyes madly rolled and shouts,
((Russian)) 'I, like a decent man, did everything you told me,
came there,
put a bottle of vodka on the table,
unwrapped the salo,
and said, ((Ukrainian)) "Christ is born!",
((Russian)) just like you told me,

and they are like, "Catch him!"[6]

Catch me, my ass!'

This is the joke.

As can be seen throughout Klara's joke, language ideologies of aggression tied to language choice and use abound. The character, Mikola, is Russian and afraid to go to Western Ukraine, which is a Ukrainian-dominant region of Ukraine (Masenko, 2009), for fear of the aggression he will face. The intertextual link to this ideology provides the setting for the joke to commence, especially as many Ukrainians are familiar with this ideology but do not believe it as truth. The linguistic cross-over between the languages provides further humor, as the misunderstanding which ensues is due to a homophonous phrase that carries a very different meaning in each language ('Let us glorify Him!' in Ukrainian, and 'Let us catch him!' in Russian).

Language Ideologies Following the Orange Revolution

While most Ukrainians do not give credence to the idea that language choice and use will frequently lead to aggression, it is still true that there is differing opinion about 'appropriateness' of language choice and use throughout Ukraine (Braha, 2011; Csernicskó, 2015; Masenko & Orel, 2014). This has also been noted by scholars to be more prevalent in the discourses of Ukrainians (20 to 40 years old) who grew up during Ukraine's gaining of independence (in 1991) and/or during the Orange Revolution in 2004. As a result, many Ukrainians within this age range have been found to express stronger ideas of national identity and what it means to be Ukrainian, including language choice and use (e.g. Shulga, 2015). This idea will be revisited in Chapter 7, along with findings that further complicate it.

As an example of the discourses of young Ukrainians, I present here the results of the pilot research of the current study, the former of which I conducted in 2009. These interviews were conducted with women in their early 20s who had been teenagers during the Orange Revolution (and the current Ukrainian war had not yet happened). Participants were chosen based on their membership in an organization of which I was also a member at the time – the Soyuz Ukrayinskykh Studentskykh Tovarystv Ameryky (SUSTA) (Federation of Ukrainian Student Organizations of America). As mentioned above, previous research in Ukraine has reported that Ukrainians' language ideologies regarding the use of Ukrainian and Russian can significantly depend on what part of Ukraine the speaker is from and which language they identify as their primary language (e.g. Bilaniuk, 2005; Masenko, 2009; Tarenko, 2007). Given this, I chose to focus on three comparatively similar speakers from three areas of Ukraine thought to be ideologically distinct from each other: Western Ukraine, Central/Kyiv capital region of Ukraine, and the Crimean Peninsula in Southern Ukraine.

For the pilot research, each interview was conducted via Skype and audio recorded onto a Sony digital hand recorder, after receiving each participant's permission. The interviews were semi-structured and roughly followed a sociolinguistic interview schedule, based on that used by Labov (1973), but with the primary focus being on education, politics and language. Each interview lasted approximately one hour, and the format was kept as conversational as possible. Interviews were conducted primarily in English, due to the fact that the interviews were also used for a phonological analysis of palatalization (see Seals, 2010 for the phonological results).

All participants were competent speakers of English, Ukrainian and Russian, so conducting the interviews in English did not appear to pose a problem (and participants were allowed to use Ukrainian or Russian when they preferred). English as the dominant language of the interview was also chosen because it was the common language that I shared with the participants that I had the most fluency in and was thus able to rely upon most to conduct a proper discourse analysis. I was weary, however, that this could potentially cause communication difficulties for the participants, so I went over this aspect with them in detail before we began the interview, assuring them that they could utilize other languages and varieties as they wanted, including in order to clarify meaning and ideas. All participants assured me that they were comfortable with this before we began. Additionally, throughout the interviews, if a word choice, idea, or meaning was not entirely clear, we clarified with each other across languages.

As shown in the following table, the participants for the pilot interviews were Olesya (from Western Ukraine, a university student studying abroad in the United States at the time of the interview), Alyona (from the Kyiv capital region, a university student in the capital region of Ukraine) and Yana (from the Crimean Peninsula, a university student who moved to the United States as a teenager).

Pseudonym	Origin in Ukraine	Current location	Gender and age	Self-identifies as
Olesya	L'viv (Western Ukraine)	United States	W20s	Ukrainian
Alyona	Kyiv (Central Ukraine)	Ukraine	W20s	Ukrainian
Yana	Simferopol (Crimea/Black Sea Region of Ukraine)	United States	W20s	Ukrainian-American

As previously mentioned, the pilot project was conducted out of an interest in the shifting, and at times strained, sociolinguistic history of

Ukraine between the usage and acceptability of the Ukrainian and Russian languages. Numerous scholars, including Bilaniuk (2003) have found that even fairly recently, Russian has been viewed as a language of status in Ukraine (especially Eastern Ukraine), with Ukrainian politicians frequently using Russian within elite circles (Csernicskó, 2017; Kulyk, 2007; Seals, 2009). However, in 1989, language ideologies shifted when Ukrainian became the state language of Ukraine, with Ukrainian independence following shortly thereafter in 1991. Since Ukraine's declaration of independence, a reverse process of Russification, termed Ukrainisation, began in the country (Seals, 2009), often at a covert level of awareness.

Scholars have argued that the development of Ukrainisation nationally led to further tension among those Ukrainian and Russian subgroups of the country who had already felt themselves polarized and/or marginalized (Bilaniuk, 2003; Chernychko, 2018; Masenko & Orel, 2014). For example, Bilianuk (2003) reports on Martyniuk's findings that 10 years after the start of Ukrainisation and just before the Orange Revolution, 40% of ethnic Ukrainians preferred Ukrainian, but 33% of ethnic Ukrainians preferred Russian (Bilianuk, 2003: 57). This divide has also historically been characterized regionally, with a strong preference by Ukrainian citizens for the Ukrainian language in Western Ukraine, a preference for the Russian language in the East and South, and a mixed preference in Central Ukraine (as discussed further in Chapter 1). While this is a superficial understanding of language politics, it is one that has been frequently drawn upon due to political and linguistic trends in these regions.

Further elaborating on this, the INTAS Project (The International Association for the Promotion of Co-operation with Scientists from the New Independent States (NIS) of the Former Soviet Union)[7] launched a research project to examine language policy in Ukraine. They reported on their website in 2009 that '[t]he most important [challenges] are: Ukrainian is the only state language, but half of the population prefers Russian in daily communication, especially in the workplace. Ukraine hosts the largest Russian minority of all former Soviet republics and the largest group of Non-Russians, declaring Russian their mother tongue'.[8] Here, official rhetoric can be found reflecting the ideology of national identity being equivalent to language used (cf. Braha, 2011; Csernicskó, 2015), with Russian speakers being positioned as a challenge to the Ukrainian national identity (Masenko & Orel, 2014). Therefore, it is not surprising that these views would be found dialogically represented in statements made by the young adults interviewed as well.

Olesya: Language is Part of the National Consciousness

Ukrainian citizens, such as Olesya, voiced frustration at having to live with the linguistic tension instilled by politicians while the politicians frequently continue to use both languages at their leisure (cf. Masenko &

Horobets, 2015). As can be seen in the example below, Olesya provides a strong example of this, as she says that Ukrainian politicians promoting Ukrainian but speaking Russian are 'gross':

Corinne: I've heard some strange stories ((laughter)).
Olesya: Oh really?
Corinne: Yeah.
Just some stories of like politicians,
um in Ukraine using,
um, Ukrainian to talk to people
and then walking off-stage and speaking Russian
and some people got upset.
Olesya: Oh!
Oh, ye- ((laughs)) yeah.
((laughs)) Okay.
((laughs)) Yea:h, uh,
they- they mostly cannot speak Ukrainian at ((laughing)) all ((laughter)).
Corinne: ((laughter))
Olesya: It's like, you know.
Corinne: Uh huh.
Olesya: They speak inappropriate Ukrainian,
so it's funny sometimes.
Corinne: ((laughs)) What do people think about that?
Or what do you think about that when that happens?
Olesya: Well, I think it's gross.
Corinne: ((laughter))
Olesya: They're-,
They're, uh, politicians.
They should know Ukrainian very well.

Olesya's descriptive word choice ('gross') is an almost visceral response to the idea of Ukrainian politicians speaking what she calls 'inappropriate Ukrainian', showing how embodied her language ideologies are for her. She continues to explain that politicians 'should know Ukrainian very well', holding them to the ideological standard that they have promoted across the country through official language policies. It is also interesting to note that purist language ideologies also make their way into Olesya's comments when she says, 'they mostly cannot speak Ukrainian at all', and 'they speak inappropriate Ukrainian'. These comments dialogically echo widespread language ideologies about 'pure Ukrainian', which is a standardized literary form and actually quite distant from the more common surzhyk spoken around the country (Del'Gaudio, 2015; Kulyk, 2011; Taranenko, 2013). Thus, while Olesya is commenting upon politicians failing to meet their own espoused language standards, she simultaneously dialogically calls upon these standards in evaluating their speech.

Later in the same interview, Olesya commented on surzhyk directly, showing her awareness of it, and again echoing widespread commentary about the undesirability of this language variety. She then continues by linking this topic to language ideologies more generally:

Olesya: Yeah, and it ((surzhyk))-

it's very funny and strange language.

It's mostly people in the villages can recite this- speak this language.

Um, very, uh, special is Crimea peninsula.

It's, uh, you know,

there are people-

there are mostly seventy- uh sixty seven percent of the population are Russians.

And they consider themselves to be in the, uh,

on the Russian territory.

So they mostly speak Russian and they don't accept,

even they don't tolerate Ukrainian spoken there.

So, yes.

This is a little bit like a rebel war,

a language war.

And, so yes,

mainly- mainly eh,

in the western Ukraine

people speak real Ukrainian.

In the beginning of the above excerpt, Olesya refers to surzhyk as a 'very funny and strange language', and she further connects its use with 'mostly people in the villages', which is a common ideology found within Ukraine – that this mixed language variety is associated with villagers (cf. Bilaniuk, 2005). By associating this language variety with villagers, this intertextually draws upon Discourses of low education and 'backwardness', further positioning this linguistic variety as undesirable.

Following this initial statement, Olesya immediately switches to talking about the Crimean Peninsula as another perceived exceptional language case in Ukraine. Before beginning to talk about language use in Crimea, she first states that the majority of the population in Crimea 'are Russians' referring to their ethnicity as well as their claimed national identity, and she dialogically voices them when she says, 'they consider themselves to be in the, uh, on the Russian territory'. By referring to Crimean residents as 'Russians', Olesya has positioned them as having less legitimate claims to their own language ideologies, as Crimea was still Ukrainian territory at that time. She then goes on to say that 'they don't tolerate Ukrainian being spoken there', which is reminiscent of the earlier example of Klara's joke showing widespread ideologies of the Russian language not being allowed in the West. She then further equates people in this area who hold Russian-dominant language ideologies as 'rebels', and she calls their preference 'a language war'. Interestingly, in referring to this situation as 'a rebel war', Olesya had no way to know in 2009 that a rebel war would in fact break out in Eastern Ukraine five years later. However, this shows how such ideologies have existed in Ukrainian Discourses for many years before the current Ukrainian war began.

Finally, Olesya brings Western Ukraine back up again in order to contrast it with Crimea. While she has positioned Crimeans' preference for Russian as less legitimate because of their simultaneous dispreference for Ukrainian, she presents Western Ukraine as the counter-example of this and as the place where 'real Ukrainian' is spoken; that is, Ukrainian with less Russian language influence. In this example, not only is Olesya dialogically echoing language ideologies found around the country, she is also intertextually connecting with past Discourses from the Orange Revolution of Russian-aligned Ukrainians as rebels, while those in Western Ukraine (where she is from) as the keepers of preferred Ukrainian-European values (Besters-Dilger, 2009; Maiboroda *et al.*, 2008; Masenko, 2004; Osnach, 2015).

Olesya directly connects her identity with the Ukrainian language in the next example. I had just asked her if the Ukrainian language is connected with her personal identity. She stated:

Olesya: Well, as I said,
it's the part of the national consciousness,
so it's-
language is the part of, my personality.

In this short excerpt, Olesya positions herself as very much aligning with the ideology of national identity being tied to the language you speak (cf. Braha, 2011). She says that 'language is the part of my personality', showing her embodiment of these ideals. She also interestingly states that language (specifically the Ukrainian language) is a 'part of the national consciousness'. This statement has very strong intertextual links to Discourses of the Orange Revolution and reflects Shulga's (2015) findings that young Ukrainians of Olesya's age were very much affected by the Orange Revolution, developing more of a sense of national identity (as opposed to privileging local city/village identity). This is further tied to language ideologies such as those expressed previously by Olesya that Ukrainians should speak the Ukrainian language (also found in Chapter 3 and Chapter 5).

Importantly, Olesya also balances the Discourses upon which she draws, possibly wary that she may now be coming across strongly as a pro-Ukrainian activist. As shown in the example below, in balancing these Discourses, she is responding to any possible challenges that I or other unknown future audiences might raise.

Olesya: Have you heard about Bandera?
Corinne: What was that? ((clarification request))
Olesya: Bandera.
Like the nationalists.
Corinne: Oh, okay.
Okay.
Olesya: They just don't XXX.
So, uh,
they're the people who think that, uh,
just Ukrainian has to be spoken in Ukraine
and they are nationalists
and they are radical people
and I don't really like it,
so, um,
I think that people have- have to have the choice,
um, which language they want to speak.
Um, except those who are working for the State.
They have to know Ukrainian.

Shortly after her previous statements relating to Crimea, Olesya initiates the topic in the excerpt. She begins by asking if I have heard of Stepan Bandera, who is a controversial historical figurehead in modern Ukraine for some pro-Ukrainian (and often anti-Russian) groups (cf. Narvselius, 2012). I provided her with a neutral answer 'okay' in the hope that she would further elaborate, which she did. She explains that the supporters of Bandera, 'the nationalists' as she calls them, believe that *only* Ukrainian should be spoken in Ukraine. She calls them 'radical people' and directly states that she dislikes this assertion, thus distancing herself from this stance and positioning herself in alignment with a more moderate viewpoint. She follows this up by stating that in her belief people should have a choice of which language to speak, though she then immediately follows this with 'except those who are working for the State. They have to know Ukrainian,' therein dialogically echoing her earlier statements regarding politicians. However, by placing these comments immediately after her self-distancing from Ukrainian nationalists, she effectively mitigates her position and her comments, framing them within a more moderate ideology of language choice and use.

Yana and Alyona: It Depends Where You Are

Some of the language ideologies present in Olesya's interview were also reflected in interviews with Yana and Alyona. However, while Olesya is a Ukrainian-dominant speaker, Yana and Alyona are Russian-dominant speakers, which brings an interesting point of comparison between their perspectives. As can be seen in the following, despite being Russian-dominant speakers, Alyona and Yana feel no less Ukrainian for it. However, despite their comfort with both languages, Alyona and Yana express a familiarity with language ideologies and resulting tensions that can be found around parts of the country, as Alyona explains:

Alyona: And, uh, here in Kyiv,
people mostly speak in- in Russian,
so I don't know,
maybe in the western part of Ukraine,
if you try to R-Russian,
everybody will look at you like,
'Hey!
Who are you?
Where are you from?
Everybody here is speaking Ukrainian,
so flee.'
I don't know,
but here in Kyiv,
you can usually speak both languages,
and other people won't say to you anything about it.

In this example Alyona expresses first that people in Kyiv were speaking mostly Russian at the time of the interview (see Chapter 5 for changes in this). She also states that in Kyiv, 'you can usually speak both languages, and other people won't say to you anything about it,' showing Alyona's very laissez-faire approach to language choice and use, which dialogically draws upon Discourses of language found in Kyiv in 2009.

However, it is interesting to note that in making her point, Alyona also chooses to contrast Kyiv against Western Ukraine. She voices an unknown other from Western Ukraine who she imagines as confronting a Russian speaker and saying, 'Everybody here in speaking Ukrainian, so flee'. This imagining of an anti-Russian language Ukrainian in Western Ukraine dialogically echoes the same language ideologies present in Klara's joke from earlier in this chapter, showing its widespread familiarity and endurance.

In fact, this same language ideology is present in Yana's interview, when I asked her if there are any parts of Ukraine where certain languages are more or less acceptable than others:

Yana: Um, well,
    in the West,
    only Ukrainian,
    no Russian.
    And anyway you speak,
    they'll know you're not from there.
    But I've never been actually there.
    I really wanted to go, but I- I still haven't.
    I will one day.
    Um, and then,
    like where you- where I live in the South,
    um, Ukrainian is not used I guess at all.
    So, um, people speak Russian only.
    So, you only use it like in school when you have the Ukrainian language or the Ukrainian literature class.
    That's the only time when it's appropriate I guess.
    Socially acceptable.
    In the South.
    And um, other times it's Russian only everywhere.
    And then um,
    well no,

there's really no Ukrainian unless you have Cable ((television)),

which most people have.

So then- then it's mixed.

And then yeah,

in the- in the North,

you speak both.

So, it depends where you are.

Both are acceptable.

Yana, a Russian-dominant speaker originally from Crimea, states without mitigation in the beginning that in Western Ukraine, you can use 'only Ukrainian, no Russian'. However, almost immediately after making this statement, she says, 'But I've never actually been there,' showing that her awareness of language ideologies around language choice and use in Western Ukraine are in fact wholly based upon previous Discourses of linguistic appropriateness, upon which she is drawing. She then follows this non-mitigated expression of language ideologies with a mitigated statement about equally divided language preferences in Crimea: 'where I live in the South, um, Ukrainian is not used I guess at all'. She further mitigates her statements about social acceptability of language use in Crimea when saying that Ukrainian is only found in Ukrainian language and literature classes. However, this is shortly followed by her statement that language use is 'mixed' and that 'both are acceptable', showing that language ideologies are much more dialogically present than discourses of actual language use.

The actual allowance of both Ukrainian and Russian languages in fact matches much more closely with the complex linguistic identities presented by the participants. This contributes to our growing understanding in sociolinguistics and related disciplines that sociolinguistic identities are not singular, nor are they static (e.g. Barr & Seals, 2018; Bucholtz & Hall, 2005; Norton, 2000, 2013; Seals, 2013, 2017b; Zimman, 2014). Furthermore, in an era of increasing globalization, transnational and translingual identities are the norm for many people around the world (cf. Seals & Olsen-Reeder, 2019). Therefore, it is crucial to acknowledge that while participants may highlight one aspect of their identity or another at any given time, these multiple aspects of identity are in fact interwoven, and the threads continually draw upon each other.

Yana's interview offers a very good illustration of the complexity of identity. Though she is familiar with the Discourses of *national identity* as singular, and *language* as a singular monolithic construct, her lived experiences as evidenced through her narratives show how flawed these popular singular monolithic constructs are. Yana grew up in Crimea, an area of Ukraine that is known for being Russian dominant in use and preference. However, Yana's narratives still present the complexity of the ideas around a 'Ukrainian' or 'Russian' identity. As the following example shows, shortly after saying that she identifies with the Ukrainian language and as a Ukrainian, Yana says the following:

Yana: I identify very much with Russian
and it's easier because you do meet a lot of people through Russian
and you say, 'I'm Russian!'
'Oh where are you from?'
'Oh I'm from Ukraine.'

As the example shows, Yana's self-identification appears to be a contradiction if we approach it from a singular, monolithic conceptualization of identity. However, Yana's self-description makes sense from a social constructionist, identity-as-multiple perspective. As she explains, how she self-identifies verbally depends on who she is interacting with. If she meets someone through the use of the Russian language, she will identify as 'Russian', drawing upon similar cultural and linguistic practices. However, when asked specifically where she is from and forced to make a geographical distinction, she will name Ukraine.

Furthermore, as previously mentioned in this chapter, when speaking with someone who is familiar with the complexity of Ukrainian identities and transnational identities, she self-identifies as Ukrainian-American, thus highlighting her national allegiances. So, while Yana continues to draw upon popular ideas of identity as singular (e.g. Ukrainian, Russian, American), she also displays the complexity of her identities by drawing upon multiple identities fluidly within a conversation.

Further Remarks

This chapter began by drawing on the frameworks of social constructionism and post-structuralism in order to explore the connections between language and identity that are currently made in the field. Within this, the concepts of subjectivity, positioning, intersectionality and performativity were explored in relation to identity. Then, the concepts of imagined communities, imagined identities and investment were introduced, and identity negotiation in Ukraine following the Orange Revolution was discussed.

Through the narrative examples presented, it is possible to locate intertextual references to past texts, as well as dialogic echoes of other Discourses in the participants' own discourse. Examples such as Klara's joke told originally in Ukrainian and Russian highlight the prevalence of ideological Discourses around language and identity in Ukraine. Meanwhile, narratives such as those from Kyrylo and Olesya highlight the rising importance of a defined national identity since the Orange Revolution, as found by Shulga (2015) and the Tsentr Doslidzhennya Suspil'stva (2014), and returned to in the remaining chapters of this book. These examples show that Discourses connecting national identity with language use are not new in Ukraine since the start of the Ukrainian war. Rather, this is a process of consciousness raising at a national level and of investing in a national imagined community that has been occurring at least since the time of the Orange Revolution ten years prior (cf. Braha, 2011). However, as explored in later chapters, it has taken on a slightly different form since then.

Additionally, the pilot research that I conducted in 2009, before the Ukrainian war, with Olesya, Yana and Alyona was introduced and explored. Through the narratives of these young women, it became clear that they were all very familiar with the ideological Discourses about language and national identity that surrounded them. Furthermore, their self-positionings in regard to alignment or disalignment with these Discourses were influenced by their social networks and the discourses they were exposed to therein. Some of these networks were influenced by the regions in which these women grew up, while other networks existed for them because of more transnational travels and communication, especially for Olesya and Yana who had moved overseas. This exposure to multiple languages, cultures, and ideologies also contributed to these three women's own discursive negotiations of their own identities and beliefs within the context of the narratives. This therefore shows the complexity of identity negotiation, especially in an era of increasing globalization where more people from a spectrum of backgrounds and ideologies come into contact with each other.

Furthermore, whether or not these women themselves aligned with any particular view, they were familiar enough with the more common ideologies that echoes of these ideologies were dialogically present in their own narratives. This is important to recognize because it highlights the continuing presence and influence of ideological Discourses for future generations in a country. Even as a country continues to develop and redevelop itself in terms of national identity, the old ideologies do not disappear. Rather, they live on through dialogic echoes and intertextual references that have become entwined in the imagined identities of those living there (Bondarenko, 2008). These previous Discourses thus live on in the words of future generations, no matter in what language, as they themselves reflect on the past and attempt to make sense of it while negotiating their own imagined identities of the future.

Notes

(1) Later parts of this chapter draw upon pilot data first presented in the following proceedings: Seals, C.A. (2010) Язык как часть национального самосознания:

Палатализация в трехъязычном межличностном взаимодействии Украинцев. Материалы 1-ой Международной научно-практической конференции «Языковая Личность в Современном Мире». Magas, Ingushetia, Russian Federation: Ingush State University Press.
(2) This discussion of post-structuralism and social constructionism was developed originally for the Masters course that I teach in interaction and identity.
(3) For more on narrative analysis, please refer to the extensive collection of research found within De Fina, A. and Georgakopoulou, A. (eds) (2015) *The Handbook of Narrative Analysis*. London, UK: Wiley-Blackwell.
(4) In this book, I have elected to use simplified transcriptions so that interested readers of all backgrounds can access them without having experience with discourse analysis. As the focus is primarily on the message conveyed and the *how* is related to the discursive ways in which things are said (not the more discrete linguistic features), this should not unnecessarily detract from meaning. I have, however, kept the intonation units (IUs) so that a sense of the conversational cadence can be maintained. The IUs used in this book draw upon the system outlined by DuBois (1993, 2005), wherein 'roughly defined, an Intonation Unit (IU) is a stretch of speech produced under a single intonation contour... The IU is said to correspond to a single focus of attention in the mind of the speaker' (2005: 1). The remaining transcription conventions are outlined in the appendices at the end of this book.
(5) The original version is told in Ukrainian and Russian, and it can be found in the appendices.
(6) The play on words here is based on homophony. The traditional Ukrainian response to the phrase 'Christ is born!' is 'Let us glorify Him!', where the verb 'let us glorify' is homophonous to a colloquial Russian verb 'we will catch/let us catch'.
(7) INTAS Project < http://www.intas.be/>
(8) INTAS Project: Language Policy in Ukraine. < http://international.univie.ac.at/en/portal/aktuelles/sprachenpolitik/>

3 Othering and Positioning During a Time of War

Reigniting Discussions of National Identity

As discussed in Chapter 2, *identity* is already a complex and complicated construct on its own. It is especially difficult to ask participants to discuss something that they are not used to having to meta-discursively consider. However, this discussion becomes simultaneously more difficult but more practiced when a major event occurs that makes individuals question what identity means. A time of war in the home country is just such an event. Individuals are then drawn into rampant Discourses of what it means to be loyal to a place, loyal to ideas and loyal to identities. They are forced to revisit what it means to claim certain identities when the popular discourses around those identities shift and change.

Tensions in Ukraine began to grow stronger from November 2013 through February 2014 when the Maidan (i.e. EuroMaidan) protests were occurring in Kyiv, and they reached an extreme turning point in February 2014 when 88 people were killed during the protests, and former President Yanukovych fled among rumors that he was being supported by Russia's government (Tsentr Doslidzhennya Suspil'stva, September 2014). Following this, Russia annexed Crimea in March 2014, pro-Russian separatists declared an (officially unrecognized) independent republic in Eastern Ukraine in May 2014, and the Malaysia Airlines tragedy occurred in Eastern Ukraine in July 2014, as a result of pro-Russian separatist missile fire.

In August 2014, data collection for the current project began, with the first interviews occurring in September 2014, and continued throughout additional war-related developments, including the election of a new Ukrainian Parliament (with a separate one elected in the East), Putin's confirmation that the annexation of Crimea was purposeful, the coming and going of additional ceasefires in the war zone, and Ukraine's banning of Soviet symbols in favor of European ones.

A timeline of key events discussed by participants during their interviews is given below:

- **November 2013–February 2014**: Maidan in Kyiv
- **February 2014**: 88 people killed in Kyiv, and former President Yanukovych flees
- **March 2014**: Crimean Peninsula holds contested referendum and is annexed by Russia – internationally not recognized as legal
- **March–April 2014**: Ukrainian troops withdraw from Crimea, and Russian troops begin to support pro-Russian occupation of Eastern Ukraine
- **May 2014**: Pro-Russian separatists in Luhansk and Donetsk declare independent republic after referendum not recognized internationally
- **July 2014**: Malaysia Airlines tragedy in Eastern Ukraine
- **August 2014**: Fighting spreads in Eastern Ukraine, now supported by Russian military
- **September 2014**: Ceasefire signed but then violated four days later
- **October 2014**: New Parliament elected; Eastern Ukrainian pro-Russian separatists hold own election
- **January 2015**: Donetsk Airport falls to pro-Russian rebels
- **February 2015**: Ceasefire signed but never occurs; another Eastern city falls to pro-Russian rebels; Russia continues to send military and weapons into Ukraine
- **March 2015**: Putin confirms purposeful plans to annex Crimea; Western countries impose new sanctions on Russia
- **April 2015**: Another ceasefire comes and goes; Ukraine announces plans to implement military conscription; G7 and EU Summit focus on Ukraine

The events preceding the current Ukrainian–Russian war, most notably the Maidan protests from November 2013 through February 2014 in central Kyiv, reignited discussions of identity for a great many Ukrainians. A number of Ukrainian researchers found empirical evidence of a rise in national identification following the events of Maidan. In particular, when analyzing a survey of 1800 residents of Ukraine conducted by the Institute of Sociology at the National Academy of Sciences of Ukraine before Maidan and shortly after Maidan, Shulga (2015) found a marked increase across all age groups in identifying nationally as a citizen of Ukraine (compared with identifying primarily as a resident of the town or region where they live). This increase in national identification was most prominent in the 18–30-year-old age group, with 58% of respondents primarily identifying with nationality in 2013 and 75% of respondents identifying this way in 2014 (Shulga, 2015: 237). Importantly, this survey provided actual empirical data for trends that had been noticed by many, researchers and non-researchers alike. The question of nationality has gained in importance for

Ukrainians, particularly younger adults (Tsentr Doslidzhennya Suspil'stva, April 2014). This is significant, as this is the generation which is coming into junior and senior leadership positions. Their perspectives on what is important for the nation will have great influence on the directions the country takes in the not too distant future. Therefore, it seems that a rise in national consciousness is not just something remarked upon by a few – rather, it is mass repositioning of a collective self set to impact national and international relations in the future (cf. Bondarenko, 2008).

Furthermore, the Institute of Sociology at the National Academy of Sciences in Ukraine also surveyed Ukrainian residents' opinions of the events of Maidan, including the EuroMaidan and Revolution of Dignity protests. Examining these surveyed opinions, Vyshniak (2015: 171–172) found that the majority of Ukrainians in all regions, except for the Donbas region in Eastern Ukraine (in the war zone) approved of the Maidan protests. Some regions, such as Western Ukraine and the Kyiv capital region had extremely high approval rates (83% and 79%, respectively). Meanwhile, the anti-Maidan events organized by Yanukovych and his supporters were only approved of by 6.5% of the entire Ukrainian population, never reaching 20% approval, even in war zone areas.

These findings regarding age and region are particularly relevant for the interviews that I conducted with Ukrainian young adults throughout 2014 and 2015. All 38 of the participants in these interviews were between 18 and 40 years old, and they come from different regions of Ukraine. They grew up with the Orange Revolution as a major event in their lives, and they felt the echoes of this through the Maidan events, which significantly took place in the same location as the Orange Revolution a decade earlier. As in the discourse-historical approach (Wodak, 1996, 2001; Wodak *et al.*, 1990), the analysis present in this book will consider relevant historical events in order to understand the full extent of people's discursive meaning making practices. Without also considering historical texts, we do not get a full understanding of current Discourses (Blommaert, 2005; Bondarenko, 2008).

The Current Study

Based on the discursive and sociolinguistic variation findings from the 2009 pilot study (discussed in Chapter 2), which connected ideologies with language use and discursive topics, the current full study was launched in early 2014 after receiving university Ethics Committee approval. Thirty-eight semi-structured sociolinguistic interviews were conducted by myself with Ukrainians between 18 and 40 years old, throughout 2014 and 2015. Participants between 18 and 40 years old were chosen because this age range means that these participants grew up during the switch from Russification to Ukrainisation policies, including the language policy changes and ensuing ideologies.

Twelve of the interviewees currently live in Ukraine (three from each of the sociohistorically politically defined regions – West, Central, East and Black Sea regions (Himka, 2015; Vyshniak, 2009, 2015)). The other 26 live in diaspora communities (12 in North America, and 14 in New Zealand). All members of the diaspora communities emigrated from Ukraine at the age of 16 years old or older. This specific detail was necessary for the phonological study but is still an interesting detail of note here. Participants were recruited via the friend-of-a-friend approach, beginning with my own Ukrainian networks and working outwards through recommendations, from which participants self-selected to participate. While this friend-of-a-friend approach undoubtedly yielded an above-average number of participants with similar views, this was not always the case. In fact, some participants in the New Zealand diaspora community referred to others by name for their 'extremely different views'.

However, it is important to clearly acknowledge that the use of an expanded network approach (i.e. friend-of-a-friend) does not allow for generalizability of results in the way that more representative sampling might. Future studies looking to be generalizable would need to extend a wider net for the goal of recruiting a participant sample more statistically representative of the Ukrainian population, and this would need to include people both inside and outside of the researcher's own networks. That being said, the current study did not seek to represent the views of all Ukrainians, but instead to locate emergent trends across participants interested in discussing these sensitive issues. Repetition of emergent discursive topics may suggest emergent Discourses for some Ukrainians, but this does not mean they are relevant to all Ukrainians. Despite the limitations of this approach, I still chose it as the preferred method, as the subject matter was sensitive in content at times, and it was important that participants know they could trust me to protect their information and to not push them in an uncomfortable direction. For many, discussing these highly sensitive political issues also felt dangerous. Therefore, it was of utmost importance that a chain of trust be established before the interviews began and continued afterwards.

Each interview lasted between 45 minutes and 2.5 hours, depending on how much the interviewee wanted to talk about each topic. Some participants found their narrative retellings of the events of Maidan to be particularly cathartic and chose to discuss them at length (they were always given multiple opportunities to change topics or end the discussion). All interviews were done individually, one-on-one with me, except for Lev and Raisa who chose to do their interview together. The full participant list can be found in the appendices.[1]

Similar to the interviews conducted for the pilot research (see Chapter 2), English was also used as the dominant language of the interviews out of necessity for the discourse analysis, as it is my language of greatest proficiency that I share with the participants. As was done for the pilot interviews, I discussed this at length with the participants before we began the interviews, and I assured them that they could use Ukrainian and/or Russian any time they would like, including to clarify meaning or ideas. While some participants made use of other languages (e.g. see Klara's joke in Appendix E), English was used the majority of the time. Whenever an issue of major importance arose, such as the discussion of terminology associated with the war (see the next section below), we spent time talking about the words and ideas being expressed to clarify crosslinguistic meaning. As a result, the excerpts drawn upon in such cases are those of which I am confident in the participants' conveyed meaning. Furthermore, if any questions arose when I was interpreting their meaning, I asked the participants, thus staying as true as possible to their intent. While there is undoubtedly variation in meaning when speaking across languages, the steps described above help to mitigate any loss or confusion of meaning.

Data coding and analysis were done using the Grounded Theory (emergent category) approach via NVivo 10 software (cf. Charmaz, 2014). The guiding theoretical approaches for the analysis were the poststructuralist view of identity (see Chapter 2) and an interactional sociolinguistic discourse analysis with a critical lens.

Interactional sociolinguistics (IS) is an approach to discourse analysis that comes from the work of John Gumperz. According to Gumperz's approach, interaction is studied through discourse to determine how people create meaning moment-to-moment (1982, 2005). Gumperz was highly influenced by work in anthropology and sociology, in addition to linguistics, which laid the groundwork for the foundational ideas of IS. Some of these foundational ideas include the fact that conversational participants rely heavily on semantic inference in the construction of meaning (Gumperz, 2005; Rampton, 2017), which also connects to Bakhtin's ideas of intertextuality (1981). Along with inferences, conversational participants provide contextualization cues, which can be used by the receiver to interpret the message (Gumperz, 2005; Rampton, 2017; Schiffrin, 1996). This is also similar to Bakhtin's idea that both conversational participants must have access to the same intertextual referents in order for the intertextual message to be interpreted (1981). Interactional sociolinguistics therefore draws upon meaning making during the entire interaction and across interactions to interpret interlocutors' discourse.

Furthermore, a critical lens is adopted for the IS conducted in this book. In applying a critical lens, both the local and larger societal contexts must be considered. As Heller (2001: 118) explains, 'Without an ability to situate those local practices in time and space it is difficult to know what to make of them.' Therefore, to maintain a critical focus, IS analysis should equally look to 'large-scale cultural forces, to local contexts of practice, and to the fine details of discursive form and content,' (Bucholtz, 2001: 166). This approach differs from Critical Discourse Analysis (CDA) (cf. Fairclough & Wodak, 1997) in that while CDA 'strongly relies on linguistic categories' (Wodak, 2009: 28), the approach taken in this book critically analyzes narratives as pieces of social interactions, through which sociocultural constructs are evidenced and negotiated through discourse. Thus, both the local and larger societal contexts influence the narratives and therefore inform the analysis. Through this incorporation of the local and larger societies, participants' realities, ideologies and identities are formed, challenged, negotiated and re-negotiated again and again, moment-to-moment throughout the course of their discursive interaction.

Naming Ideologies by Naming Events

When looking at participants' retelling of events of the Ukrainian war, even the naming of the events as a 'crisis', 'conflict', or 'war' carries with it a particular positioning and associated symbolic value (Ellis, 2006). As argued by Pavlyuk (2015), by occupying Crimea in 2014, Russia officially violated Article 2 of the 1949 Geneva Convention and entered into an act of war. However, semantically calling something a 'war' tautologically implies that there is an outside political aggressor, while calling something a 'crisis' implies an event originating from within the country upon which it is impacting, and calling something a 'conflict' implies equal responsibility between the two parties. Therefore, calling the events in Ukraine a 'conflict' would appear to assign equal responsibility to Ukraine and Russia, while calling the events a 'crisis' would imply that it is primarily Ukraine's responsibility to resolve these issues. Most importantly, perhaps, calling the events a 'war' assigns responsibility to Russia as the aggressor on Ukrainian soil. As Pavlyuk (2015) argues, this issue of terminology has been something of which political and media outlets in Ukraine and Russia are very much aware, as they have received many financial resources from various parties to further the public's uptake of particular terminology (Pantti, 2016).

During the interviews, I alternated between terms during the questions, so as to see what terms the participants would choose to use themselves. Some participants matched my own terminological alternations, signifying no one particular preference. However, more often than not, the participants had very strong views about the appropriate terminology that should be used and would correct me. In one such example below, Maxim corrected my terminology, directing me to use the term 'war'. Maxim is 31 years old and is from the central Kyiv-region of Ukraine, still lives there, and identifies as Ukrainian.

Corinne: um, and
what are your feelings,
about the current,

	political situation and war,
	in Ukraine
Maxim:	uh current political situation and war?
Corinne:	yeah
Maxim:	uh you mean about the war?
	uh in Eastern part?
Corinne:	yeah um,
	just however,
	I always like to leave it open to however you want to call it
	so ((laughs))
Maxim:	ah
Corinne:	whether you
	feel more comfortable calling it war or political situation,
	conflict,
Maxim:	well it is true,
	there is a war,
	in the Eastern part,
	and uh, we need to,
	to understand that,
	everybody knows it,
	but due to some, specific moments, in the policy
	u:h our politicians u:h
	don't say it uh like
	clearly that there is a war

As can be seen above, when I referred to the events in Eastern Ukraine as 'the current political situation and war,' therein offering up two possibly alternating terms, Maxim questioned my use of both terms. He then continued on to correct me, saying, 'uh you mean about the war?' Noticeably, not only does Maxim correct my terminology to *war*, but he also uses the definite article 'the', indexing the assumed shared intertextual referent to the current events that had taken center stage in Ukrainian consciousness as *the* war.

Another important point to note about Maxim's correction of my terminology is that while correcting someone has the potential to other them (Dervin, 2012; Fine, 1994; Hatoss, 2012), that is not the approach that Maxim takes. Rather, he phrases the correction as a question, implying that I have misspoken: 'uh you mean about the war?' Additionally, by indexing the assumed shared intertextual referent, as mentioned in the previous paragraph, Maxim is highlighting our assumed shared knowledge of the events taking place. Likewise, he connects with the unknown, yet assumed, mass population saying, 'everybody knows it'. However, this is quite different from how he positions politicians in the lines that follow. He begins by setting them up in opposition through the use of 'but' at the start of the turn, and he continues to say 'u:h our politicians u:h don't say it uh like clearly that there is a war.' In this statement, Maxim is continuing to align with the masses through the use of 'our', even while positioning the politicians in somewhat of an opposition because they don't say clearly that there is a war. This positioning of 'us' (the people) versus 'them' (the politicians) occurred frequently throughout the interviews (cf. Beliaeva & Seals, 2019).

When Friends Become Enemies

Another common feature of the interviews was the linear progression that marked individuals as 'those who used to be friends but who then became enemies'. Effectively, this progression allows participants to quickly and simply access a narrative of tragic betrayal and loss, that of the 'friend become enemy'. Furthermore, by discursively invoking an implied timeline ('then' to 'now'), the interviewees are also able to imply that these events happened alongside the development of the war, the timelines therein paralleling each other. This time and space construction indexes stories of the war by placing the timelines alongside each other, while also personalizing the experience by referencing people the interviewees personally know. Thus, personal narratives draw upon the chronotope (Bakhtin, 1992 [1981]) of the Ukrainian war, bringing the individual stories together into a more powerful collective experience. As Bakhtin (1992 [1981]: 84) defines the chronotope:

> ...spatial and temporal indicators are fused into one carefully thought-out, concrete whole. Time, as it were, thickens, takes on flesh, becomes artistically visible; likewise, space becomes charged and responsive to the movements of time, plot and history. This intersection of axes and fusion of indicators characterizes the artistic chronotope.

The concept of chronotope thus allows for a socioculturally contextualized merging of space and time, such as how people cognitively process events, spaces and places together as one. As further explained by Liebscher and Dailey-O'Cain (2013), the chronotope is a useful construct in particular for understanding how those in diaspora or transnational communities connect with multiple places and times: 'when people migrate from one place to another, they bring such a sense of their place of origin with them, and they use it in the construction of local immigrant spaces by indexing aspects of it in their positioning' (Liebscher &

Dailey-O'Cain, 2013: 18). Through the discursive connection with this chronotope, Ukrainians are able to share in the collective experiences of being affected by the Ukrainian war, even if they themselves are not currently in Ukraine.

An example of drawing upon and contributing to the shared chronotope is shown below in a story told by Lyuba, (25 years old, from Eastern Ukraine, living in New Zealand). In the following example, Lyuba discursively moves between times and places, at times retelling her mother's story, and at times placing events in the present.

Corinne: Mhm and um

Do you know any people directly involved in the events?

Lyuba: Well, my- my parents obviously still live in, the Sloviansk,

which is where, the whole action's happening,

so that's pretty scary

and they had to: run away at some stage um…

And it was- it's- it's quite a unique, um, set of events

because, all of a sudden it divides people into these two distinct categories and…

just to give you an example

my parents live in an apartment building which is about ten stories high

and one of my mum's best friends lives in the building next door.

Well, my mum's friend supports the movement towards Ukraine becoming closer with, Russia and,

you know,

promoting closer economic ties

and so on and so forth.

Um, so she's been attending all the,

events

for basically the rebels,

and um she ended up,

giving them the key to the rooftop of the apartment building

where they placed a couple of snipers when, things were really, getting bad.

And so they-

that's the kind of thing that really…

((exhales loudly)) tests a friendship and-

and really draws you into

one camp or the other

and: you just kind of-

you have to choose

and then it doesn't matter that you've been friends for ten years or whatever.

All of a sudden,

you're just on, different sides.

In this example, Lyuba begins by talking about her parents and where they live. She then references her current emotions ('so that's pretty scary'), drawing herself into the story. Lyuba then continues by briefly telling of a past event when her parents had to run away, which she then quickly brings back into a present tense, beginning with 'it was' and self-corrects to 'it's quite a unique, um, set of events'. This then leads into the more universally generalizing statement, 'all of a sudden it divides people into these two distinct categories', commenting as an omniscient narrator on the events that have occurred.

To then highlight her point, Lyuba initiates a narrative, following a structure that fits well within that outlined by Labov and Waletzky (1967): 'just to give you an example'. She then establishes the setting and tells a story in the present tense of her mother's friend and next-door neighbor who has been attending pro-Russian events. However, up through this point, any evaluation of her mother's friend's behavior is intertextual and depends on prior knowledge of Lyuba's own position on the events that have taken place in the war, as well as background knowledge of key players and events in the war to date. However, the 'friend to enemy' complicating action begins in the narrative when Lyuba switches tenses in the next few lines to tell what her mother's friend did: 'Um, so she's been attending all the, events for basically the rebels, and um she ended up, giving them the key to the rooftop of the apartment building where they placed a couple of snipers when, things were really, getting bad.' In the previous lines, Lyuba has now constructed her mother's friend as the 'other' who has now betrayed Lyuba's family, using evaluative terms such as 'rebels' and 'really, getting bad', as well as terms that draw semantically upon war and danger, such as 'snipers'.

Lyuba then summarizes, concluding her narrative and evaluating the events by saying that such things are what 'tests a friendship', places you 'in one camp or the other', and 'you have to choose'. Most powerful is Lyuba's concluding statement: 'and then it doesn't matter that you've been friends for ten years or whatever. All of a sudden, you're just on, different sides.' This statement again highlights the timeline of friend to enemy over the course of the events of the war, such that even 10 years of friendship

Othering and Positioning During a Time of War 51

cannot outlast the events of the war. Even through Lyuba is telling her mother's story and is not physically present at the location herself, she is able to draw upon the chronotope of the Ukrainian war to bring the listener into the events of the war, intertextually drawing upon master narratives, including those of friend turned enemy.

Likewise, Gleb (38 years old, from Eastern Ukraine, living in New Zealand) drew upon the Ukrainian war chronotope. His narrative also shows how time and space become one transportable, accessible whole when discussing the complexity involved in narratives of the 'other' wherein friends become enemies.

Gleb: I feel pain for them because I'm one of them.

But it's- it's a social science,

if you're moving towards eighteenth century, you will be colonized.

They don't understand that,

and they like-

and instead of saying like 'Oh, what made you Ukrainian,'

you know,

'you are my friend,

you are normal guy,

what made you say we Russians are fascists?

Maybe there's something going wrong,

maybe we should look around,

maybe we should- maybe we should-

Russians should come together and discuss.'

Instead they saying me like

'Why you calling me fascist?

We didn't- we didn't vote for- to tanks went to Ukraine.'

Well, but if you think we are bro- friends and brotherhood nation,

I never heard you voice of opposite.

You- so instead of saying like w-

instead of posting something like

'What a horrible story,

my Ukrainian friend called me fascist,

isn't it freaking alarming?'

He don't post this,

he send me like

'Why do you call me fascist,

why are you abusing me?'
They don't understand.
What your nation is doing you're responsible for that,
it's not um, it's not some aliens doing it,
it's not Putin's doing himself,
it's not Putin running in Ukraine and- and- and, and doing that.
They don't understand.
…
But I mean it's horrible to say,
because it's- it's my brothers,
like they're same brothers,
I am same XXX Russian,
and again I have Russian culture,
but I see my c- my, both my people,
both my nations are in huge trouble.
This one becau- because of this attack,
and this one because of the schizophrenia.
And like- and as I said,
both of them,
it's like so painful.

Immediately, Gleb positions himself as both the same and as different from Russians, as he is a Russian-dominant speaker himself and thus feels a personal connection through the language. As he states, 'I feel pain for them because I am one of them.' While relating himself emotively and experientially with Russians, Gleb simultaneously distances himself by continually referring to 'them', rather than using the construction 'we' or 'us' (Fligstein, 2008; Wodak & Boukala, 2015). He continues with this discursive distancing by saying 'they don't understand that', with 'they' meaning Russian people.

Gleb continues his discussion, bringing time and space even closer together by voicing the individuals he is discussing. Furthermore, he also voices what they could have potentially said in dialogue, therein bringing the possible into the actual, joining together narratives of what could have occurred with what has actually occurred. Through Gleb's voicing of his interlocutor, he positions himself as 'normal', while at the same time revealing that this conversation could occur as the result of him saying 'Russians are fascists,' which is a very interesting juxtaposition indeed. He then comments on this constructed dialogue, saying, 'Instead they saying me like, "Why you calling me fascist? We didn't – we didn't vote for – to tanks went to Ukraine,"' wherein the constructed dialogue of what he actually experienced lacks the claiming of responsibility and softness found within the constructed dialogue of what could have possibly been said. Even though both the possible and the actual are in response to a heavy, direct comment from Gleb, the focus of Gleb's narrative is not on what he said himself. Rather, the focus is on his perception of his interlocutor's self-positioning, which he expresses as a simultaneous self-re-positioning from ally to non-ally.

The juxtaposition of what did happen versus what could have happened continues with another constructed dialogue immediately after. Following this second dialogue, Gleb again directly positions Russians as outsiders, as the 'other', stating 'They don't understand. What your nation is doing you're responsible for that.' Once again, the discussion of responsibility plays a major role in how Gleb positions his interlocutor. By denying responsibility for events of the war, Gleb sees his Russian interlocutors as distancing themselves from the master narrative of shared loss and grief found within the Ukrainian community's chronotope of the Ukrainian war. As such, the Russian interlocutors become the 'other' and are discursively positioned as such by Gleb. He furthers this point by specifically stating, 'it's not Putin's doing himself,' again highlighting the role of the individual and showing how, for Gleb, individual responsibility is key, as it is individuals who are sharing the master narrative of grief and loss.

Finally, Gleb shows how complex this othering from 'ally' to 'non-ally' can be for one's own self-positioning. As discussed in Chapter 2, identity is always multi-faceted and complex. An event such as a war in the home country highlights this complexity, as war with others also can become war with self. In the example above, Gleb says, 'But I mean it's horrible to say,' reflecting a dialogic echo of how others could perceive his negative preceding statements. He furthers this by saying that the aforementioned Russian interlocutors are his 'brothers', and he emphasizes his sameness with them through a shared Russian culture, therein aligning currently high-stakes aspects of his identity with theirs. He then says that 'both my people, both my nations are in huge trouble.' While simultaneously aligning in this statement with both Russian and Ukrainian monolithic cultures, Gleb is able to also highlight a binary divide through the use of 'both'. Therefore, while he has long identified with the Russian language, which is itself used by many Russian and Ukrainian-identifying people, the focus has now shifted from what is shared to what is divided. By highlighting this divide, the shared experience of 'being Ukrainian' during a time of war is reinforced by simultaneously constructing Russian-identifying individuals as the 'other' who do not experience the same master narrative losses and pain.

Crucially, the othering that occurs through a negative naming event such as 'fascist' is not unidirectional. Rather, this word itself has come to stand for the intertextual dialogues of lack of empathy and fighting espoused by all sides (usually discussed as the 'two sides'). Lesya (28 years old, from Western Ukraine, living in the United States) tells her own story of how the term fascist was used against her, rather than by her. Her narrative also includes the discussion of 'brothers' turned 'enemies'.

Lesya: I- yeah,
> I- I don't understand how that is possible
> because up until last year we were brothers, you know,
> brotherly countries,
> um and now, you know,
> suddenly we are fascists.
> I mean how the heck is that even possible?
> And this other friend of mine,
> she was like 'yeah you guys discriminate against Russians'
> and this and that
> and 'you hate foreigners,'
> like what are you talking about?
> I went to a foreign-
> I went to a Polish school,
> I grew up with Russian parents living in the heart of Lviv,
> which is considered to be, you know,
> the nationalist city quote un-quote.
> I mean it's completely not true
> and everybody knew about it,
> but suddenly since this conflict started, you know,
> we're the enemy
> and I don't know if it's the propaganda is that good
> or Russians are just used to being told what to think from years and years of communist rules, you know,
> maybe that's why,
> but um yeah,
> it's- it's ah-
> it's frustrating
> and mind boggling that they don't- that they're- the-
> that Russians have this diffic- different opinions all of a sudden
> and all of a sudden they need to ah show their s- strengths to the US
> and all this stuff,

and you know I- I- I asked some of my friends, you know,

if you like Russia so much go back and live there?

You know, go back to Russia and support your president, you know,

put your mouth where you mind is

or your money is-

I don't know the expression, but whatever,

ah yeah,

but no,

they still live here.

They hate Ukraine

and they love Russia

so it's very frustrating, yeah.

Notably, Lesya's narrative begins with an evaluative orientation (Labov & Waletzky, 1967) very similar to that found throughout many of the Ukrainians' narratives – that is, a seeming suspension of reality where the individual doesn't 'understand how this [war] is possible.' Such a statement speaks to the importance that a vast number of individuals had placed on the shared commonalities, including shared heritages, on either side of the national border between Ukraine and Russia. The war currently taking place calls into question for many this heretofore assumed reality of commonality superseding difference. The resulting identity struggle (Norton, 2000) and conflict that takes place is discursively constructed as a lack of understanding and/or belief.

While Lesya is providing her orientation, she also makes an interesting shift in position, wherein 'we' goes from being inclusive of Ukrainians and Russians, to 'we' meaning just Ukrainians: 'we were brothers'… 'suddenly we are fascists' (cf. Beliaeva & Seals, 2019). Through this transition of semantic meaning, Lesya also merges time and space, again drawing upon the chronotope of the Ukrainian war, creating a perceived reality in which all individuals throughout Russia and Ukraine experience this event collectively, no matter where or when they are.

As Lesya's narrative continues, she takes on the defensive stance. Discursively constructing her friend as the aggressor, Lesya voices her friend as being the first to do the othering, by saying, 'Yeah you guys discriminate against Russians,' and 'You hate foreigners.' This then allows Lesya to respond defensively to the other positioning she has experienced, calling into question the believability of such othering: 'like what are you talking about?' She then provides her own backstory as a way to self-position as a transnational, transcultural, translingual individual, intertextually drawing upon Discourses of openness and willingness to accept others that go along with such positionings.

Lesya continues her narrative, expressing her disbelief at being positioned such that 'suddenly we're the enemy', with 'we' continuing to stand for her and other Ukrainians. She then begins an attempt at reasoning aloud, saying she's not sure why this has happened, that maybe it's the propaganda (meaning Russian propaganda), or maybe 'Russians are just used to being told what to think from years and years of communist rules, you know.' In this latter statement, Lesya has named Russians as the other, while also assigning responsibility of this divisiveness to the Russian government, not the people themselves.

However, after this mitigated think-aloud, Lesya then presents a still mitigated ('you know'), yet also more direct, response to the other-positioning that she has expressed thus far, when she states that she asked her interlocutors why they don't return to Russia. While Lesya has named her interlocutors as friends, the speech that she indirectly reports, while mitigated, is still othering and confrontational, reflecting the conflict experienced by an unexpected situation of friends becoming enemies, and of fluid borders becoming rigid.

The disbelief and sense of displacement expressed in the interviews as a result of the war is further discussed by Ruslana (28 years old, from Eastern Ukraine, still living in Ukraine) who was both emotionally as well as literally physically displaced by the war. At the time of the interview, Ruslana was living in another country on an internship that she had secured before the war began.

Corinne: So, you're on an internship for a few months there,
and where- what city did... you come from,
and where will you go back to when you're done?

Ruslana: Er, actually, it is a very tough q- question,
because I came from, er, Lugansk,
but my city is... right now it is closed, er...
because of the rebels.
They have their own requirements, their own regulations,
and people there wait to return back to their homes.
For example,
my parents and I,
we left Lugansk, uh, at the end of July,
and, er, then we couldn't ret- return back home,
because all trains and all buses,
they were canceled,
and we gathered to- to live, er, in Kyiv,
in our capital,

in my sister's apartment, er, for one month,

then I, er, went to... [country],

and my parents,

they are still, er, in Kyiv.

So, I don't know where we'll return back,

I- I hope that it will be Lugansk,

but I'm not sure.

Ruslana's story was emotionally difficult to learn, as she lost so much in the events of the war (discussed more in Chapter 7). As Ruslana explained during the course of her interview, not only was she experiencing the struggle of physical displacement from the events of the war, but she also lost access to her heretofore imagined future and has to decide on new future goals. The events of the war forcibly erased her planned future trajectory, requiring her to process the current events and simultaneously plan a new future for herself. This turn in events brings identity struggle (Norton, 2000) and renegotiation (Seals, 2013) to the forefront of Ruslana's daily live, and subsequently to the forefront of her discourse.[2]

In telling her story, Ruslana connects with the Ukrainian war chronotope, merging time and space into one so that her reality is transported to the recent, current and future struggles she faces in Eastern Ukraine, even though she is not currently in Ukraine herself. She also shows the struggle she faces, especially in regard to having both allies and enemies in the same location – the place which she calls her own home. First, it is interesting to note that every time Ruslana names her city, she uses the Russian version of the name – Lugansk (Luhansk is the Ukrainian version). She shows her embodied connection with the city, calling it 'my city'. She then positions the pro-Russian Ukrainian separatists within the city as not belonging to the city in the same way that she does, referring to them as 'rebels' and stating that the city is closed because of them, therein making it so that she cannot return to her own city and home. She further distances herself from the rebels, specifying that 'they have their own requirements, their own regulations', which are different from the ordinary residents who want to return home. Therefore, while the rebels are occupying the city, they are preventing the ordinary 'people' and her co-residents from returning to their homes. Even though many of the rebels are from within Luhansk also themselves, they are positioned as no longer having a rightful claim to the city, having violated the rights of the ordinary people to live there.

Ukrainians but not Ukrainians

For many of the interviewees, the acts of the rebels in violating the rights of ordinary citizens of Ukraine were too much to accept. For these interviewees, the rebels had revoked their right to be considered Ukrainians and could no longer be identified as such. As such, the rebels were called many things, but 'Ukrainian' was not one of them. The denial of this identity label further contributed to the interviewees' discursive othering of the rebels as a way to build further figurative distance between them. An example of this is given in the interview with Larysa (31 years old, from Eastern Ukraine, still living in Ukraine).

Larysa: Because, the people who left there,
they are from, er… cl-
like those Ukrainians with Ukrainian passports,
yeah, because they are also participating in this
but as I said I can't call them Ukrainians,
I don't have any respect for them.
Er, they are coming from smaller towns,
er… from… er, mine towns,
er… th- they- they don't want to perceive any other… occupation
and they just got the guns in their hands,
and they feel like the kings.
So, there is a lot of robbery, erm, violence,
just like this,
because now they have the gun,
they used to have not much,
maybe some money for beer, er,
but ((laughing)) now they could have everything,
so there is a lot of… apartment robbery… ((smacks lips))
Er… such things.

In this example, Larysa first establishes the national original and technical identity of the rebels of whom she is about to speak, referring to them as 'those Ukrainians with Ukrainian passports'. In so doing, she establishes that she is not currently talking about rebel fighters who come from anywhere else other than Ukraine (such as Russia). She then says that, however, she 'can't call them Ukrainians' because she doesn't have respect for them. For Larysa, Ukrainian identity is a bonded identity, tied to mutual respect for one's countrymen/women. By violating the rights of Ukrainian citizens to reside in their own homes, and by attacking pro-Ukrainian views and ideals, the rebels are also seen to have violated the mutual respect expectation, thus losing the right to call themselves Ukrainians.

However, what arises next in Larysa's argument is a multi-voiced echo of stereotypes that have surfaced regarding who the rebels are. While the stereotypes may be true for some, they are not true for all. However, the nature of the stereotypes, such as 'coming from smaller towns... mine towns... don't want to perceive any other occupation... guns in their hands... feel like kings... robbery... violence... used to have not much... maybe some money for beer...' makes it easier to discursively paint the rebels as the enemy other. By assigning all socially unacceptable behaviors and characteristics to the rebels, they are repositioned as the undesirables of society and thus very different from anyone whom Ukrainians would want to call their own. Therefore, the behaviors of the rebels become less shocking, and simultaneously, it becomes easier to discursively distance them from all other Ukrainians.

One Nation, One People

Occurring alongside the Discourse of rebels losing the right to call themselves Ukrainians is the Discourse of 'true' Ukrainians establishing and reinforcing between each other a collective impression of what it means to be Ukrainian. Within this Discourse is also the underlying dialogic echo of the ideology that 'if you're not with us, you're against us.' Presupposed is that if you are not part of this new ideological 'one nation', then you are not Ukrainian; you are an 'other'. Ilya (33 years old, from the Black Sea region of Ukraine, still living in Ukraine) explains this in his interview.

Corinne: What do you think um has been what-
what are the main ah factors that led to the changes recently?

Ilya: ... ah I think that Ukrainians have become one nation
ah according to the definition nation,
is just the people having a political will to live together,
and ah we have never had this political will.
If you take for example our ally XX,
the last century for instance,
ah there you know-
there were a-always Ukrainians who didn't know that they are Ukrainians-
that they were Ukrainians,
and ah for example
if-if you take this XX period
...
then there still times where Russia try to intervene Ukraine-

to attack Ukraine,
um for the first time XX history,
then many Ukrainians just didn't know what state they lived in.
Um er, and now everything looks different,
Er, you know,
just- um Ukrainians have understood-
understood that they are together,
ah I think Dnipropetrovsk, Mykolaiv, or XX,
so I feel that we are united,
and ah I've been to Kyiv recently,
and er the first thing that I noticed er
was the number of people ah speaking Ukrainian.
Ah mm so we in Kyiv er never look so,
XX the majority of Kyiv inhabitants er spoke Russian.
Now it's different, um ((laughter))
Ok.

Ilya explains that previously, a shared national political identity was not seen as an important part of being Ukrainian. Ilya's sentiment is reflective of the previously mentioned findings in recent Ukrainian research, detailing the rise in importance of national identity for young people in Ukraine (Shulga, 2015; Tsentr Doslidzhennya Suspil'stva, April 2014). Ilya further confirms these findings by stating that within the last century there were always Ukrainians who did not consciously know that they were Ukrainian, meaning that national identity was not as important as local identity (Shulga, 2015; Tsentr Doslidzhennya Suspil'stva, April 2014).

Ilya's discussion of the rise in importance of national identity becomes further complex when he introduces a complicating factor in the form of Russian interference: 'then there still times when Russia try to intervene Ukraine – to attack Ukraine.' He then creates a cause and effect relationship, explaining that he sees Russia's attacks on Ukraine as the reason why Ukrainians did not have a strong shared national identity: 'then many Ukrainians just didn't know what state they lived in.' However, Ilya then compares this continuous past to events of the present, saying that 'now everything looks different… Ukrainians have understood… that they are together… that we are united', therein showing the importance placed by some Ukrainians in a perceived shared national identity.

Notably, Ilya's narrative then ends by drawing language into the equation, saying that on a recent trip to Kyiv, he noticed 'the number of people ah speaking Ukrainian.' Ilya explains that traditionally, the Russian language featured much more prominently in Kyiv than did the Ukrainian language, which has been confirmed by statistics (see Chapter 1) as well as by other interviewees. This same connection between the rise of a shared national identity and a change in linguistic practices is further commented on by Larysa (31 years old, from Eastern Ukraine, still living in Ukraine).

Larysa: It's like everybody of us wa- was pushed to think,
yeah, it's, er, absolutely personal thing of course, er,
to think of who they are,
on what side they would ((laughing)) like to be.
Er, as- er, we don't have a- any civil war going on here,
it's, er, it's occupation.
But, er, you just start thinking about those questions,
because they are becoming… pr- pra- primarily.
Er, it's not economics, or wage, or… workplace,
but it's like who I am,
what language I need to speak,
what language I would like to prefer to speak.

Similarly to Ilya, Larysa positions Russia as an outside driving force that mobilized the Ukrainian people into developing one shared national identity – 'Ukrainian'. While Larysa removes a direct responsible actor in the sentence 'It's like everybody of us wa- was pushed to think', this comment comes in the midst of the portion of her interview discussing the Ukrainian war. She then follows this by saying people had to decide 'on what side they would like to be', implying that there are definitely separated 'sides' that are at war. However, she then further clarifies that she does not see these sides as existing within Ukraine and between the Ukrainian people. Rather, she states that there is no civil war; rather, 'it's occupation'. By specifically negating that the fighting is a civil war and instead calling it an 'occupation', Larysa is drawing upon the semantic meanings of these words to indicate that she sees the war as a taking of territory by an outside nation, which is also reflective of the intertextual master narrative of Russia attacking Ukraine. So, while some of the occupiers are from within Ukraine, Larysa sees them as outsiders belonging to Russia and as not having any internal allegiances to Ukraine or to the Ukrainian people.

Also similar to Ilya, Larysa then brings language into the discussion of national identity. When talking of identity ('to think of who they are'), she separates professional and socioeconomic identity from linguistic identity, relating language specifically to identity by saying, 'it's like who

I am, what language I need to speak, what language I would like to prefer to speak.' Interestingly, Larysa has also separated need from desire: 'need to speak' versus 'like to prefer to speak'. However, for her, both aspects of language (needing and preferring) still factor into identity. Therefore, both language preference and use contribute to linguistic identity. This aligns with previous research findings into language and identity that have found that both language preference and use contribute to multilinguals' identities, as well as current and future language investment (Norton, 2000, 2013; Norton Peirce, 1995; Seals, 2013, 2017a, 2017b). Therefore, growing up in a multilingual country and having national identity directly challenged by the war are two factors that have contributed to some Ukrainians' views of language preference and use as also being an integral part of identity (cf. Osnach, 2015).

Being Ukrainian is Speaking Ukrainian

Furthermore, an important component to being part of the national 'us' (meaning Ukrainian people with the right to call themselves Ukrainian) for many of the interviewees, was specifically the ability and willingness to speak the Ukrainian language. This Discourse was common throughout some of the interviews, but there was also caution around this idea presented in other interviews (discussed later in the chapter). For both viewpoints, a dialogism exists within and between them, such that when each person gave their personal views on this issue, they were responding to past historical events that they have learned about, responding to recent events and discourses that they have heard, and were anticipating future reactions based on their position on this delicate issue.

For participants who ascribe to the belief that being Ukrainian means being able to speak the Ukrainian language, they are drawing largely upon Discourses of national identity, as well as those of official language policy. As mentioned previously in Chapters 1 and 2, Ukrainians have had a tumultuous linguistic history, many times during which the Ukrainian language was not allowed. Therefore, claiming the Ukrainian language as part of Ukrainian national identity firstly serves to enhance and protect the status of the language (cf. May, 2006; Ricento, 2006). Secondly, it also allows Ukrainian speakers to push back against prior Discourses of the Ukrainian language as rural, lower in status, undesirable, etc. (Bilaniuk, 2003). Thirdly, tying language to nationality is a seemingly natural and expected occurrence among young people in a country who are finding more importance in the idea of a shared national identity and what that might look like (cf. Braha, 2011; Shulga, 2015).

This third idea in particular is shared by Klara (30 years old, from Central Ukraine, still living in Ukraine). In her interview excerpt, below, she too ties linguistic identity to a developing national identity, as well as attributing both of these to the push-events in the previous year of the Ukrainian war.

Klara: With this situation that's going on right now,

with the political situation,

and with the society to beg- to being... more grown up, in the last-

becoming more grown up in the last year,

people are more willing to, er, start learning Ukrainian,

and using.

Klara attributes the Ukrainian society 'becoming more grown up' to the events of the Ukrainian war during the year preceding the interview. She views the political turmoil as having been responsible for pushing Ukrainians together into a more unified national whole. As such, she equates this unified national identity with national maturity – 'growing up'. Furthermore, Klara also equates the formation of a unified national Ukrainian identity with learning and using the Ukrainian language. By saying 'to start' learning the language, she implies that until that point, many Ukrainians had not known or used Ukrainian, which is in fact true (Paniotto & Kharchenko, 2015). As discussed in Chapter 2, the number of Ukrainians who self-reported speaking abilities in the Ukrainian language rose after the Ukrainian war began (Paniotto & Kharchenko, 2015). Like Klara, many Ukrainian people saw speaking Ukrainian as a necessary part of a 'true' Ukrainian national identity, and therefore began to learn and/or use it more than they had previously (Csernicskó, 2017).

Similarly, Larysa, comments on the expectation that people living in Ukraine speak the Ukrainian language:

Larysa: Because it is Ukraine,

and we have only one national language, er,

which is Ukrainian,

it was always like this, er,

the constitution, er, never got changed…

But just for me this is the right way of things,

and er then there is no controversy.

By drawing upon political Discourses (e.g. national language and constitution) in the establishment of her expectation, Larysa is also giving her opinion more institutional symbolic capital (Bourdieu, 1986). She is drawing upon the power of political establishments when she draws upon their discourse in order to symbolically support her position. It is often harder for people to disagree with institutional symbolic capital than it is to disagree with a simple opinion or personal experience (i.e. embodied symbolic capital) (Bourdieu, 1986; Meadows, 2009). Therefore, Larysa is dialogically drawing upon similar past and present discourses, while intertextually linking them to political Discourses, therein positioning herself in a more powerful, knowledgeable position through which to share her opinion. Simultaneously, Larysa denies voice to any alternating opinion of powerful languages throughout Ukraine's past and present history by clearly saying, 'we have only one national language... it was always like this... the constitution never got changed... this is the right way of things... then there is no controversy.' By eliminating space for the counter-discourse, Larysa has further supported her own position that a part of the national Ukrainian identity is the use of the Ukrainian language.

At the same time, by equating the knowledge and use of the Ukrainian language with national identity, this simultaneously implies that someone who does not speak the Ukrainian language is not 'as Ukrainian' as someone who does speak and use the language. This position can be found embedded in Larysa's discourse above, and it is also found in Kalyna's discourse below. Kalyna (37 years old, from Western Ukraine, still living in Ukraine) presents a view found among some of the participants, but a view familiar to many more.

Kalyna: Well uh I think that being Ukrainian is uh speaking Ukrainian language.

Corinne: Mm-hm.

Kalyna: It's absolutely naturally.
And uh, uh I told you uh later-
before that that uh I can't understand uh,
people who call themselves Russian-speaking Ukrainians.
Well, uh I told them,
you know, you should call yourself people who live in Ukraine and speak Russian.
But I can't uh, take you like, a-
accept you like Ukrainians but don't uh, who, who don't speak uh Ukrainian language.
It's, it's such a mm, controversial thing for me,
I- I- I just can't accept this.

Kalyna begins by describing a view very similar to that of Larysa – that 'being Ukrainian is speaking Ukrainian.' She then more directly states, however, that 'I can't understand uh, people who call themselves Russian-speaking Ukrainians,' therein positioning Ukrainians who speak Russian as unusual, unexpected and not the norm. However, what is interesting about this is that given Ukraine's linguistic history, it is actually the linguistic expectation that linguistic oppression via Russification would lead to language shift for many people, resulting in more speakers of Russian (Del'Gaudio, 2011). Additionally, increasing globalization in the world makes it more likely that people are moving across borders, and therefore more likely that Russian speakers would be living in Ukraine (whether Russian speakers due to recent relocation or past family heritage). Yet, there is an expectation in Kalyna's discourse that in order to be Ukrainian, you must have the Ukrainian language as your dominant language, such that this is the language people hear you speaking on the street or in the home.

As phrased by Kalyna, there are some Ukrainians who view Russian-dominant speaking Ukrainian people as 'people who live in Ukraine and speak Russian', i.e. not 'true' Ukrainians. This discursive distinction is also interesting – that living in a place is not enough to give a person access to the national identity of that place. Rather, language also becomes a key requirement for full access to the shared national identity.

Lesya (28 years old, from Western Ukraine, living in the United States) provides more insight into the dialogic nature of where this linguistic identity othering came from. At the time of this interview, Crimea was still officially part of Ukraine; it had not yet been annexed by Russia. Even since, many Ukrainians still refer to Crimea as part of Ukraine, not accepting Russia's illegal annexation of the territory.

Lesya: When you go to the Eastern or the Crimea,

um everybody sp- spoke Russian,

still speaks Russian in the East and in the Crimea,

and sometimes because I'm so used to speaking in Ukrainian when I'm back home,

I would speak Ukrainian to them.

They would look at me and answer rudely in Russian,

and you know, I felt kind of discriminated against for using the national language.

In this example, Lesya speaks in the present tense, 'when you go', which suggests that her experience is seen as a universal occurrence, existing outside of any specific timeframe, that it would be expected to happen at any point in time. In the line that follows, she also self-corrects from the past tense 'spoke' to the present tense 'still speaks' to again suspend time in her narrative. In Lesya's story, she went to the Crimean peninsula where she spoke the Ukrainian language to the people of Crimea, which is linguistically Russian dominant (see Chapter 1; Del' Gaudio, 2011).

Within Lesya's narrative, two major things are occurring. The first is that she is recalling a negative experience that impacted upon her own language ideologies and became part of the dialogic narrative upon which she draws when defending her right to use the Ukrainian language. The second thing that is happening in her narrative is that she is again drawing upon institutional symbolic capital to support her own position as a Ukrainian speaker and to 'other' the Russian speakers who reacted negatively towards her. She does this by describing their actions as 'rude' and by using words such as 'discriminated', while also reminding the listener that in legislation Ukrainian is the national language of Ukraine. Therefore, since Crimea was part of Ukraine at that time, there was an expectation that the people of Crimea would also use the Ukrainian language, or at least not react negatively towards someone else for doing so. Since the people of Crimea responded negatively towards a Ukrainian speaker (Lesya), they are then positioned by her as being in the wrong. This further reinforces the ideology that being Ukrainian means speaking Ukrainian.

Crimea and Eastern Ukraine (both Russian occupied areas during the war) were referenced many times throughout the interviews as examples of places that were in the wrong and not 'truly' Ukrainian because of their preference for the use of the Russian language. In a later part of Klara's interview, she brings up Eastern Ukraine as a counter example to the majority rest of Ukraine when it comes to language preference and use.

Corinne: Um, so, what do people in Ukraine think about the Ukrainian language?

Klara: ... Well, there are several opinions.
Erm... First of all...
not all of them speak Ukrainian.
Er, wh- the people who speak Ukrainian,
they respect this language,
and they... want it to be... more... involved,
and more used.
Erm, and many people who-don'- who doesn't speak,
they would like to speak better,
or- speak- or speak better Ukrainian, um...
Er, but I also... met... people,
mostly from Eastern region,
where the- again, war is,
who... who are not really willing to... learn... Ukrainian.
Er, but they also are not really willing to live in Ukraine.

It is first notable how in answering my question about thoughts on the Ukrainian language, Klara begins by setting up a dichotomy between people who speak Ukrainian and people who do not. Therefore, immediately it is implied that the use of the language is connected to attitudes towards the language. She then states that 'the people who speak Ukrainian, they respect this language.' Therefore, again, use is assumed to be tied to attitude, wherein all speakers of Ukrainian also respect Ukrainian. On the other side, Klara states that there are also people who do not speak the language, but here use is not directly tied to attitude. Rather, it is intention of use which is tied to attitude. For example, Klara specifies that there are many people who don't speak Ukrainian, but 'they would like to speak better.' This group goes without further comment. However, they are compared against the next group through the beginning conjunction 'but', which implies that the group who would like to speak better Ukrainian is also a positively positioned group because it is intent that matters.

The last group is described by Klara as including 'people, mostly from Eastern region' 'who are not really willing to... learn... Ukrainian.' Immediately, Klara has positioned this group in a more negative light due to their perceived unwillingness to learn the Ukrainian language. Klara also positions them negatively, while specifically mentioning that this is the war zone, without that actually being directly relevant to her point, therein showing that she is drawing upon the negative semantic connotations associated with the war zone. Finally, Klara connects this group's perceived unwillingness to learn Ukrainian to their status as 'others' (i.e. not 'true' Ukrainians) by saying, 'but they also are not really willing to live in Ukraine.' This last statement is a very powerful indicator of this group's outsider status, as through it they have been figuratively relocated outside of the ideological national border of Ukraine.

Focusing on the Individual

It is important to note that the ability and willingness to speak Ukrainian was not a requirement in the eyes of all of the interviewees. In fact, the majority of interviewees, no matter where they were from, stated that it was much more important that a person internally and consciously feels Ukrainian, no matter what language that person uses. While statements of language proficiency being equated with national identity proliferate ideological Discourses, there are many societies and cultures which do not feel that language proficiency is necessary to claim an in-group identity (e.g. Māori in New Zealand, cf. Ngaha, 2004). Therefore, it is not surprising to find many people, especially those who identify transnationally, focusing more on individual self-identification, regardless of language use or preference.

Lana (early 30s, from the Black Sea region of Ukraine, now living in New Zealand) is one such person who expresses this view, as shown in her interview excerpt:

Corinne: ((laughing)) Um, and,
so how do you identify yourself,
you said Ukrainian,
is that both nationally and ethnically?

Lana: ((sighs)) Er, I-w-...
yeah I think I:...
Mmm, ((smacks lips)) when I was living in Russia,
and you know when, I wasn't really thinking about like, well,
which- which culture I belong to,
because I think it's most...
recently when it was,
all that revolution took place and...
you really think that who you are and which side you support,
and... u:m, and I made a decision that I am more Ukrainian
because all-
I have like a lot of friends,
Russian- Russian guys,
but... um,
I found that,
it's something wrong there,
you know, when you're talking to people,
and you understand that you not really on the same wave?

Corinne: Yeah.

Lana: So,
and then when I met Ukrainians in New Zealand,
I understand that,
that's community I belong to actually,
((laughing)) so...
Yeah, so my: eth-
let's say, um, ethnitical,
identity happened,
really like in late twenties,
((laughing)) my late twenties.
((inhales)) Not like when I was a teenager.
Because I think at that time it wasn't really... like that...

critical to think,

are you Russian or are you,

Ukrainian?

But now I think it's- it's time to made-deci- er,

make a decision for yourself.

Lana begins approaching her answer to my question about self-identification by first telling a short narrative. This functions to give more experiential and embodied symbolic capital (Bourdieu, 1986; Meadows, 2009) to her claims, which is especially important in her construction of self as a transnational individual. An additional part of this is Lana's placement of herself as having lived in Russia, which positions her as being able to speak knowledgably not just about Ukraine (where she is originally from), but also about Russia, and the encompassing ideologies associated with each. She in part uses this experiential discourse to mitigate the next part of her narrative where she de-identifies with Russian culture: 'I made a decision that I am more Ukrainian' and that the more she socialized with Russian friends, the more she decided that she did not identify with Russian culture in the same way as them. Crucially, Lana also points to the events of Maidan and of the Ukrainian war as being her 'awakening' point to this new sense of self, wherein her Ukrainian identity came to the forefront.

Simultaneously, Lana then continues establishing her transnational identity by next bringing her story to New Zealand and talking about the Ukrainians she met in New Zealand. By focusing on her identity narrative of being Ukrainian while transporting across time and space to New Zealand, Lana is able to blur physical borders, which contributes further to the establishment of a transnational identity (cf. Piller & Takahashi, 2011). Furthermore, Lana's invocation of the Ukrainian community of New Zealand in itself is a transnational positioning, as the New Zealand Ukrainian community welcomes speakers of Russian, Ukrainian, English and those who feel some connection with Ukrainian culture regardless of their personal backgrounds. It is this transnational Ukrainian-New Zealander community to which Lana refers when she says, 'that's the community I belong to actually.'

At the end of Lana's narrative, she again stresses the importance of critically deciding on consciously claimed identities, no matter what those identities might be. This conscious claiming of identities dialogically echoes the claims of other young Ukrainians in this chapter about what they see to be the important emergence of conscious identification (cf. Braha, 2011). Lana further emphasizes this by saying, 'But now I think it's- it's time to... make a decision for yourself,' therein intertextually drawing also on the discourses of the Ukrainian war pushing young Ukrainians to renegotiate identities (Tsentr Doslidzhennya Suspil'stva,

April 2014). However, it is just as important to notice that throughout this discussion of self-identification, Lana never mentions language. In fact, Lana herself is a Russian-dominant speaker who is working on developing further Ukrainian language proficiency, along with several other languages. She identifies with the New Zealand Ukrainian community, which has accepted people from a wide range of national, cultural and linguistic backgrounds. Lana reflects these views in her own discussion of identity, explaining that for her, what is most important is consciously identifying with something/someone, regardless of specifics such as languages spoken.

Another interviewee from within the New Zealand Ukrainian community also expressed this same opinion. Denys (37 years old, from Central Ukraine, living in New Zealand) also regularly expressed his transnational identity throughout his interview. Affiliated with both the local Ukrainian and Russian communities in New Zealand, he connects these to the master narratives of conflict between Ukraine and Russia that are discussed internationally.

Corinne: How about between the communities themselves?
 The Ukrainian and Russian communities.
Denys: Ah the thing is that um
 so if- if- even if you take the people who identify themselves as Ukrainians,
 doesn't mean that they are in one community,
 and the same as about Russian community.
 We have a lot of Russian friends,
 they are don't-
 they don't- ah-
 so if we talk about the Russian community as a community,
 which was organized by the embassy,
 it's one group of people.
 I know another group of people who trying to not ah kind of touch-
 ah like trying to isola- isolate themselves from this group,
 ah and-
Corinne: Makes sense.
Denys: So especially at this moment,
 ah today when all this stuff happening in Ukraine and in Russia,
 ah ((4 seconds)),
 yeah so,
 and I have lots of friends who- who are natively Russian,

lots of friends here,

so it's- ah we communicate on a personal level,

ah doesn't mean that we communicate on a- ah community level.

Corinne: Yeah, yeah.

Denys: So it's- community's-

Ukrainian community is more community of friends than community of Ukraines,

ah therefore even on- ah before-

before Christmas we had this Christmas party in [city] centre,

lots of ah Russian friends were invited just to spend time with children,

so it doesn't really matter ah which community you belong to.

It's on a personal level.

In this excerpt, Denys begins his discussion of community by first establishing the complexity of identification and belonging. As he says, 'even if you take the people who identify themselves as Ukrainians, doesn't mean that they are in one community,' and he says it is the same for those who identify as Russian. In fact, Denys has drawn upon ideas that sociolinguists have long associated with communities of practice (CofP) – namely, that people belong to many different CofPs and interactionally highlight different aspects of their identities within any given context, which are often different for different CofPs (cf. Wenger, 1998). Denys also draws upon post-structuralist conceptions of identity, especially as multiple, fluid and dynamic (Bucholtz & Hall, 2005; Norton, 2013). By highlighting the negotiable aspects of individual identity, including the aspect of struggle associated with at times conflicting identities and ideologies (Norton, 2000), Denys is able to further focus on the dynamic nature of identity, which is especially highlighted within transnational communities, such as the Ukrainian and Russian communities of New Zealand.

Denys further emphasizes interpersonal identity, as opposed to monolithic conceptions of identity, similar to Lana's discussion in the previous example. As Denys says, 'Ukrainian community [in New Zealand] is more community of friends than community of Ukraines.' By making this distinction, Denys is specifically downplaying the importance of national identity in favor of interpersonal relationships and identities, which he further emphasizes with his summative statement: 'so it doesn't really matter ah which community you belong to. It's on a personal level.' Since Denys has emphasized the importance of interpersonal relationships, it also makes sense that he has not discussed any one language as being more important than another either. As further confirmed at other points with

72 Choosing a Mother Tongue

Denys, he does not see language use as connected with national identity. Rather, for Denys, as for many Ukrainians, identity is fluid, and as such, does important relational work with others, which is discussed further in Chapter 7.

Further Remarks

Beginning by revisiting the events of the Maidan protests and the Ukrainian war to date, this chapter then continued by connecting the war events to the period of time during which the participants for the main study were interviewed. While Chapter 2 introduced and discussed the participants of the pilot study in 2009, this chapter introduced the participants of the full study, who were interviewed throughout 2014 and 2015. The beginning of this chapter also included further background information about the study, such as who the participants are, why and how they were chosen, and the methods used in this study. A focus was particularly given to the choice of Interactional Sociolinguistics with a critical lens and exactly what this means.

The chapter then transitioned into a discussion of how the Ukrainian participants talk about the war. In particular, this chapter has focused on how Ukrainians discursively 'other' individuals and groups seen to be in ideological opposition to themselves. One such way this is done is by first of all specifically naming the recent events in Eastern Ukraine as a war. By naming events as a war, rather than as a conflict or as a crisis, responsibility is discursively placed upon an outside party attacking the region (in this case, that responsible party is Russia) (Pantti, 2016; Pavlyuk, 2015). Therefore, the terminology used is a powerful indicator of individuals' positioning and stance in regard to the events taking place (Ellis, 2006).

In further analyzing discursive othering, it was found that the events of the war have a clear disrupting effect upon interpersonal relationships and identity negotiation (Beliaeva & Seals, 2019). Border wars make the individuals affected question what they had previously assumed to be a fairly stable reality. In this case, participants questioned their previous assumption of commonality and shared history superseding difference. Rather, their focus fell to the chronotope of the war, which discursively and cognitively connected all Ukrainians and Russians due to a shared time-space longitudinal experience, regardless of when or where they currently were (Bakhtin, 1992 [1981]). It is this discursive connection with the chronotope of the war that enabled the Ukrainian participants to collectively share in the experience of being affected by it, even if they were currently living outside of the country itself (Liebscher & Dailey-O'Cain, 2013).

Additionally, participants discussed the idea of who had the right to call themselves Ukrainian. In these discourses, being Ukrainian was much more than where a person lives. Rather, it also involves an investment in and upholding of shared ideals (cf. Norton, 2000, 2013; Seals, 2013,

2017a, 2017b). Where these ideals were violated, the violators were discursively positioned as outsiders, no longer able to call themselves Ukrainian. Therefore, the shared experience of the war also had the effect of highlighting ideas of what it means to be Ukrainian. For some, what is means to be Ukrainian also includes speaking the Ukrainian language (cf. Osnach, 2015), and they drew upon intertextual references to institutional symbolic capital (such as state language status) to make this point. For others, being Ukrainian also means focusing on the individual and the embracing of transnational identities and experiences, for which participants usually drew upon narratives of personal experience, therein making use of embodied symbolic capital (Bourdieu, 1986; Meadows, 2009).

The responses from participants also highlight the important reminder that not everyone from the same region, from the same age group, now living in the same location, or even speaking the same language agrees on all aspects of the war in Ukraine. However, what many tend to do is to find ways to identify with those like them. Furthermore, some individuals further identify with those like them by highlighting the differences of those unlike them and then using these differences to 'other' the latter group (cf. Bucholtz, 1999; Seals, 2017b). This then makes it easier to position the other as automatically different and therefore easier to disagree with.

Finally, as discussed by Fialkova and Yelenevskaia (2016), it becomes easier for people to surround themselves with those like them nowadays with social media, such that people (including those within the diaspora) often see only a majority of like-minded views reflected back at them. This includes the type of information and news sources that are shared, therein influencing the development of opinions and Discourses (Fialkova & Yelenevskaia, 2016; Voolaid, 2013). This then takes us into Chapter 4, where the focus becomes how participants position these others whom they see as responsible for the war.

Notes

(1) Although 38 people took part in the interviews, not all of their interviews are represented in the current book, due to the necessity of keeping focus on a limited set of topics. That being said, no voices are silenced either. Their opinions and experiences are echoed in excerpts found throughout this book, just stated in a more illustrative way by other participants. Those interviewees who do not appear in the current book have still shown up in conference presentations and will continue to appear in future publications.
(2) Throughout Ruslana's interview, I was amazed at how composed and forgiving she was. Even though years of study and her planned future had just been lost, she was willing to forgive and move forward into the unknown. Her interview was a true example of the strength and positive outlook of the Ukrainian people, including those who took part in this project.

4 Who's Responsible? The Politics of Language

Metonymy and Russian Responsibility

In examining the discursive construction of national identity, De Cillia *et al.* (1999) find that one of the linguistic devices upon which people draw when focusing on an imagined national identity (rather than an individual) is that of metonymy. As they state, 'metonymies enable the speakers to dissolve individuals, and hence volitions and responsibilities, or to keep them in the semantic background' (De Cillia *et al.*, 1999: 165). Furthermore, Rattcliffe (2005) finds that this dissolving of individuals through metonymy is exactly how many people discursively construct the 'other' or out-group. Much of the discursive construction of allies and enemies that occurred in the interviews in fact drew upon metonymy. Rather than mentioning all of the politicians, policy makers, generals, etc. of (most frequently) the Russian Empire, participants usually referred to 'Russia'. As an alternative to 'Russia', interviewees also frequently referred to 'Putin' as a figurehead, using the current Russian president to represent political corruption and deviousness in Russia. Interestingly, in this creation of allies and enemies, while 'Russia' was used to refer to the many referenced political and military villains, 'Ukraine' was much more often used to refer to the citizens and general population of Ukraine.

An example of metonymy where Putin is named in place of all forces behind Russian aggression is given in the interview excerpt below. In this example, Lesya (28 years old, from Western Ukraine, living in the United States) discusses her feelings and frustrations about the Ukrainian war, including who she feels is responsible for the war.

Corinne: Um and so what are your feelings about the- the current war in Ukraine?

Lesya: Well ((laughter)) my feelings about the current war,
um I just really wish that Putin would ah disappear, you know,
because as soon as he- as long as he is in power,
Russia is going to back him up.

I mean his- his support is something ridiculous,

I don't know,

it's like ninety-nine percent or-

I don't know what it is,

but everyone is unanimous in supporting his actions,

and without Putin,

this war wouldn't have happened.

Ah yeah, so I'm extremely frustrated,

and when everything just started I was angry.

I was- you know,

so many-

like it's kind of hard to believe that in the twenty-first century,

and ah this- this could happen, you know?

While Putin is arguably acting in a very powerful position in the Russian government, it is important to keep in mind that a single individual cannot enact a war without others willing to follow orders. However, as Putin is in the top leadership role and has never shied away from claiming responsibility for the political decisions that are made, he has come to symbolize all actions taking place on behalf of the Russian government. In this way, Putin's name functions as a metonym for the Russian government and underlying political bodies. Therefore, when Lesya says, 'I just really wish that Putin would ah disappear, you know,' she may in part mean the actual man himself, but she is also referring more broadly to political corruption and scandal that has been associated with his regime. Similarly, when Lesya says, 'as long as he is in power, Russia is going to back him up,' she is referring to the general population of Russia, not of the land itself. In this instance, the use of 'Russia' in this way means Russian citizens, including politically and military affiliated individuals, as they are from where Putin's power comes.

By using metonymy in this way, it is also easier (psychologically and linguistically) to relegate a category of people to the other who is also the aggressor (cf. Rattcliffe, 2005). Therefore, 'Russia' and 'Putin' become seen as responsible for the Ukrainian war, instead of the individual citizens in Russia who support the Russian government's actions, and the political and governing bodies who pass orders and laws allowing for the resources which are used in aggressive acts against the Ukrainian people. This use of metonymy is not uncommon in people's discourse. This especially makes sense in highly straining and emotional events where cognitive function may already be strained (Beliaeva & Seals, 2019). Additionally, as narratives are told again and again, they are simplified through common literary devices such as metonymy, which allows a bundle of intertextual information to be encoded within a single word. This is precisely what makes them such a popular device for media outlets, which further spread these metonymous discourses (Catalano & Waugh, 2013). Thus, all of the events, feelings and prior and anticipated discourses associated with the Ukrainian war are compressed, and responsibility is assigned to metonymous actors.

Another function of metonymy in the interviews is that it allows emotions and human characteristics to be drawn upon without naming any specific names. In this way, collective identities are able to be formed and referenced, as demonstrated in an excerpt from an interview with Lilia (27 years old, from Western Ukraine, living in Canada).

Lilia: Er... I hope that the war ends tomorrow,
and everyone goes home and continues with their peaceful life,
but... that's ((laughing))- that's not happening.
I- I think the war will... continue on,
because Putin does have a lot of people he doesn't care about,
and can send to get killed in Ukraine.
And... No one- no other... s- er... world leader... seems to understand the threat,
and, er... willing to... ((smacks lips)) openly... er... step into this... conflict.
So Ukraine is basically there on- on- on its own,
and... will have to... carry on,
I don't think Putin with- just withdraw and...
stop... doing what he's- he's been doing.
So it's totally up to... Ukrainian leaders, and... Ukrainian people to just,
((exhale)) carry on, and... show that, er...
they can still prevail.

The story painted by Lilia is a bleak one, but it is also a view held by many Ukrainians, including the majority who took part in this project. As in Lesya's excerpt, Lilia uses Putin's name both to symbolize the man and all of the powers that he directly and indirectly controls. Lilia positions Putin as a cold, calculating man, which is indeed how he is portrayed throughout much international media, therein dialogically reflecting the international news outlets. This positioning is furthered when Lilia discursively removes agency from the soldiers, saying instead that they will be sent to be killed in Ukraine. This reassignment of agency also discursively indicates that Lilia's anger is with the political and governing bodies of Russia, not with the Russian people themselves.

In fact, Lilia's frustration appears to be directed to world political bodies, in general, which was again reflected in many of the interviews for this project. As Lilia says, no other leader seems willing to help, 'So Ukraine is basically there on- on its own.' This frustrated statement also dialogically echoes news reports of the many sanctions that other countries imposed upon Russia for the Ukrainian war, which seemed often to have little to no effect (e.g. Christie, 2015; Rettman, 2016; RT Staff, 2016). The inability or unwillingness of international political bodies to intervene in more serious ways has been a source of frustration and despair for many Ukrainian people, which is dialogically echoed throughout Lilia's statements.

Finally, when Lilia refers to 'Ukraine' when she says 'Ukraine is basically there on- on its own', she is referring to the Ukrainian politicians as well as the Ukrainian people, especially the Ukrainian citizens who are experiencing the brunt of Russian aggression. This is evidenced by Lilia's near-repetition of this statement shortly after, during which time she also mentions Ukrainian politicians and the general population individually: 'So it's totally up to… Ukrainian leaders, and… Ukrainian people to just, carry on, and… show that, er… they can still prevail.' Lilia's final statement, of prevailing, also clearly discursively marks Ukrainians as victims and Russians as aggressors in the war, therein assigning responsibility for the war once again to Russia.

Other literary devices were also found to be helpful to the interviewees in discussing their feelings and perceptions of the war, especially when it came to who is responsible. In the next example, married couple Lev (late 30s, from Eastern Ukraine, living in New Zealand) and Raisa (late 30s, from Eastern Ukraine, living in New Zealand) make particular use of personification in explaining their views of what Ukraine is experiencing during the war.

Corinne: What do you guys… think will happen,
and what do you hope will happen?
Lev: What I- I'm afraid… will happen… Mmm… Is…
well, u- I-have-
I've read that… ((smacks lips))
one of… goals of Russia in this conflict is…
just make… permanent wound on the b-body of Ukraine.
So Ukraine will suffer f-from this constant conflict…
and will not raise,
will not hit… even… average country…

	will be just... below everything ((inhales)).
	And that's... what... I am thinking wi- really will happen because...
	they have resources to- to make this happen.
	Er... and Ukraine from its side cannot fight... er, in X war...
	Because... we're smaller country,
	we cannot fight... on political... arena... really...
	We tried with... er... European Union, USA...
	And in-
Raisa:	They're just concerned.
Lev:	They're concerned.
Raisa:	((laughter)) ((inhales)) And it helps.
Lev:	And then again concerned.
Raisa:	Mm-hmm... Yeah,
	and they warn... again... that it will be sanctions... against-
Lev:	Yeah, they will talk about sanctions again.
Raisa:	[Mm-hmm.]
Lev:	[They will talk.]
Raisa:	And again concerned.
Lev:	S-so... we, erm... well,
	we as Ukraine, er,
	we are alone.

When Lev first begins explaining his views of what might happen in the Ukrainian war, he first mentions having read the forthcoming information (assumedly from news outlets). Mentioning this before telling his opinion serves two purposes. First, it allows him to draw upon institutional symbolic capital in addition to embodied symbolic capital, therein adding more perceived weight to his opinion (Meadows, 2009; Seals, 2011). Second, this allows Lev to prime his listeners to dialogically connect with the many recent stories of Russian aggression against Ukraine, including the many internationally illegal acts that had been reported at that time. Lev then makes use of personification to give very strong visual weight to his opinion, saying that Russia's goal is to make a 'permanent wound on the b-body of Ukraine. So Ukraine will suffer f-from this constant conflict... and will not raise.' This personification brings to mind a person who has been beaten to the point that they can no longer stand, a gruesome and powerful image of violence. Lev then continues by explaining that because Ukraine is a smaller country, it cannot fight on equal terms, therein further personifying Ukraine as a smaller person who is unable to fight back as they are beaten.

After this powerful imagery, Lev begins to explain that Ukraine has asked for help from larger political bodies such as the European Union and the United States. Raisa then joins Lev in this description, co-constructing this expression of frustration and hopelessness. Double-voicing the previous statements made by the aforementioned larger countries, Raisa says, 'They're just concerned,' which Lev repeats. They in fact repeat the statement 'and again concerned' four times within ten lines, showing through repetition the perceived pointlessness and insincerity of these countries' statements of concern after so long without further actions. Lev and Raisa cement this point by then stating once again, 'we as Ukraine, er, we are alone,' reflecting an in-group sentiment shared among many who identify as Ukrainian and who are personally invested in Ukrainian affairs.

The Government but Not Necessarily the People

Other interviewees were careful to specify that not all Russian people support the war in Ukraine. More specifically, many of the participants attributed responsibility directly to those in the Russian government and were careful to distinguish between the Russian people following the Russian government's influence and the Russian people who are not so swayed. An example of this comes from Anatoliy (mid-20s, from Central Ukraine, living in New Zealand).

Corinne: What... er, are your feelings about the current... political situation in Ukraine?

Anatoliy: Well, it is actually quite worrying... erm... unfortunately,
quite disturbing...
Er, of my first thought was about my parents.
Er, luckily, they are in central part,
and the actual... conflict, the war, hasn't, er, reached, er, that part.
And hopefully it will not, er...
unless people... stop doing what they are doing, erm...
And, er... I definitely... disapprove... erm...
and probably condemn... er, this... this propaganda,
which is... er, coming from Russia,
and which is orchestrated by Putin...
Erm... I do... believe that...
this is, erm... human... erm... specificity... er,
or this is how brain works,

that we... do deny things, er, which are uncomfortable...
but do not... cause us big problems... now...
So we'll procrastinate until it gets really really bad,
and then we wake up and open our eyes.
So I think this is what's happening with many Russians...
Erm, I do know that many Russians do not support war,
and they... do not... er... approve what-Russia-is-, er,
what Putin is doing.
Er... and, erm, I noticed... a very interesting... division... er...
in Russia...
Although, I think this is probably... different question,
er, so, yeah,
your question was about... er, what I feel about it.
Yeah, so, yeah, I- I- I- I- I'm-... I don't feel... comfortable about it,
erm... and I do hope that it would- er... will stop.
Er, I'm happy to see that international community... er, does support Ukraine,
and they were not fooled...
((sighs)) erm... er, by Putin...
Although, the fact that, er,
there was... no official... statement from,
actually... anyone, really,
saying that,
yes, there are Russian soldiers... fighting in Ukraine...
I do s-... see that people are kind of trying to use it as an excuse...
Er... because, erm... If there is no... evidence that there-
there are Russian... soldiers... fighting against Ukraine,
there is no war... between Russia and Ukraine.
Erm... So it is kind of still... as if... internal conflict.
They kind of understand,
and they say that it's not really internal conflict,
but nobody says in black and white that Russia is fighting with Ukraine.

When Anatoliy begins his story, he first connects discursively across time and space to the Ukrainian war chronotope through his parents who still currently live in Ukraine. In discussing their location and experiences with recent events, Anatoliy self-corrects from using the term 'conflict' to the term 'war'. As previously mentioned in Chapter 3, the terminology used carries much semantic weight in regard to assigned responsibility (Pavlyuk, 2015). By self-correcting from 'conflict' to 'war', Anatoliy is emphasizing Russia's responsibility in the aggressive events that led to the war.

Anatoliy further emphasizes Russia's role as the aggressor in the war by stating his clear disapproval of actions orchestrated by the government and carried out by the Russian military: 'And, er… I definitely… disapprove… erm… and probably condemn… er, this… this propaganda, which is… er, coming from Russia, and which is orchestrated by Putin…' Anatoliy is careful with his word choice, saying that he definitely disapproves of the Russian propaganda related to the war. He also says that he 'probably' condemns it, which indicates Anatoliy's awareness of the strength of a word such as 'condemn', and his careful use in applying it. Furthermore, by mentioning Russian propaganda in particular, Anatoliy is drawing intertextually upon the type of messages that have been espoused by some major Russian media outlets, referring to Ukrainians as fascists and neo-Nazis (cf. Chalupa, 2014; Walker, 2014), similar to what Gleb discussed in Chapter 3. By making this intertextual connection, Anatoliy is able to dialogically respond to these claims, which he has heard repeated many times by some Russian-identifying people, especially on social media outlets. Noticeable, however, is that Anatoliy does not condemn the Russian people repeating the statements from this propaganda. Rather, he blames Putin and the government officials working under him who have approved the printing of this negative propaganda towards Ukraine, once again indicating that it is the Russian government, not the ordinary Russian people, who are viewed as responsible for the Ukrainian war.

This point is further elaborated on in the next part of Anatoliy's discourse when he says that he believes 'this is how brain works, that we… do deny things, er, which are uncomfortable… but do not… cause us big problems… now… So we'll procrastinate until it gets really really bad, and then we wake up and open our eyes.' Through this more psychologically focused discourse, Anatoliy effectively absolves the general Russian people from any conscious responsibility in supporting Russian aggression in the Ukrainian war. Rather, Anatoliy says that this is an aspect of all human nature. In so saying, Anatoliy also creates more discursive bridges between the everyday Russian people and other general populations broadly, including Ukrainians. This is further evidenced by Anatoliy's use of 'we' and 'us' in his discussion of human nature.

Throughout the next part of Anatoliy's discourse, he is careful to continue avoiding a general lumping of all Russian people together. Rather, he talks about those who support the war and those who do not: 'Erm, I do know that many Russians do not support war, and they... do not... er... approve what-Russia-is-, er, what Putin is doing. Er... and, erm, I noticed... a very interesting... division... er... in Russia...' In this excerpt, Anatoliy is careful to talk about 'many Russians' instead of Russians in general. He talks about the many who do not support the war, as well as a second group of many for whom 'this is what's happening'. That is, the second group who support the war are not directly blamed by Anatoliy; rather, he has already attributed responsibility for their position in the war to the propaganda created by the Russian government. Therefore, it is once again the Russian government, not the people themselves who bear primary responsibility for the war.

Notably, Anatoliy's discourse again shifts to discuss the perceived lack of genuine effort by other countries to assist Ukraine, similar to the discussion had by Lev and Raisa. It is interesting to note that like Lev and Raisa, Anatoliy is careful in how he talks about other world powers, indirectly criticizing these countries' lack of sincere assistance. Anatoliy begins by saying what he is thankful for, therein positioning these other world powers in a positive light in the beginning. However, Anatoliy then subtly shifts position, stating, 'Although, the fact that, er, there was... no official... statement from, actually... anyone, really, saying that, yes, there are Russian soldiers... fighting in Ukraine...' Beginning with the contrastive discourse marker 'although', Anatoliy has interrupted the expected positive narrative continuation to offer instead a subtle criticism of these countries for not doing in fact what one would expect, which includes an official statement acknowledging Russian soldiers' presence in Ukraine. This statement by Anatoliy intertextually draws upon the many stories from world news at that time that carefully avoided ever directly stating that Russia had broken international law, something heavily criticized by many Ukrainians.

Anatoliy further presents his mitigated criticism by first not pointing to any specific countries, instead using the general term 'people', and then explaining why this lack of sincere effort on the part of other countries is actually hurting Ukraine: 'I do s-... see that people are kind of trying to use it as an excuse... Er... because, erm... If there is no... evidence that there- there are Russian... soldiers... fighting against Ukraine, there is no war... between Russia and Ukraine. Erm... So it is kind of still... as if... internal conflict.' As Anatoliy explains, because other countries have purposefully avoided acknowledging Russia's breach of international law and militant occupation of Ukrainian territory, there is no official acknowledgment that a war is taking place. This can be understood as a strategic move on the part of these countries because they are thus avoiding sending their own resources to aid in the war effort, and they are also avoiding directly taking one side or another in a highly explosive situation. However, as Anatoliy points out, through this avoidance, these countries are also participating in a construction of the war as an internal war for

Ukraine, which it is not. As previously mentioned, if it is seen as an internal war, then it is also seen as Ukraine's problem, and therefore the other countries are not required to respond. Yet, it is not an internal war, and the lack of acknowledgment of this by other countries denies Ukraine of needed support as it is engaged in war with Russia.

This last point is reinforced once again by Anatoliy through repetition of ideas, when he says: 'They kind of understand, and they say that it's not really internal conflict, but nobody says in black and white that Russia is fighting with Ukraine.' Here Antoliy explains that the representatives from these other world powers understand the effect their avoidance is having, though he again mitigates his criticism of these foreign powers by using 'kind of'. He then once again begins by giving some positive credit to these country representatives when he explains that they acknowledge it is not an internal conflict for Ukraine. However, he then once more subtly criticizes these countries' avoidance by beginning with 'but' and then explaining that still none of these country representatives are directly making the statement that Russia is attacking Ukraine, therein allowing the unsaid to be further avoided in discourse and in practice.

For some of the interviewees, the focus of responsibility for the war rests solely with government, whether this be only the Russian government or whether it also include the Ukrainian government. For Kalyna (37 years old, from Western Ukraine, still living in Ukraine), blame for the Ukrainian war also sits with the Ukrainian government. Therefore, responsibility for the war is still outward looking, but in a different way. For her, those in the Ukrainian government who have been involved in the war are not of the people and are therefore part of 'them' and not part of 'us' (cf. Csernicskó, 2017; Fligstein, 2008; Tsentr Doslidzhennya Suspil'stva, April 2014; Wodak & Boukala, 2015).

Corinne: Um, so- so what,
uh y- you've- you told me some,
some about the current uh war
and what are your feelings about um everything that's happening right now?
Um, and how closely do you follow it every day?

Kalyna: Well.
The situation in Ukraine is very dramatic.
Because we have not only external um, uh, enemy
like uh Putin and uh uh this Russia pr- Russian propaganda.
We have all uh even uh very uh strong uh internal uh enemies.
Like um uh, some officials who are- uh who are paid by Kremlin.
They are uh officials in all the branches,

like in police, in army, in uh government,
so they uh do their best to to spoil everything,
to stop some uh good initiatives
to stop um, mm uh different help for Ukrainian army.
So, we have to fight uh to the, to in- in the two directions.
S- well, I don't know when, when will it fi- ((exhales)) stop.
And some people say that it could be a big and uh massive war and everything is only uh coming.
Um, another people say that everything uh will uh end
uh there on Donbas,
and nobody's uh planning to co- to come here.
Well you know,
When- when you fight uh against uh ill uh person,
uh, like Putin you-
you cannot predict what- what is in his head.
We- we can't uh know w- what's there.
Well, we's- we are concentrated in uh daily needs,
and we- we do our best to- to- to- to make something
to help to keep situations- situation
and I have an idea (xx) will be there.

Kalyna begins by describing the situation in Ukraine as 'very dramatic', therein positioning events as already more intense than would be expected. She then goes on to explain that the reason events are dramatic is 'Because we have not only external um, uh, enemy like uh Putin and uh uh this Russia pr- Russian propaganda. We have all uh even uh very uh strong uh internal uh enemies. Like um uh, some officials who are- uh who are paid by Kremlin.' Similar to Anatoliy, Kalyna also specifically points out Russian propaganda and positions it as creating a problem by further contributing to the Ukrainian war. In fact, she mentions Russian propaganda alongside Putin, therein discursively drawing comparisons between them and drawing upon intertextual references to Putin and his administration's role in the war, as well as the role of the Russian propaganda of which Putin's government has approved. Kalyna then continues by saying that there are also internal enemies, which she describes as 'very strong', therein positioning them as powerful and difficult to remove. She provides an example in the form of some Ukrainian officials who are paid by the Kremlin, meaning through metonymy that these officials are paid by the Russian government. Kalyna has thus detailed an indeed distressing situation, where top members of the Russian government have paid powerful members of the Ukrainian government to aid Russia in disrupting Ukraine.

Kalyna then continues, providing more details as to who these powerful officials are: 'They are uh officials in all the branches, like in police, in army, in uh government.' The branches that Kalyna names include those known for carrying power and having the ability to carry out aggressive acts when ordered to do so, such as the police and army, as well as those who do the ordering in the government. Kalyna explains that these officials are paid to attempt to stop any initiatives that would help the Ukrainian army, which she implies includes actions such as fighting against Russian aggressors in the war zone. By not fully stating this, Kalyna is expecting that I will fill in the gaps by drawing upon the intertextual threads that link her meaning to the many narratives existing about corrupt individuals interfering in Ukraine's ability to fight in the war zone (with which I was in fact familiar). Kalyna then emphasizes again the exhaustive, dramatic nature of this two-way internal/external fight, saying, 'So, we have to fight uh to the, to in- in the two directions. S- well, I don't know when, when will it fi- stop.'

Kalyna next draws dialogically upon Discourses that were (and still are) circulating among the Ukrainian people. She says, 'And some people say that it could be a big and uh massive war and everything is only uh coming. Um, another people say that everything uh will uh end uh there on Donbas, and nobody's uh planning to co- to come here.' Drawing dialogically upon the unknown mass voices of 'some people', Kalyna relates one view that is that the war is only beginning and that it will get much larger, which also dialogically reflects many past Discourses throughout the centuries of wars spreading suddenly and unexpectedly, something that the Ukrainian people are familiar with from the Soviet era. She also dialogically expresses a second view that the war will not progress beyond the war zone, which has centered in the region of Donbas in Eastern Ukraine. Notably, Kalyna does not present a third view of Russia withdrawing or of international allies stepping in, as neither one of these are major Discourses in Ukraine, the hope of each of these having ended for most Ukrainians prior to Kalyna's interview (Russian occupation of Donbas had been going for six months by this point). It is still impossible to say what the outcome will be at the writing of this book; even though Kalyna's interview took place several years ago, the Ukrainian war is still ongoing.

The final part of Kalyna's excerpt again mentions Putin, both as the individual and as metonymy for the Russian government and officials operating alongside him. As she says, 'When- when you fight uh against uh ill uh person, uh, like Putin you- you cannot predict what- what is in his head. We- we can't uh know w- what's there.' By mentioning mental illness, Kalyna is drawing upon stigmatizing Discourses of people with mental illness as unpredictable to position Putin as such. Additionally, she is dialogically drawing upon discourses among some Ukrainian people and within some Ukrainian news outlets speculating as to whether or not Putin is ill, which at times has included mental illness.[1] Once again, though, Putin is also named as a metonym for the Russian government and officials condoning the Russian war, as a single man would not be able to fight against the Ukrainian army alone. In both meanings, Kalyna is pointing to the government, and not the general population, as being responsible for the Ukrainian war.

The General Population as Responsible

While most of the participants named various governments as responsible for the Ukrainian war, some of the participants specifically pointed to individuals from outside of the government as retaining responsibility for the events of the war. One such case can be found in an excerpt from the interview with Lana (early 30s, from the Black Sea region of Ukraine, now living in New Zealand). In this excerpt, Lana begins by immediately focusing generally on people and more or less maintains this focus while including a discussion of larger nation-states.

Corinne: Yeah.
And, what are your feelings about, um,
what's going on with the war in Ukraine right now in general?
Lana: U:m, ((smacks lips))
I- I have really-
really big regret that the best, erm,
((smacks lips)) the best men of Ukraine,
they're just dying in that,
stupid war? ((sighs))
And, um, so,
and Ukraine just losing the chance to change,
or to become this, um,
swapping to Eu- to European, u:m, values,
to European, erm, w- way of life
and they're just losing their, erm,
((smacks)) all efforts,
just, like you know
just dying,
for nothing?
And, er,

and I mean like from,
let's say like, er,
Russians,
they send not the best people,
they send,
like prisoners,
like former prisoners or,
people who we:re, like, with-
have some, erm,
((smacks lips)) problems with law?
They just give them guns and illegally transfer them to Ukrainian territory and say
'Okay, you can do whatever you want?'
A:nd um, and all those people who:,
like poor- poorly educated, or,
have, er, have no values of any other life,
they just kill for nothing.
They don't have eh
it's like, they-
I- I'm- I'm sure that they don't want, like, don't want to,
bring freedom or bring Russia to: this Donbas?
But just erm,
they- they just like,
they just like to: have a power,
to have a gun in their heads and-, hands and
d- do the robbery and, mmm,
ch- took whatever they like, and,
I know that some- some families who: erm run from Donetsk?
and the:y, mm,
all their belongings were taken.
So, th- they left their flats?
And their flat now robbed?
And, th- and those, they-
they took whatever they want,
like TV,

> so any, like, so, it's-
>
> it's not really like, for something good,
>
> they're not fighting for something good,
>
> for bringing something good,
>
> but just for dest- for destroying.

When I asked Lana to talk about her feelings relating to the Ukrainian war, she begins by talking about the individual Ukrainians who are fighting with the military in the war. Lana calls these Ukrainian soldiers 'the best men of Ukraine', positioning them positively and in fact valorizing them. She then addresses what she perceives to be the futility of the war, saying that these soldiers are 'just dying' in the war, which she calls a 'stupid war'. By including 'just' and 'stupid', Lana clearly positions herself as against the war, with the war being positioned as a pointless event.

Lana then increases the stakes of what is being lost, bringing the discussion to a national level that affects all Ukrainians. By saying that Ukraine is 'losing the chance to change', Lana dialogically draws upon the Discourses of EuroMaidan which largely focused on Ukraine entering the European Union as a strategic move to embrace Western European values and ideologies and to further separate from Russia. She even connects with these Discourses at a more direct level by mentioning 'swapping' to European values and way of life, meaning moving from a more Russian-aligned position to a more Western European-aligned position. When Lana then references 'all the efforts', she is intertextually referencing the many years that Ukraine had spent working with the European Union since 2008 in an attempt to draft an agreement by which Ukraine could become part of the European Union (Ukrainian Independent Information Agency, 2008). Lana then once more comments on the futility of the war, expressing that all of these efforts will be lost 'for nothing', showing her clear positioning against the war.

Following this discussion of what is at stake, Lana then returns to a focus on the individuals involved in the war, saying that 'Russians, they send not the best people.' By 'Russians', Lana is clearly referring to the Russian government officials, who she says are not sending the 'best people', referring to the soldiers being sent to fight in the war zone. Interestingly, in saying that the government is 'sending' these individuals, and not that the individuals are going themselves, Lana is also very much holding the Russian government responsible for Russian soldiers going to the war zone. Lana then continues with a lengthy description of the type of people she believes are going to fight, a description that is very similar to that given by Larysa in Chapter 3, including a lack of education, low socioeconomic status and a penchant for violence, including robbery and a fondness of weapons. This repeated description shows that this narrative of Russian villains has become a master narrative in discussions of the Ukrainian war, which is easily intertextually drawn upon by Ukrainians who are against the war. In addition to this description of the Russian soldiers allowing Lana to easily other these individuals, by having this description follow the valorized Ukrainian soldiers, Lana creates a clear divide between them. Furthermore, this divide, focused on the soldiers themselves, allows Lana to place more direct blame for the violence occurring on the individual Russians fighting in the war zone. Lana has described their perceived undesirable qualities in detail, thus placing much importance on identifying them as the responsible parties.

To further emphasize Lana's villainy of the Russian soldiers, she then recounts a short story of Ukrainian families who lived in Donbas (the war zone), fled when the fighting started, and were robbed by the Russian soldiers. Interestingly, this story is a general recounting, again dialogically drawing upon stories that Lana has likely heard from a number of sources: 'I know that some- some families who: erm run from Donetsk'. However, drawing upon these events in a narrative format brings more voices and experiences directly into Lana's argument, therein allowing her to draw upon embodied symbolic capital, even if not hers, in order to further strengthen her argument for her audience. This narrative of delinquent villains stealing from defenseless Ukrainian citizens who must flee also serves the purpose of further placing full responsibility for the Ukrainian war on the Russian individuals who are fighting in the war zone.

All as Responsible

Finally, there was another, yet much less prominent, position taken by some of the participants when discussing responsibility for the Ukrainian war. For some of the participants, both Russians and Ukrainians are responsible for the war. This responsibility includes not just the Russian and Ukrainian governments, but also the Russian and Ukrainian people. Klara (30 years old, from Central Ukraine, still living in Ukraine) was one of the people who held this view, as expressed in her interview excerpt.

Corinne: Thinking about, um, the war that's currently happening in Ukraine,
um, how closely do you follow the situation,
and what are your feelings about it?
Klara: ... Well... I'm trying to...
all the time... stay... er, ne-n- loyal,
or neutral, or-
and just see people... behind... the countries.
Because... ((sighs))

I actually was thinking about it a lot.
What we are blaming Russians for, is… basically… following- for-following the… propaganda,
that they hear on the TV,
and losing their… their people's values.
They- some of them are, er…
starting to… er,
to be glad or happy when… bad things happen to Ukraine.
Some of them are actually-
have so much anger that they are willing to go and fight against Ukrainians with… with their guns.
And even those who are not doing either one,
they still… already building some borders in their… themselves,
in- in- like, in their,
I would say… soul, if-you-can-s- if- if we can talk about it.
And… I'm just afraid to … ph… to… become the same,
and start being happy when something bad happens in Russia.
Because no one in-, n- no one…
It-will- it will not… be better for anyone, if- if people are hurted- ar- are hurt.
But… Well… I- it is hard to- s- to stay neutral in this situation,
we- do- I do feel like…
there is aggression against… my country,
and… people who are actually my friends, er,
or some people who are- I just n- hardly know, but I…
But these are pe- these people who I actually know…
have to- to fight, and… and possibly die… for-
I… really don't understand for which reason.
Why this is happening in twenty-first century,
li- it just doesn't feel- s-seem to… to… to be possible in twenty-first century.
There is a lot of aggression… er, in the society,
and it's… obvious, for obvious reasons,
but definitely Ukraine is growing up.
The soc- Ukrainian society is growing up,
there- is- a- there are volunteers…

> They are helping a lot,
> there are volunteers to actually fight.
> There are... er, there is a lot... of discussion going on,
> and the society is becoming... more grown-up,
> in terms of... f-...
> in terms of, first of all, defining ourselves as Ukrainians.
> Not... former Soviet-Unions-ners,
> not... Russian friends, or not friends,
> but actually Ukrainians who have their own path.
> And... we finally,
> we-... Ukraine...
> wanted to have good relationships in- with Russia for so long...
> And... w- were- w-was willing to give up... n-
> little and big things to stay friends...
> is finally willing to- to not stay friends and not give up anything,
> because- because the... stocks... are... our lives already.
> You can't give up your life to stay friends.

Corinne: Yeah. And... do you think that- that that's, um, an important step that Ukraine has made?

Klara: Yes.
> I- We actually- we were forced to make this step.
> Maybe we would never had courage to make it ourselves.
> But... we were helped,
> and we are making it.

Klara's position on who is responsible, likely stems from her own self-positioning in regard to the war, evidenced when she says, '... Well... I'm trying to... all the time... stay... er, ne-n- loyal, or neutral, or- and just see people... behind... the countries.' Interestingly, Klara first says 'loyal' before she self-corrects to 'neutral', which are two seemingly opposing terms in political discourse, as 'loyal' implies clearly taking one side over another. However, Klara then continues in her discussion of remaining neutral, saying that for her this means focusing on individual people and not on monolithic nation-states. Before beginning to explain further what she means, Klara first states, 'I actually was thinking about it a lot.' This positions Klara as having spent time giving considerable thought to her opinion, therein giving it more symbolic weight than an opinion which is thought to be spontaneous. This discursive positioning further foreshadows Klara's presentation of an idea that may be controversial for some.

In further setting up the presentation of her own opinion, Klara first dialogically draws upon more frequent discourses among Ukrainian identifying people: 'What we are blaming Russians for, is… basically… following- for- following the… propaganda, that they hear on the TV, and losing their… their people's values.' In fact, this statement clearly echoes the opinions given by several other interviewees earlier in this chapter. However, Klara positions herself as still one of them, not against them, by referring to 'we' and including herself in these discourses of blame, thus not absolving herself of any blame either. She then explains that some Russians are fighting in the war, due to 'so much anger' within themselves, therein positioning these Russian individuals as acting reactively, not without personal reason. This reactiveness further implies that something has happened to cause this anger, which differs from other Discourses of the Russian soldiers being pure villains (see earlier in this chapter and Chapter 3). In this statement, Klara is dialogically drawing upon these Discourses and subtly disagreeing with them.

After mentioning some Russian individuals who are happy about the war and others who are willing to fight in the war, Klara then says, 'And even those who are not doing either one, they still… already building some borders in their… themselves, in- in- like, in their, I would say… soul, if-you-can-s- if- if- if we can talk about it.' This comment is notable for several reasons. The first is because Klara is making allowances for Russian individuals who are neither happy about the war nor wanting to fight, which is an allowance not made by many of the Ukrainian interviewees. The second is that Klara reflects on the effect that the war is having for Russian people, which is similar to that which is happening for Ukrainian people. The comment about building borders within themselves is a very insightful, metacognitive comment, which also draws more commonalities between the Ukrainian and Russian experiences of the effects of the war. Third, Klara mentions the soul and then says 'if we can talk about it', which dialogically echoes the history of the Soviet Union, during which time religious talk, including discussion of concepts such as the soul, were not allowed and were even dangerous (cf. Hroch, 1999). This past history has strong echoes throughout former Soviet countries, with some people still very uncomfortable talking about anything viewed as religious. By commenting upon the allowance of such a topic, Klara is dialogically drawing upon these past experiences and still present discourses, therein merging the past shared Soviet history with the present Ukrainian and Russian fighting.

Klara further draws connections between the Ukrainian and Russian experiences by saying, 'And… I'm just afraid to … ph… to… become the same, and start being happy when something bad happens in Russia. Because no one in-, n- no one… It-will- it will not… be better for anyone, if- if people are hurted- ar- are hurt.' The negative views that she mentions being expressed by some Russians, such as joy at seeing Ukrainians hurt, are no longer something only possible in the 'other'. Rather, Klara says that she is afraid of the possibility of feeling the same way, thus implying that this is something that anyone could experience, including herself, regardless of her identity as a Ukrainian. She also says that the violence does not benefit anyone, which reinforces her neutral position, while drawing upon and negating Discourses of retaliation.

While attempting to remain neutral in her views, Klara explains why this is still something that she finds difficult to do: 'we- do- I do feel like… there is aggression against… my country, and… people who are actually my friends, er, or some people who are- I just n- hardly know, but I… But these are pe- these people who I actually know… have to- to fight, and… and possibly die… for- I… really don't understand for which reason.' Klara references Russian aggression against Ukraine, calling the latter 'my country', therein showing her allegiance to Ukraine and clear self-positioning as Ukrainian. This statement also serves to place primary responsibility for the war on Russia as the aggressor. She then further elaborates on the struggle she feels by drawing upon embodied symbolic capital to explain how friends of hers are dying in the war. She amends this to include other people who she does not personally know, emphasizing how many Ukrainians are dying in the war. However, she then returns to a focus on people who she personally knows, therein reinstating her embodied symbolic capital and personal losses in the war. Like Lana, Klara emphasizes the futility of the war when she says that there appears to be no particular reason for the death of her friends. Klara further emphasizes her feelings about the senselessness of the war by saying that she does not understand how this could happen in the twenty-first century – a statement which intertextually references historical references to wars in 'less sophisticated' times, as well as positioning modern Ukrainian and Russian societies as contexts that should be beyond such wars.

While this previous part of Klara's discourse emphasizes Russian responsibility for the war, she does not renege on her previous sentiment of neutrality. Klara's next statement assigns responsibility once again also to Ukraine: 'There is a lot of aggression… er, in the society, and it's… obvious, for obvious reasons, but definitely Ukraine is growing up.' In this statement, Klara refers to aggression in Ukrainian society, intertextually referencing the Ukrainian Discourse against Russian people regarding the war. By using the same term for both Russian and Ukrainian societies ('aggression'), Klara semantically assigns responsibility for the fighting to both societies, albeit in a subtle way. However, Klara notably then excuses Ukrainians for behaving aggressively, saying that it is for obvious reasons, by which she intertextually references the topic of this part of the interview (the Ukrainian war) and dialogically echoes the many Ukrainian voices assigning responsibility for the war to Russia. Continuing to pardon Ukrainian individuals for this position, Klara connects these events to Ukraine 'growing up', which is another master narrative that has run throughout Ukrainian discourse, including many of the interviews in this book (cf. Bondarenko, 2008; Osnach, 2015; Tsentr Doslidzhennya Suspil'stva, September 2014).

During the next part of Klara's explanation, she elaborates on how Ukraine is seen to be growing up. Again drawing on master narratives of Ukrainian identity development, which have been found to be especially prominent among Ukrainian young adults (see Chapters 2 and 3; Shulga, 2015; Tsentr Doslidzhennya Suspil'stva, April 2014), Klara states, 'in terms of, first of all, defining ourselves as Ukrainians. Not... former Soviet-Unions-ners, not... Russian friends, or not friends, but actually Ukrainians who have their own path.' By contrasting the identity of 'Ukrainian' against other nation-state related identities, Klara emphasizes the newly stressed importance of a national identity (Tsentr Doslidzhennya Suspil'stva, April 2014). Therefore, when she refers to 'Ukrainian who have their own path', she is emphasizing the national aspect of the identity marker Ukrainian over the cultural or linguistic aspect (though these are not mutually exclusive). She then says, 'we-... Ukraine... wanted to have good relationships in- with Russia for so long.' By beginning with 'we' and then self-correcting to 'Ukraine', Klara is both including herself in the definition of Ukraine and drawing upon more institutional symbolic capital in addition to her own embodied symbolic capital. In so doing, Klara also is able to dialogically access Ukraine's long history with Russia to make a stronger point by drawing upon a greater historical timeline. This statement also echoes the past tumultuous history between Ukraine and Russia, while simultaneously positioning Russia as once again in a position of being the one at fault by not being willing to cooperate in upholding a good relationship.

Klara ends this discussion by comparing the 'previous' Ukraine with the 'current' Ukraine, by personifying Ukraine and saying that previously the Ukrainian people would make many sacrifices for the sake of friendship with the Russian people, as well as for a positive international relationship between the two countries. Klara then dialogically echoes her and others' previous discourses of the rise of a Ukrainian national identity (Bongarenko, 2008; Shulga, 2015; Tsentr Doslidzhennya Suspil'stva, April 2014). Connecting time and space, bringing them together to access the chronotope of the Ukrainian war, Klara says that Ukrainians are no longer to give up everything for the sake of a good relationship with Russia 'because the... stocks... are... our lives already. You can't give up your life to stay friends.' Through this statement, Klara again intertextually draws upon the Ukrainian war and the many lives that have been lost. Simultaneously, Klara acknowledges Ukraine's role and responsibility for fighting that has occurred in the Ukrainian war. Even though she condones it, therein breaking her neutral stance, she does so while positioning Ukraine as necessarily taking part in the war, therein holding some of the responsibility.

Finally, following the final question that I posed to Klara, her succinct answer again joins the events of the Ukrainian war with the rise in importance of Ukrainian national identity. As Klara states, 'I- We actually- we were forced to make this step. Maybe we would never had courage to make it ourselves. But... we were helped, and we are making it.' The step Klara refers to is two part - establishing a national Ukrainian identity and breaking ties with Russia, both of which have been connected in Klara's discourse. Klara begins this final statement by saying Ukrainians (in which she includes herself through 'we') were forced, therein assigning responsibility again to Russia. However, interestingly, Klara sees this step as beneficial for Ukraine and something that Ukraine may not have 'had courage' to do itself, further personifying Ukraine, and positioning the aggressive actions from Russia as a not altogether bad thing since there was, in her view, a positive result for Ukraine. In this way, she says that Ukraine was 'helped' by Russia. However, she then ends by assigning Ukraine, and therefore the Ukrainian people, more agency by saying that now they are taking this necessary step themselves. Thus, while Russia is not without responsibility, Ukraine is also not without agency.

Further Remarks

Many different arguments have been made of who is responsible for the war in Ukraine, ranging from those who believe that responsibility comes from outside of the country with Ukraine being used as an international political tool (e.g. Fursov, 2016) to those who believe that political extremists from within Ukraine itself are responsible (as detailed in Risch, 2015). The participants in the current project were likewise divided on the issue of to whom or what responsibility should be attributed.

A key factor in establishing responsibility resided in how participants positioned themselves and others in their narratives. This positioning led to the various arguments that responsibility resided with the Russian government, with various governments but not with lay people, with the general population of a given country, or with everyone. Across all of the arguments of responsibility, the interviewees drew upon similar linguistic strategies, including the use of metonymy, personification, repetition, dialogism and intertextuality, as well as the aforementioned discursive positioning.

For the individuals who were arguing that politicians and governments are responsible for the war, metonymy was a particularly useful device. Through the use of metonymy, they were able to discursively form collective identities which they then continued to reference throughout their discourse under a metonymous referent (Catalano & Waugh, 2013; Rattcliffe, 2005). In this way, 'Putin' or 'Russia' came to mean much more than just the man or the country; they became symbols of political responsibility and aggression (Beliaeva & Seals, 2019). By pointing to them specifically, it also became possible to subsume individual identities of other people involved, thus drawing more upon institutional discourses, which are not as emotive as personal discourses (cf. Ratcliffe, 2005).

Furthermore, other governments were not without responsibility either. Many of the participants named the lack of support from international governments, but they did so indirectly through the use of linguistic devices. Repetition was one of the devices used, enabling participants to emphasize the futility of these countries' espoused efforts and to instead indirectly criticize these countries' lack of genuine effort in supporting Ukraine. In making this argument, participants also found personification useful, as it allowed them to evoke more emotion for Ukraine's situation. In particular, Lev's description of Ukraine as a smaller person beaten helpless on the ground painted a very powerful image of the helplessness and hurt that they feel for their country.

For the participants who argued that individual people are also responsible, dialogism and intertextually were particularly useful in supporting their position. One such way this was achieved was through the voicing of others not present (whether named or unnamed). This voicing of the other in a narrative format directly brought more voices into the account being told, therein drawing upon even more embodied symbolic capital than what would exist for the teller alone (Bakhtin, 1986, 1992; Bourdieu, 1986; Meadows, 2009; Todorov, 1984). Historical references were also intertextually drawn upon, bringing more institutional symbolic capital to the argument and positioning the speaker as speaking from a more knowledgeable space (Bourdieu, 1986; De Cillia *et al.*, 1999; Meadows, 2009).

Finally, responsibility was also shown through sequencing in discourse. When participants wanted to clearly assign responsibility, they found success in juxtaposing characters who represented valor with those who represented villainy. This was particularly useful for Lana in comparing her discursively constructed Ukrainian heroes against Russian villains to make her point. However, Klara also made use of sequencing, this time in order to construct a give and take of responsibility in her attempt to negotiate her desired position of neutrality. It is through this assortment of linguistic devices that participants were able to position and reposition themselves and others in discursively constructing responsibility for the war.

Note

(1) Due to the highly controversial and potentially dangerous nature of these posts, I have chosen to not name any specific articles or outlets here. However, readers can conduct a simple internet search and will retrieve many relevant printed news items.

5 Renegotiating Identity and 'Changing Your Mother Tongue'

A common theme throughout the interviews, and one that became more common as time went on, was the discussion of 'changing your mother tongue.' On the surface, this unique turn of phrase appears to be in part due to translation of the term 'рідна мова' into English. In Ukraine, the term 'рідна мова' has multiple meanings, depending on how it is being used and by whom. These meanings range from language of national identity to the language one grew up speaking; however, even individuals in Ukraine disagree on the exact meaning of this term in Ukrainian (Shimeki, 2007; Vyshniak, 2009). However, the meaning of the term 'mother tongue' in English as used by the participants in the phrase 'changing your mother tongue' focuses more on the projected transition into a regular, dominant usage of the Ukrainian language. More specifically, the participants used this term to refer to the case wherein a person (sometimes even themselves) actively worked to shift their dominant language used from Russian to Ukrainian, and to simultaneously internally shift the language they most identified with from Russian to Ukrainian.

The idea of 'changing your mother tongue' as the participants discuss it is highly reflective of a commonly discussed belief in Ukrainian life that there is a strong binding tie between experiences and language. As stated by activist Sergiy Osnach (2015, n.p.), 'Мова та історична пам'ять — дві взаємопов'язані складові ідентичності' (language and historical memory are two interconnected identities).[1] This belief has led to several language related movements in the wake of Maidan and the Ukrainian war, including the bilingual day of solidarity, centred in Lviv and Odessa on February 26, 2014 (cf. Csernicskó, 2017). On this day, people participating in the event in Lviv (Western Ukraine) spoke in Russian, and those in Odessa (Southern Ukraine) spoke in Ukrainian. For most participating in the event, this meant using a non-dominant language in their regular interactions that day as a way to show solidarity across the country and to highlight the importance of a single Ukrainian national identity (cf. Shulga, 2015; Tsentr Doslidzhennya Suspil'stva, April 2014). Yet, public

Discourses of bilingualism do not sit well with everyone, as evidenced by prominent Ukrainian sociolinguist Larisa Masenko arguing that the current bilingual campaigns hurt the Ukrainian-speaking minority who live in Russian-language-dominant areas of Ukraine (Masenko & Orel, 2014).

The complexity of views in Ukraine regarding language make the 'changing your mother tongue' concept even more fascinating. On a theoretical level, this perceived concept of being able to change one's mother tongue has implications for our understanding of how language is embodied and how the conscious awareness of this embodiment can serve as a tool for the individual in their attempt to reposition themselves in their view, as well as in the views of others. Furthermore, connections between embodiment, language shift, conscious language use and sociolinguistic identity further contribute to a narrative that redefines what it means to actively belong to a particular community of practice – in this case, self-identifying Ukrainians who position themselves as aligned with Ukraine and disaligned with Russia during the ongoing Ukrainian war.

Embodied Language

Research into how language is embodied has brought much understanding to what people have felt for a long time without necessarily having a way to talk about it. I will always remember giving a talk on heritage languages as embodied, and person after person coming up afterwards to tell me their stories and how much this concept resonated with them. Bucholtz and Hall (2016) in particular, have made a huge contribution to this field of inquiry recently. As they describe, language is quite literally embodied – that is, it is the body itself that allows us to produce language in order to communicate. Furthermore, they cite research on indexicality (e.g. Carr, 2011; Silverstein, 2003, 2005) to show how 'sociocultural beliefs about language rely on indexical iconization… such as when speakers perform stereotyped "gay speech" through the flap of a limp wrist or parody "teenage girl talk" with the accompanying embodied posture of taking a selfie with a cellphone' (Bucholtz & Hall, 2016: 178). They also cite research on the voice itself and stylistic features of the voice indexing perceived social categories and membership of those (e.g. Podesva, 2007, 2013; Zimman, 2013).

Perhaps the most poignant part of Bucholtz and Hall's (2016) article for the current book is when they discuss embodied discourse and how we quite literally talk the body into being (Bucholtz & Hall, 2016: 181; see also Goodwin, 2000 and Zimman, 2014). It is this third mentioned point which resonates so strongly with other work with multilingual speakers and embodied language.

For example, in research with multilingual youth of migrant families, Krumm (2001, 2004, 2010) found evidence of how even youth are so conscious of their embodied multilingualism that they represent their languages visually within a 'stick figure portrait' of a body itself. As Krumm

(2004) notes when discussing these linguistic identity portraits, 'Many migrants have developed multilingual identities, that is, the languages they have acquired during the migration process are no longer felt to play a conflicting role, but have become part of their lives and personalities' (Krumm, 2004: 65). In repeating the linguistic identity portraits, but with young children, Seals (2013, 2017b) likewise found that even young children already felt a sense of embodied language, filling in blank figures to reflect an inner presence of each language (societally dominant as well as heritage languages) with which they identified. Children were also able to narrate their drawings, such that this think-aloud activity helped provide insight into how children conceptualized their relationship between language and identity through internalizing languages in the body itself.

However, as discussed in this chapter, researchers need to be mindful to not allow embodied languages in the multilingual context to appear static. Rather, as this chapter shows, even an internalized sense of languages can shift and change, reflecting ideologies and contextual positionings. Through the 'changing your mother tongue' narratives in this chapter, it becomes clear that even a multilingual sense of embodied languages should be thought of as indexing other sociocultural ideals and aspects of identity.

Dialogic Echoes

Throughout the discourses of changing their mother tongue, the participants connect dialogically with aforementioned master Discourses, such as the Ukrainian language being connected to Ukrainian identity (cf. Braha, 2011), and the rise in importance for young Ukrainians in identifying nationally as Ukrainian (cf. Shulga, 2015). The interviewees living in the Ukrainian diaspora also have intertextual dialogic echoes of home country Discourses in their diasporic Discourses, though each is still its own. To illustrate this point, an excerpt is presented from an interview with Ilona (35 years old, from Western Ukraine, now living in the United States).

Ilona: With Ukrainians,
    most of them speak Russian,
    but um, lately we've been making a point of,
    um if, people understand Ukrainian,
    I, only speak Ukrainian.

When Ilona begins, she unexpectedly discursively positions Ukrainians on the outside of herself, naming the group and then saying that 'most of them speak Russian'. This indicates that in this instance, she is referring to Ukrainians still in Ukraine. She then repositions herself, however, as a member of the Ukrainian group of whom she is now speaking, shifting focus to talk about what 'we've been making a point of'. She then continues this shift, discussing personally the actions that she is taking. As she says, the point that she and other Ukrainians (broadly) have been making if that 'if, people understand Ukrainian, I, only speak Ukrainian.' Therefore, while Ilona begins by drawing intertextually on the historical practices of many Ukrainian people in Ukraine, her discursive positioning shifts to allow her to dialogically include her own voice as well as those of Ukrainians globally. Her final shift to a more personal focus ('I') still carries with it the previous intertextual references she has just made in setting up her point and allows her to draw upon the home country master narrative of Ukrainian language use being a part of Ukrainian identity. The dialogic connection with home and host country Discourses during discussions of changing a mother tongue become even clearer in other interviews, which are discussed throughout the remainder of this chapter.

A Previous History

One of the ways in which many participants in the diaspora, as well as in Ukraine, legitimized stories of changing the mother tongue was to focus linearly on what they saw as the historical nature of this movement, therein providing more symbolic capital for what some consider a controversial move. This was particularly common for those who positioned themselves on the periphery of the movement. That is, these participants were taking part in the actions while expressing some resistance to the idea of fully aligning with more obviously political aspects of the movement, such as drawing direct connections between language use and political identity. Rather, a subgroup of participants within the larger group of those actively changing their mother tongue saw their own efforts to change their mother tongue as being connected longitudinally to historical practices of Ukrainians in Ukraine (cf. Bondarenko, 2008). An example of this positioning can be found in the excerpt from an interview with Denys (37 years old, from Central Ukraine, living in New Zealand).

Denys: Ah nationally yeah,
I- I at the moment, I identify myself as Ukrainian,
p- probably like ten years ago I- I wouldn't care.
Corinne: Yeah.
Denys: Um now yeah,
I- I identify myself as Ukrainian,
even so my f- ah probably my grandmother was-
my grand- grandmother from Poland,
and other grand- grandmother was from Russia,
and so all kinds of blood.

Corinne:	Yeah.
Denys:	And all kinds of relatives,
	all nationalities,
	but ah yeah, I was born in Kyiv so.
Corinne:	Yeah, and so you mentioned it's more important now to identify yourself as Ukrainian,
	could you talk a little bit more about that?
Denys:	Yeah, so ah basically,
	when- when I came to Kyiv at the age of fourteen,
	it was like- like three last years of my school,
	and er I didn't know U- Ukrainian at all.
Corinne:	Oh really?
Denys:	Yeah, and it was a Ukrainian environment,
	so it was rather hard for me to get into it,
	but ah it's not the language,
	'cause Ukrainian is my second language,
	it's not the first one,
	like I- that all- it just that I hav-
	I heard it, ah like, I w-
	I started to live in Ukrainian society ah bit late in my life,
	but ah- but I can understand it freely,
	and I can talk,
	and I try to talk sometimes, and ah yeah,
	my wife tells I'm getting better at it.
Corinne:	[((laughs))]
Denys:	[((laughs))] ah it's not really that hard,
	and I- 'cause you know, when yo- er,
	there's probably a lot of people in e- in ex Soviet Union ah,
	they didn't have nationality,
	especially if you can see from- from your face,
	it's ah- therefore it was-
	I- I think for every person,
	it's kind of important at some point in life to identify yourself,
	so that's- that's probably the reason why I started thinking about ah,
	it's not because of-

> I identified myself as Ukrainian probably before the oldest er Maidan,
>
> ah in- happened in two thousand and thirteen probably,
>
> ah- probably even before the Maidan in two thousand and four,
>
> ah but ah yeah I- I-
>
> I remember that ah in two thousand and four,
>
> I just kind of formulated this idea that,
>
> yeah I am Ukrainian,
>
> it's- it's not- it's just- ah it was a straight idea,
>
> just,
>
> I have a nationality,
>
> ah before that,
>
> I just you know,
>
> I just normal person,
>
> I don't care.

Denys begins by first drawing a more common distinction found within the interviews – between 'then' and 'now'. As Denys says, 'at the moment, I identify myself as Ukrainian, p- probably like ten years ago I- I wouldn't care.' By beginning his self-identification with 'at the moment', we see Denys's clear understanding of identity as constantly shifting, which also matches the rest of his interview. Furthermore, by then stating, 'I identify myself as Ukrainian,' followed by information about his family's connections to Russia and Poland, Denys shows the complexity of identifying in any particular way in a post-Soviet space. By drawing upon his family's multicultural background, Denys also highlights that he could choose to identify with any of these places, but he has currently chosen to identify with Ukraine.

Then, in comparing the present time to 10 years prior, Denys draws upon intertextual references to current Discourses of the increasing importance of national identity for Ukrainians (Tsentr Doslidzhennya Suspil'stva, April 2014), as well as providing an intertextual link to the Orange Revolution, which occurred a decade prior. While some Ukrainians point to the Orange Revolution as the first time they consciously identified with a national identity, other Ukrainians point to the recent EuroMaidan events as this consciousness raising event. However, after indexing the importance of the current events in Ukraine for establishing a current positioning in regard to Ukrainian national identity, Denys continues by further drawing connections to the past and attributing his consciousness raising to events in his life that occurred before either EuroMaidan or the Orange Revolution. These connections serve to contextualize the current events and rising importance of national identity in Ukraine as something that has been developing, not something that occurred suddenly from nowhere.

Denys relates his Ukrainian identity negotiation story through a narrative that begins when he was in secondary school and had just moved to the capital city of Kyiv. As Denys explains elsewhere in his interview, his family moved around a lot, much of which was in Eastern Ukraine and Russia, so he also encountered many different people, cultures, languages, dialects and ideologies. Denys begins by explaining that when he moved to Kyiv as a teenager, 'it was a Ukrainian environment, so it was rather hard for me to get into it, but ah it's not the language, 'cause Ukrainian is my second language, it's not the first one.' While having difficulty integrating into his new environment at first, Denys is careful to specify that it was not the language that was a problem. This explanation also requires an intertextual understanding of Kyiv to know what Denys is referring to. In Kyiv, both Russian and Ukrainian languages are frequently used. Since these two languages were first and second languages for Denys, he would not have had a problem with the use of both in Kyiv.

Denys then continues to explain this, saying, 'I started to live in Ukrainian society ah bit late in my life, but ah- but I can understand it freely, and I can talk, and I try to talk sometimes, and ah yeah, my wife tells I'm getting better at it.' The reference Denys makes to living 'in Ukrainian society… late in life' again draws upon intertextual knowledge shared during the interview, that Denys spent much of his life in Russian-dominant regions of Ukraine and in Russia. Therefore, this comment is one of many found throughout the interviews that speaks of the importance of an approach such as interactional sociolinguistics that foregrounds interpreting discourse in the context of the entire interaction, as well as drawing upon prior known knowledge of the participants to interpret their discourse. Denys's reference to trying to sometimes speak Ukrainian is another example of this. At the time of the interview, Denys was already using Ukrainian often, especially due to his wife's encouragement, and he and his wife, Vira, had already been pillars of the local Ukrainian community during that point, a place where they both made use of the Ukrainian language. It is this shared prior knowledge upon which we both drew, which led to our shared laughter in the line following Denys's comment.

In the next part of Denys's narrative, he then draws upon more intertextual references to Soviet history, as well as to larger Discourses of ethnicity and phenotype found internationally: 'there's probably a lot of people in e- in ex Soviet Union ah, they didn't have nationality, especially if you can see from- from your face.' The reference Denys makes to not having a nationality is reflective of the fact that when the Soviet Union collapsed, each nation-state that was then formed also chose its own policy in regard to who would be granted citizenship and how that would happen. Citizenship was not automatically granted for residents in all of these new countries. Notably, in countries such as Latvia and Lithuania, new requirements had to be met if people wanted to be granted citizenship in these countries. For other countries such as Armenia, citizenship laws did not take effect until years after the collapse of the Soviet Union, therein affectively leaving people 'without nationality' (Makaryan, 2006).

Denys then returns to a reflection of his own moment of Ukrainian identification. First, Denys is careful to specify that his own consciousness raising occurred before either national movement – EuroMaidan of 2013 and the first Maidan that is associated with the Orange Revolution of 2004. However, 2004 still remained an important year for Denys in terms of national identification. As Denys explains, 'I remember that ah in two thousand and four, I just kind of formulated this idea that, yeah I am Ukrainian, it's- it's not- it's just- ah it was a straight idea, just, I have a nationality.' This particular dating of events is interesting because Denys has also been careful to separate his own self-identification moment from the national movements in 2004. While the events occurring in Ukraine in 2004 undoubtedly contributed to influencing Denys's establishment of a national identity, it is important for him to position these events, and subsequent events such as language choice and use, as personal, rather than political.

During this excerpt, Denys also establishes his ideological position, that 'it's kind of important at some point in life to identify yourself.' While Denys mitigates the directness of this statement through the use of 'kind of', his position is still clear. However, this mitigation and Denys's own historical narrative show that while he aligns with the idea that self-identification is important (in this case national identification), he still positions himself on the periphery of the national identification and changing you mother tongue movements.

Constructing a historically situated narrative was also a discursive technique used by Kyrylo (early 20s, from Eastern Ukraine, now living in the United States). This is evidenced in an excerpt from Kyrylo's interview below, when he brought up the language shift that had occurred within his own family in Ukraine.

Corinne: mm hmm

Kyrylo: So my dad who is from Dnipropetrovsk and uh,
he spend all his childhood in village,
um he:-
like he is Ukrainian,
totally Ukrainian,
but he- his level of Ukrainian language is not so strong as my mom's
who has Russian roots,

	and uh never talked Ukrainian language,
	but right now,
	she make incredible uh success with Ukrainian language so,
	she can speak it fluently almost.
Corinne:	Yeah and what do you think about that?
Kyrylo:	It's- it's, amazing,
	and I want to- I want to- people in Ukraine use this language,
	not only official- uh as official language,
	but also uh, their kids,
	even though like my family for example,
	if my mom dad and my sister?
	She's uh right now, uh eleven years old.
Corinne:	mm hmm
Kyrylo:	S:o she speak to her friends at school in Ukrainian language,
	and uh, at home they speak uh uh Russian language ((laughing)) with my sister,
	and she's answering in Russian language,
	though she can't uh write uh Russian language.
Corinne:	[mm hmm]
Kyrylo:	[She can] write only Ukrainian,
	because they-
	I- I'm not sure does they have uh uh Russian language at school?
	I'm pretty sure that they don't have it?
	But, she can she fluently speak Russian language,
	and uh feel like it's first language for her?
Corinne:	mm hmm
Kyrylo:	Because she was born in Dnipropetrovsk.
Corinne:	mm hmm
Kyrylo:	And uh, at school?
	She start school and uh kindergarten uh in Kyiv?
	And all, kids and uh, teachers speak with these kids only Ukrainian language,
	which is uh strategically really really good for Ukraine.
Corinne:	mm hmm
Kyrylo:	So then after, twenty: thirty years,
	these kids will rise to young professionals,

	and in their professional um, fields they will speak Russian,
	and u:h Ukrainian language, not Russian language so,
Corinne:	[Yeah],
Kyrylo:	[But because],
	I'm, the generation who is like in between Russian and Ukrainian language,
	and uh for example,
	it just how- how strong,
	your motivation is to speak Russian or Ukrainian language.

Kyrylo chose to begin his story by first realigning the chronotope of his narrative to an earlier time and space – that which is connected with his parents' childhood. He explains, 'So my dad who is from Dnipropetrovsk and uh, he spend all his childhood in village, um he:- like he is Ukrainian, totally Ukrainian.' By first orienting his father to a life in a Russian-language-dominant Ukrainian city and emphasizing that his father is 'totally Ukrainian', Kyrylo is dialogically anticipating and pre-emptively responding to any criticisms arising from the master narrative of needing to speak Ukrainian to be considered Ukrainian, with which his father does not align. However, Kyrylo has also used this example to emphasize his mother's story, which as he says, 'his level of Ukrainian language is not so strong as my mom's who has Russian roots, and uh never talked Ukrainian language, but right now, she make incredible uh success with Ukrainian language so, she can speak it fluently almost.' Through this example, Kyrylo emphasizes the unexpected result of his mother, who has Russian roots and never grew up speaking Ukrainian, becoming nearly fluent in Ukrainian as an adult. Through this short story, Kyrylo has drawn dialogically upon Ukrainian expectations that most Russians do not speak Ukrainian, as well as the current narrative of changing one's mother tongue to further align with the ideology that most Ukrainians do or should speak Ukrainian. Since Kyrylo's family lives in Ukraine, Kyrylo also implies through his story that his mother at least partially identifies as Ukrainian, as a person living in Ukraine who has learned Ukrainian. This is further emphasized by Kyrylo's phrasing, stating that his mother has 'Russian roots', not that she herself identifies as Russian.

When I asked Kyrylo what he thinks of his mother learning the Ukrainian language, he replies very enthusiastically: 'It's- it's, amazing, and I want to- I want to- people in Ukraine use this language, not only official- uh as official language, but also uh, their kids.' Kyrylo positions the action of learning Ukrainian as a very positive one, which aligns again with the ideology that Ukrainians should know and speak Ukrainian, at least for official and business purposes. However, Kyrylo also uses his story as an example of what he sees to be positive language shift within families towards the Ukrainian language. This statement continues to intertextually reference the rise in the perceived importance of national identity for young Ukrainians (Shulga, 2015), which is seen as embodied and enacted through the use of the Ukrainian language.

Kyrylo then continues his story of language shift among Ukrainian youth by giving the example of his young sister who has been raised at home speaking Russian but who uses Ukrainian at school, and as a result speaks Russian dominantly but writes in Ukrainian. Kyrylo ties these linguistic events to regional locations, which is another common Discourse in Ukrainian society. He explains that she speaks Russian 'because she was born in Dnipropetrovsk,' which is in Eastern Ukraine, but she writes in Ukrainian because 'she start school and uh kindergarten uh in Kyiv,' which is the country's capital city, located in the center of Ukraine. As discussed in Chapters 1 and 2, Kyiv historically had the regular presence of both the Ukrainian and Russian languages. However, with Ukraine's declaration of independence in 1991, there also came an expectation from the public that Ukrainian should be used at the official level, which includes the capital city of Kyiv. Therefore, it is upon this history and these Discourses that Kyrylo intertextually draws when he makes regional comparisons, with Dnipropetrovsk being the city of Russian language and Kyiv being the city of Ukrainian language.

Kyrylo further aligns with the master Discourse that Ukrainians speak the Ukrainian language by stating that this language shift among Ukrainian children is 'strategically really really good for Ukraine.' He then continues emphasizing his focus on full language shift, not multilingualism, by predicting that in the future 'after, twenty: thirty years, these kids will rise to young professionals, and in their professional um, fields they will speak Russian, and u:h Ukrainian language, not Russian language so…' While at first Kyrylo mentions multilingual use of Russian and Ukrainian, he self-corrects to say the Ukrainian language but not the Russian language, therein implying language shift among the current young people of the country.

After discussing what he sees to be the ideal situation of language shift in Ukraine, Kyrylo then returns to the present and to his own language abilities, saying, 'I'm, the generation who is like in between Russian and Ukrainian language, and uh for example, it just how- how strong, your motivation is to speak Russian or Ukrainian language.' Interestingly, while Kyrylo had positioned the children of Ukraine as influenced by an outside force (education) which can lead them through language shift, Kyrylo discusses his own generation's linguistic abilities as embodied but also as tied cognitively to motivation. Therefore, for Kyrylo, and for many Ukrainians, language is seen as not a stable force. Rather, the language you speak is seen as tied internally to motivation, which is also the supportive reasoning behind the ideas present in the movement to change one's mother tongue.

An example of this reasoning and of how it is seen as having been enacted in practice comes from Ilya. Ilya (33 years old, from the Black Sea region of Ukraine, still living in Ukraine) grew up speaking Russian and identifying as a Russian speaking Ukrainian. However, as he explains, he subscribes to the changing one's mother tongue ideology that is growing in presence among Ukrainians.

Ilya: Originally I am a Russian speaking Ukrainian,
now I just ah-
now we have shifted to Ukrainian-
and speak Ukrainian in everyday life and ah forever ((laughter))
...
on purpose
...
now everything looks different er, you know,
just- um, Ukrainians have understood- understood that they are together
...
so yes I am trying to change my mother tongue.
...

Corinne: Um I've talked to some people who have said that they are-
that on purpose they're trying to change their mother tongue from Russian to Ukrainian.
Is that something that you are doing as well,
or is it not quite that much?

Ilya: XX so yes I am trying to change my mother tongue,
but you know, I always felt this controversy in myself
ah my, ah parents for example,
ah well are Russian speaking,
although my mother er now-w- also tries to- to shift to Ukrainian,
ah she has really problems with that because er um
her education in Ukrainian was- was quite poor in Soviet times,
mm and so my relatives a-always claimed that they were-
and they- they are Ukrainians,
and er they spoke Russian,
so I always believed that Russian is er- is not the very mother tongue of mine and my-
by the way my grandpa my grandma,

they were Ukrainian-speaking ah people from the Voronezh region,

which is in Russia um and ah,

so y-y-y-

what else,

but what's er characteristic of that ah is that

when they moved from a small city-

from Voronezh region to Kharkiv,

which is in Ukraine actually,

they ah ah they turn to-t-to Russian, you know,

so it is ah there's XX habits of Ukrainians ah to switch to Russian when they move to a big city

because XX it was um- was something- something- you know- know,

s- something X tradition about Ukrainian,

so it was er conceived as a rural language,

as something provincial and some- something uncivilized,

and so on and so forth.

Ilya begins his narrative by establishing a 'before' and 'after' trajectory, not unlike the structure used in conversion narratives (Castillo Ayometzi, 2007; Griffin, 2009). In so doing, Ilya is able to disconnect from his 'previous self' and instead re-position himself in light of his current actions and beliefs. For Ilya, this includes the shift from speaking Russian to speaking Ukrainian: 'Originally I am a Russian speaking Ukrainian, now I just ah- now we have shifted to Ukrainian- and speak Ukrainian in everyday life and ah forever.' By naming himself as previously 'a Russian speaking Ukrainian', Ilya is dialogically echoing the negative positioning of this identity label, as was seen presented by Kalyna in Chapter 3. He then states that 'we' (he and his family) have shifted to Ukrainian, speak Ukrainian every day, and will do so 'forever', thus speaking to Ilya's re-positioning of himself as a Ukrainian speaker, which he sees as an important enough part of his identity to continue doing so 'forever'. He then pauses and says that this switching from using Russian to using Ukrainian in everyday life is 'on purpose', therein further speaking to the importance with which he views being a Ukrainian-dominant speaker for his identity.

In further explaining his goal to change his mother tongue, Ilya explains that 'now everything looks different er, you know, just- um, Ukrainians have understood- understood that they are together.' Through this statement, Ilya expresses the perceived importance of embodying a particular sociolinguistic identity, that of the Ukrainian speaking

Ukrainian, in order to belong to the 'together' in-group of positively positioned Ukrainians (Braha, 2011). This also draws dialogically upon the ideological master narrative that 'real' Ukrainians speak Ukrainian, which was seen throughout Chapters 3 and 4.

Ilya further demonstrates how dominant language use has become an embodied component of those attempting to change their mother tongue to Ukrainian. As Ilya says, 'I always felt this controversy in myself ah my, ah parents for example, ah well are Russian speaking.' Ilya explains that he felt an internalized identity struggle (cf. Norton, 2000) due to identifying as Ukrainian but speaking Russian, a language that his parents also use and that he therefore grew up speaking. As Ilya relates, speaking Russian but identifying as Ukrainian caused him a sense of internal conflict, which in part motivated his decision to attempt to embody a Ukrainian speaker identity, therein attempting to resolve this struggle within himself.

To further justify his self-positioning, Ilya draws upon his family history in a very interesting way. First, he excuses his mother's dominance in Russian by attributing it to poor Ukrainian language teaching during the Soviet era. Since the Soviet Union (the central governing region of which is now the Russian Federation) was responsible for Soviet era education, this contributes to a further distancing from Russia for Ilya, as he blames them for his mother's low Ukrainian language abilities: 'so I always believed that Russian is er- is not the very mother tongue of mine and my- [family].' In this way, the former Soviet Union is positioned as responsible for denying his family the linguistic identity of Ukrainian language speakers, which is something that Ilya feels is his right. As evidence of this, Ilya explains further about his family linguistic history: 'by the way my grandpa my grandma, they were Ukrainian-speaking ah people from the Voronezh region, which is in Russia.' Interestingly, even though Ilya mentions that his grandparents were born in Russia, this is not the focus of his example, and this is not even an allowance that he makes in regard to their positioning or identity. Rather, his focus is on them being Ukrainian language speakers. Even though they lived in what is today Russia, they spoke the Ukrainian language, and therefore Ilya feels that speaking Ukrainian is part of his heritage.

Ilya then continues to tell his grandparents' story, as a means of explaining why he did not grow up speaking Ukrainian. He explains that even though his grandparents ended up moving to a city in Ukraine, the fact that it was a city and not a town or village meant that the trend then was to use the Russian language. This in fact has been supported by linguistic research, showing that Soviet ideologies resulted in a construction of the Ukrainian language being perceived as 'backwards' and 'rural', while the Russian language was constructed as 'forward moving' and 'urban' (Bilaniuk, 2003; Kulyk, 2011). It is in part in response to this positioning that the current 'speak Ukrainian' movements in Ukraine have taken place and why they have gained so much force, as advocates attempt to overcome the negative positioning of Ukrainian from past Discourses. These are the historical events and ideologies which Ilya is referencing. However, he then joins the dissenters of these past ideologies by trivializing this past view through his statement: 'and so on and so forth,' which is a discursive equivalent of 'blah blah blah,' therein denying legitimacy to the claims associated with this statement. Thus, Ilya has once again re-aligned with the pro-Ukrainian language position.

A Recent Event

Other participants who discussed the 'change your mother tongue' ideology emphasized the recent events that led to this position. For these participants, past events were not emphasized nearly as much as recent events, if at all. Therefore, they attributed the 'change your mother tongue' ideology directly to the events that they themselves recently experienced (as opposed to those retold by older family members). In particular, the events of EuroMaidan and the Ukrainian war were named as leading to this unique linguistic ideological movement. Milena (20 years old, from Eastern Ukraine, still living in Ukraine) provides an example of this in her interview excerpt.

Corinne: Do you think there's been... any...

    change in opinion... recently,

    or in the last couple of years?

Milena: Mm-hmm, like, er...

Corinne: [About... Russian and Ukrainian.]

Milena: [Yeah. Yes, right.]

    Mm-hmm.

    I think, yes, especially... due- to- th-

    due to the... mmm, situation in Ukraine,

    what happened, like, three months ago...

    and, yeah...

    Also, I want to say about patriotism.

    Mmm, because, for example... er...

    when... somebody ask you one year ago,

    where- where do you from, er, all people, er, answered them, like... erm... modestly,

    that they are from Ukraine,

    and almost nobody knows- no- almost nobody kno- knew, where is Ukraine.

> And right now, erm, almost everybody… er, has the… the f- mmm, the national flag…
>
> some national, er, dresses,
>
> and they- they started to speak in Ukrainian.
>
> Because, even, er, when-I- er, when I came to my university,
>
> all my tutors, er, tutors are speaking… Russian.
>
> But due to the situation in Ukraine,
>
> they started to er, to… speak in Ukrainian,
>
> like, in order to respect- in order to support Ukraine, so…
>
> something like that.
>
> So yeah,
>
> I think that… situation change,
>
> and real change.

Before delving into a discourse analysis of Milena's interview, it is important to first acknowledge that her answer was in response to the question I posed to her, which focused on recent years. However, while there is a possibility that some of her response may be due in part to my prompting, it is important to note that nearly half of the respondents answered this question in the negative and proceeded to explain that the language ideologies present now had been so for a long time. Therefore, this prompt was a way to get participants to discuss language ideologies directly, especially as tied to a timescale, whether past or present.

The excerpt above begins with me asking Milena if she thinks anything has changed during the past few years in regard to the Ukrainian and Russian languages. She answers affirmatively and then narrows the time focus even further to the past few months. Since Milena's interview was held in October 2014, she is referencing the events of the Ukrainian War and Maidan. As Milena states, 'I think, yes, especially… due- to- th- due to the… mmm, situation in Ukraine, what happened, like, three months ago…' Specifically, Milena points to the period approximately three months prior, which is the time during which the Ukrainian war first escalated. During the period Milena refers to, the war zone in Eastern Ukraine (including Donetsk and Luhansk) declared themselves to be an independent republic, the Malaysia Airlines tragedy happened in Eastern Ukraine, and fighting in the war zone intensified, supported by the Russian military. Milena points to this period of intensification as the time during which she also sees opinions about the Russian and Ukrainian languages significantly changing.

Milena then continues by relating the topic of changes in language ideologies to national ideologies and identification: 'Also, I want to say about patriotism.' As Milena is in Ukraine, and we are talking about

Ukraine, we can understand that Milena is referring to patriotism as related to Ukrainian patriotism. By also stating 'I want to say about...' without simply talking about patriotism, Milena has made a clear move to take the conversational floor (cf. Shaw, 2000) in her topic initiation (cf. Sacks *et al.*, 1974). This taking of the floor allows Milena to continue her discussion of patriotism uninterrupted, which makes sense as a discursive strategy because, for some, patriotism in the context of Ukraine is a controversial topic.[2] Therefore, by making this conversational move, Milena is simultaneously intertextually referencing the potential controversial nature of this topic, and dialogically anticipating and responding to any of these concerns.

Milena then provides an example of what she means by patriotism and why she has connected this concept to my question of recent language perception and ideologies. She begins her example by reorienting our timeline to one year in the past: 'when... somebody ask you one year ago, where- where do you from, er, all people, er, answered them, like... erm... modestly, that they are from Ukraine, and almost nobody knows- no- almost nobody kno- knew, where is Ukraine.' In the context of Milena's example, 'somebody' and 'them' refer to those outside of Ukraine who are not already familiar with Ukraine. This is a common story related by Ukrainians – that when interacting with non-Ukrainian identifying people outside of Ukraine, more often than not the latter have no idea where Ukraine is located or what it means to be Ukrainian (see Chapter 6). Therefore, Milena is drawing upon this common narrative to situate the contrast between 'then' and 'now' which she is setting up. Noticeably, Milena also states that Ukrainians would answer this first question 'modestly', therein further setting up a counter example to the idea of patriotism. Furthermore, this discussion of modesty intertextually draws upon other common Discourses in Ukrainian culture, in which Ukrainians frequently position themselves as gentle, kind, soft-spoken and peace-loving people.

This previous positioning is then contrasted by Milena with what she sees as a shift in ideologies, identification and self-presentation, with national identity coming to the forefront for Ukrainians. This aligns with previous findings of the rise in importance of national identity for young Ukrainians (see Chapters 2 and 3). Milena discursively illustrates this change in identification and positioning by pointing specifically to the changes in both visible appearance and language use, therein drawing a connection between the two and further showing the embodied nature of language choice and use during this time of war in Ukraine: 'And right now, erm, almost everybody... er, has the... the f- mmm, the national flag... some national, er, dresses, and they- they started to speak in Ukrainian.' The national dress that Milena is referring to is the vyshyvanka embroidery – a particular style of embroidery unique to Ukraine, which has also risen in symbolic importance as being representative of

Figure 5.1 Photo of Ukrainian embroidery[4]

Ukrainian identity, as shown in Figures 5.1 and 5.2 (cf. Brown, 1994). For Milena, and for many Ukrainians, speaking Ukrainian has become as symbolic a sign of Ukrainian national identification as wearing vyshyvanka embroidery.

Milena then provides a second example that stresses what she sees as an ideological shift across domains of language use: 'Because, even, er, when-I- er, when I came to my university, all my tutors, er, tutors are speaking… Russian. But due to the situation in Ukraine, they started to

Figure 5.2 Photo of Ukrainian girls wearing vyshyvankas and traditional vinok flower crowns at a celebration[5]

er, to... speak in Ukrainian, like, in order to respect- in order to support Ukraine, so... something like that.' In this example, Milena draws upon a more formal setting – that of the university context. Furthermore, she does not focus on language use between friends, but rather the language used by her tutors,[3] who have a higher level of authority. As Milena explains, she perceived all of her tutors to primarily use the Russian language, but she says that they have recently switched to using Ukrainian. She directly attributes this to the events of Maidan and the Ukrainian War ('the situation in Ukraine'). Milena sees the change in preferred language use as being sociopolitical and as directly tied to Ukrainian national identity. Through this example, Milena connects again intertextually to the Discourse of the Ukrainian language as being tied to Ukrainian national identity, and she positions a switch in preferred language use as being located fairly recently in time, being universal across people in the Ukrainian space, and being tied directly to the Ukrainian war (Shulga, 2015; Tsentr Doslidzhennya Suspil'stva, April 2014).

In another example, Denys (37 years old, from Central Ukraine, living in New Zealand) also sees a change in preferred language use as being a recent event, though he does not locate it in time as near to the present as does Milena. Rather, Denys describes this change in preferred language use as something that has developed within a particular generation of Ukrainian people.

Denys: Well I think that ah we have a new generation of people,
who are like between their twenties and ah thirty-five or fourties,
and I know many people who specifically ah ((4 seconds)) started to sp-
like they- they declared that they will speak Ukrainian.

Corinne: Mm-hm.

Denys: XX- and they started to learn it,
and to speak solely into Ukrainian,
and switch to other languages only when they need to
a- according the- the situation,
if someone doesn't understand them or different environments,
but in- ah in the companies.
And ah at work,
ah home parties and everywhere,
it's- they- they specifically choose to- to speak Ukrainian,
so it's like-
call it patriotism or whatever.

Corinne: [Yeah ((laughter))].

Denys: [(((laughter)))]

Ah some of them tell me- told me that they like it just- just because that they-

they want to learn it,

and that's the best way to learn if you force yourself to speak.

In this excerpt, Denys points to a very specific age range of people whom he sees as being those taking part the most in the effort to change their mother tongue. The age group that Denys points out ('like between their twenties and ah thirty-five or fourties') also matches the recent sociological research published in Ukraine of Ukrainians who have placed more emphasis on national identity (e.g. Shulga, 2015), as well as the demographics of those who were interviewed for this study. Furthermore, as shown throughout this chapter, as well as in the previous chapters, there are a number of people from all different regions and demographics within this age group who attribute a conscious preference for the Ukrainian language to a rise in Ukrainian national identity. Therefore, it is not surprising that the vast majority of participants in this research are familiar with the effort to change one's mother tongue taking place among Ukrainians, and that some are even taking part in this effort themselves. As Denys mentions, even though he himself is not taking part in this effort directly, 'I know many people who specifically ah… started to sp- like they- they declared that they will speak Ukrainian.' By also self-correcting from saying individuals merely started to speak Ukrainian to saying that individuals 'declared' they will speak Ukrainian, this also speaks to the consciousness of this effort for those taking part.

Denys then further elaborates on his explanation, saying that those taking part in this effort to change one's mother tongue 'started to learn it, and to speak solely into Ukrainian, and switch to other languages only when they need to.' This aspect of switching to the Ukrainian language, wherein individuals use only the Ukrainian language and only switch when necessary again dialogically echoes the Discourse of 'real' Ukrainians speak the Ukrainian language (Braha, 2011), as well as the Discourse of the Ukrainian language being a marker of Ukrainian national identity (Shulga, 2015). However, there is also another intertextual reference implied in Denys's statement, and that is of the long history of the Ukrainian people accommodating to others if other people do not understand the language they are using. Researchers have documented the Ukrainian people's well-intentioned non-accommodation, such that individuals will continue using their preferred language in an interaction, but only so long as others can understand them (cf. Bilaniuk, 2010).

This behavior of friendly non-accommodation comes from a long history of multilingualism in the country, such that people could understand multiple languages, and it was therefore not a problem to hold a multilingual conversation, with each participant maintaining their language of choice. However, the terminology ('non-accommodation') as well as the description of this behavior during interaction has often been misinterpreted as being ill-intentioned and as an unwillingness to accommodate. Yet, as explained, it is not ill intention, but rather unnecessary for the interaction. Rather, each participant would rather that their interlocutors use the languages with which each is most comfortable. Linguistic accommodation (Giles & Coupland, 1991) is therefore only utilized when a language in use is not understood in the course of the interaction. However, while this has been a long-standing practice in Ukraine, it has not had the same level of conscious language choice about it. Therefore, it is better explained as having previously been *translingual interaction*, with the current more conscious practices being explained as *friendly non-accommodation*. It is the latter behavior which is referenced by Denys when he talks about people only switching from Ukrainian to another language 'when they need to'.

As the excerpt above continues, Denys explains that the Ukrainian language is also what is being used across domains of language use: 'but in- ah in the companies. And ah at work, ah home parties and everywhere, it's- they- they specifically choose to- to speak Ukrainian, so it's like- call it patriotism or whatever.' An interesting aspect of Denys's discourse here is that he began this section with 'but', which is usually used when contrasting ideas. However, it is not immediately clear what ideas he is contrasting, since he continues to talk about the preferred use of Ukrainian. This, however, is when Denys again draws upon a shared intertextual understanding of sociolinguistic interaction in Ukraine in order to create this contrast.

As previously explained, Ukrainians have historically engaged in translingual interaction, and many of those taking part in the conscious use of Ukrainian now engage in friendly non-accommodation. However, as also previously mentioned, friendly non-accommodation still focuses on the interaction between individuals and pays mind to the linguistic needs of the individuals engaged in this interaction, therein still implying that shifts in language (e.g. from Ukrainian to Russian) may still occur in the course of the conversation, even by those practicing friendly non-accommodation.

This contrasts with the second part of Denys's explanation (following 'but') in which he is discussing conscious language choice and use not between specific individuals, but within an entire domain, and in fact across domains. Therefore, it is across the domains of work, home and 'everywhere' that these Ukrainians are asserting their preferred language, rather than passively taking part in translingual interaction or negotiating the use of friendly non-accommodation. Therefore, while language choice and use may be negotiated in individual interactions as needed, this does not preclude the asserted preference for the Ukrainian language across domains of language use. It is this asserted preference across domains that Denys refers to as 'patriotism'.[6]

Notably, Denys ends this explanation by providing room in Ukrainian use for another group of people – those not taking part in conscious, purposeful language use for political purposes nor taking part in the efforts to change one's mother tongue. Denys explains that this additional group 'they like it just- just because that they- they want to learn it, and that's the best way to learn if you force yourself to speak.' By using the mitigator 'just', Denys implies that this referenced group does not have the same political motivations as the other groups. Rather, there are still Ukrainians who are consciously using the Ukrainian language in an effort to learn it because they have never previously acquired it (see Chapter 1 for a brief linguistic history of Ukraine). Denys is careful to be clear that this does not, however, mean that this group of Ukrainians learning Ukrainian are doing so for any specific political reason, therein dialogically responding to any arguments that might be made against his previous discussions of sociopolitical motivation behind using Ukrainian.

This attribution of political motivation in beginning to speak the Ukrainian language is what Ksusha (36 years old, from Central Ukraine, living in the United States) references below.

Ksusha: And um, some people make a conscious effort to start to speak Ukrainian,

it's just a political statement…

political cultural statement.

As evidenced by Ksusha's excerpt, there is a prevalent Discourse among Ukrainians, especially those of the young adult generations, who see the 'conscious effort' of beginning to speak the Ukrainian language at this time in Ukraine's history as a 'political cultural statement'. That is, language is seen as tied to political positioning and cultural identity, both of which contribute to the rising Ukrainian national identity (Braha, 2011; Shulga, 2015; Tsentr Doslidzhennya Suspil'stva, April 2014). For many young Ukrainians, making the conscious effort to learn and use the Ukrainian language at this time is seen as a deliberate self-re-positioning in alignment with the rise of Ukrainian national identity.

As further evidence of the conscious identification with a particular language being perceived as a simultaneous identification with the rising Ukrainian national identity, Ruslana (28 years old, from Eastern Ukraine, still living in Ukraine) discusses in this excerpt her deliberate attempt to change her mother tongue. As Ruslana was working in another country on an internship at the time of her interview, the reference to 'back home in Ukraine' also references her daily lived experiences outside of the scope of her internship.

Corinne: So, and, um, back home in Ukraine,
  what languages do you use?
Ruslana: Umm… ((smacks lips)) at home I used to speak Russian language…
  before the war.
  Then, uhm… it was just a protest,
  um, I started speaking Ukrainian.
  And also, um,
  I had, er, a mission, abroad, and, er,
  I was very… unsatisfied when people mixed me with Russian, er,
  with Russian citizen because I was speaking Russian language.
  And that was so unpleasant for me,
  that I decided just to change my mother tongue and just to start speaking Ukrainian.
  Because I, er, don't want that people… could mix me with Russian… um, citizen.
Corinne: [So, er…]
Ruslana: [Because…]
Corinne: [²Sorry, go ahead.]
Ruslana: [²Yeah.]
  Because, of course,
  language, it, erm, identifies… the person,
  and if a person speaks Russian, er,
  everybody will think that he is from Russia.
  But, I don't want-
  I don't want that.

As mentioned previously in this chapter, participants often initiated a discussion of language shift, especially as related to the Ukrainian war, without my direct prompting in this area. In the case of Ruslana's excerpt, my question had to do with the languages she uses in Ukraine, which triggered a response from her about language shift and the Ukrainian war, therein showing the semantic relationship between these topics. That is, my mention of language use in Ukraine cognitively primed connected events for Ruslana, which in this case means the Ukrainian war and language shift. As explained by Ruslana, 'at home I used to speak Russian language… before the war. Then, uhm… it was just a protest, um, I started speaking Ukrainian.' Ruslana begins like many of the Ukrainian participants, orienting the story to a period of time before the Ukrainian war and then pulling it forward towards the present time, therein showing the notability of this particular event in their chronotopic reconstruction of space and time. Furthermore, Ruslana related her initial use of the Ukrainian language as a protest action, therein showing the political nature of language shift for many of these participants.

Ruslana then gives an example of an event that motivated her to join in the attempt to change her mother tongue. As she explains, she went overseas, and people thought she was Russian because she was speaking the Russian language, 'And that was so unpleasant for me, that I decided just to change my mother tongue and just to start speaking Ukrainian.' This dialogically echoes many Ukrainians' stories of being abroad (such as Milena's narrative earlier in this chapter) and being mistaken as Russian. However, while once this implicit erasure of Ukrainian identity was not particularly poignant for many Ukrainians, the rise in national identity has meant that many Ukrainians, such as Ruslana, now find this mistaken identity 'so unpleasant'.

Ruslana attributes this mistaken identity to the fact that she was speaking the Russian language. In fact, it would not be uncommon for speakers of Russian from other countries outside of Ukraine to not know exactly where Ruslana was from, as Russian is one of the most spoken languages in the world with over 267 million speakers, including native speakers from throughout the Russian Federation, as well as from countries such as Ukraine, Georgia, Kazakhstan, Belarus, Israel, Latvia, Poland, Slovenia and the United States, to name only a few (Simons & Fennig, 2017). However, while this may not be an uncommon event, it was unpleasant enough for Ruslana that she says she then decided to change her mother tongue to Ukrainian. Her identity as a Ukrainian citizen (and not as a Russian citizen) was seen as more important to her than using a more widely spoken language internationally. Through this decision, Ruslana shows her clear positive identity practices towards Ukrainian and simultaneous negative identity practices towards Russian (cf. Bucholtz, 1999; Seals, 2017b). Through these identity practices, language has once again become symbolic of sociopolitical identity and national allegiance.

Ruslana herself makes the direct connection between language practices, sociolinguistic identity, sociopolitical identity and national allegiance. She does this most clearly at the end of her excerpt when she states, 'Because, of course, language, it, erm, identifies... the person, and if a person speaks Russian, er, everybody will think that he is from Russia. But, I don't want- I don't want that.' Ruslana's statement that language identifies the person has two meanings. First, this statement expresses the idea that language is tied to identity – a very common concept across cultures and languages, frequently commented on by people of all walks of life, especially those with a personal connection to a particular language, such as a multilingual speaker whose first language is a minority language in their current setting (Braha, 2011). The second meaning of Ruslana's statement is that people draw upon social constructs of language, especially in regard to culture, nation and ethnicity, when positioning others in interaction. Therefore, within interaction, interlocutors will often identify and position others in part according to the language used by that person. This is the exact situation upon which Ruslana comments in this excerpt from her interview. Recognizing the habit of people to position others in this way, and herself trying to disassociate with the Russian identity label, Ruslana decided to adapt Ukrainian as her primary language of use.

Views from the Diaspora

As mentioned at the beginning of this chapter, discussions of changing one's mother tongue take on an additional layer in the Ukrainian diaspora. These Discourses dialogically reflect the home country Discourses, while simultaneously reflecting the needs and experiences of the host country diaspora communities. As a result, while still intertextually connected to the home country Discourses, the underlying motivations for changing one's mother tongue take on a slightly different character, reflecting the different challenges faced by diaspora communities, particularly regarding the character of language shift.

An example of the changing mother tongue Discourses from within the Ukrainian diaspora communities can be found in the excerpt below. Gleb (38 years old, from Eastern Ukraine, living in New Zealand) discusses his ideas about the efforts to change one's mother tongue and the additional considerations that he has as a member of the Ukrainian diaspora in New Zealand.

Gleb: Well, like, Russian is naturally because I grew up with this-
with it,
so I use it naturally at home,
and trying to speak more with my kids,
so they have strong Russian language too.
But now I'm thinking about maybe switching them to Ukrainian.
It's a bit hard practically
...
But I'm thinking about maybe teaching my daughter Ukrainian
...
Uh, so I want her to understand like um f-
to XXX herself more to Ukrainian culture.

As Gleb explains, Russian is the language that he grew up speaking, therein making it the language that he feels is most natural for him to use, especially since he did not move outside of a Russian-speaking region until he was already an adult. However, the next part of Gleb's excerpt is where his story shifts slightly from those who still live in Ukraine: 'and trying to speak more with my kids, so they have strong Russian language too.' If Gleb still lived in a Russian-speaking region, there would not be such a concern of his children not being able to acquire the Russian language themselves as well. However, because Gleb and his family now live in New Zealand, and the dominant language of New Zealand is English, Russian is now a heritage language and no longer a societal language. Therefore, as Gleb implies, it is not assumed that his children will automatically have strong Russian language skills, and it is instead his responsibility as one of their parents to use Russian in the home with them if he wants them to be able to use it also (cf. Seals, 2017a).

The next part of Gleb's excerpt then dialogically echoes Discourses of both the home and host countries: 'But now I'm thinking about maybe switching them to Ukrainian. It's a bit hard practically.' The first sentence about 'switching' his children to Ukrainian is an echo of the change your mother tongue efforts in Ukraine. The second sentence, however, also echoes common concerns for people living in the diaspora – that is the question of how to help their children acquire, use and maintain the heritage language(s). In this case, switching from Russian to Ukrainian would also mean that Gleb would be facing the challenge of supporting his children's heritage language use in his non-dominant language. Therefore, he would be facing the difficult challenge of helping them acquire and maintain it while simultaneously working to strengthen his own abilities in the language. Furthermore, there are far more Russian language teaching materials and resources than there are Ukrainian language materials and resources, given the relatively larger number of speakers in diaspora communities around the world. It would thus also be more of a challenge to find and acquire supporting resources in Gleb's efforts to strengthen his children's Ukrainian language abilities (Seals & Olsen-Reeder, 2017).

However, as Gleb continues to explain, challenging as it may be, he is still carefully considering the option of taking part in the Ukrainian change your mother tongue efforts due to his view of the Ukrainian language being an embodied component of Ukrainian culture: 'But I'm thinking about maybe teaching my daughter Ukrainian… Uh, so I want her to understand like um f- to XXX herself more to Ukrainian culture.' For Gleb, teaching his daughter the Ukrainian language will also allow her to access more of the Ukrainian culture and to feel more closely tied to Ukrainian culture. Therefore, changing mother tongues from Russian to Ukrainian is not just a question of sociopolitical identity or of national identity, it is also a question of which heritage language to promote from within the home in a host country where neither language is spoken by a majority of the population.

A final point of note from Gleb's excerpt is that it is his daughter whom he specifically mentions. However, Gleb has both a daughter and a son. This specification also intertextually draws upon historical ideologies of language in Ukraine. As Bilaniuk (2003) has explored and explained in-depth, traditionally in Ukraine, Russian was seen as the language of progress, of business outside of the home, and of men. The Ukrainian language was traditionally seen as the language of tradition, of family inside of the home, and of women. Women have also traditionally been seen as the keepers of the Ukrainian language. Therefore, it is interesting to note that Gleb has specifically mentioned his daughter in the context of switching to the Ukrainian language. Whether consciously or not, Gleb has intertextually drawn upon another historical Ukrainian Discourse around language ideology, embedded within the context of the more recent changing your mother tongue Discourse.

In another interview, Lana (early 30s, from the Black Sea region of Ukraine, now living in New Zealand) also discursively illustrates the dialogic echoes from home and host country that occur in her narrative about changing her mother tongue. As shown in the example, Lana's account has a similar focus to that of Gleb, illustrating the dual considerations that members of diaspora communities must make in heritage related matters.

Lana: U:m:, uh I just made, this decisi- decision for myself,
I don't know is there any movement and what kind of help they can,
provide for that but…
Erm, and my boyfriend,
his native language is Ukrainian.
So, but he also speaks er Russian?
And sometimes we speak Russian,
then, 'Oh, we should stop that,
let's- let's speak Ukrainian',
and we swap to Ukrainian,
so… er, and I think when- when I, will have kids,
I think I definitely will try to speak them,
Ukrainian,
and English,
and try to exclude Russian.
I know that, it's-
it's maybe sounds a bit mean but,
um, yeah,
they should really know who they are.
((laughter)) [I think so.]

Corinne: [Yeah, and-]
And, um, what do you think is-
what is, er, really driving that decision for you,
do you think?
Lana: Er, yeah,
as I mentioned before I think it's because, um,
when you speak language,
that language, er, make up your consciousness?
So, i- it makes your minds- your mind.
And... yeah,
and e- especially,
when I came, in New Zealand,
and when I met a lot of people from a lot of different, er, backgrounds?
Like, Chinese, Indian, Nepalean, a:nd Arabian, other,
and I wa- and I have- um l-
one of my supervisor,
he is from, um-
he is from... um, Basel,
it's Switzerland?
And- and he ki-
he speaks with his kids in er, German,
and, for me it was just amazing how,
this just simply, s- sound,
interactions,
so just think like if you think about physical,
like physical part or scientific part,
it's just sound waves.
And how those sound waves?
Help to communicate with er people,
it is amazing ((laughs))
So, yeah,
and, um, sorry I forgot the question.
Corinne: The, reason behind, switching for you is?
Lana: Yeah, I think that I-

I just want to feel, er that I'm more Ukrainian.

And, er, because I missed a lot,

of that culture,

I want to catch up,

and, I want to,

become, Ukrainian.

((laughs)) Like, proper Ukrainian.

When Lana begins talking about her choice to change her mother tongue (in response to my previous question 'I've heard some people talking about a movement to change their mother tongue. Have you heard about that at all?'), she says, 'U:m:, uh I just made, this decisi- decision for myself, I don't know is there any movement and what kind of help they can, provide for that but...' For Lana then, the decision to change her mother tongue was a personal decision that she does not attribute to any outside movements nor to any particular direct influences from other people. For her, the decision to change her mother tongue is a personal one. This is interesting because while this decision reflects underlying ideologies also found in Ukraine such as language being tied to identity (as she discusses later in the excerpt), her decision has not, at least consciously, been affected by the changing mother tongue Discourses found in the home country.

Lana then continues her explanation by providing an example from her everyday life in New Zealand: 'Erm, and my boyfriend, his native language is Ukrainian. So, but he also speaks er Russian? And sometimes we speak Russian, then, "Oh, we should stop that, let's- let's speak Ukrainian", and we swap to Ukrainian.' As Lana comes from a part of Ukraine that is Russian language dominant, she herself grew up speaking primarily Russian. As she explains, her boyfriend in New Zealand has Ukrainian as a native language but also speaks Russian. Therefore, Lana and her boyfriend share Russian as a common language, and it thus makes sense that they would use this common language for everyday interaction. However, as Lana explains, she is now making a conscious effort to use the Ukrainian language instead. In fact, as she voices herself in this example, she issues a directive ('we should stop that'), which is rather direct pragmatically in New Zealand English and is often associated with stopping a negative behavior. This thus positions the act of speaking Russian as a negative behavior for Lana, which is remedied by speaking Ukrainian instead.

The next part of Lana's explanation closely mirrors Gleb's excerpt above, and in fact mirrors many of the motivations explained by the Ukrainians whom I interviewed in New Zealand, the United States and Canada. As Lana explains, her future plans for her children do not include the Russian language: 'so... er, and I think when- when I, will have kids, I think I definitely will try to speak them, Ukrainian and English, and try to exclude Russian. I know that, it's- it's maybe sounds a bit mean but, um, yeah, they should really know who they are.' When Lana imagines her future children, she constructs their imagined identities (Kanno & Norton, 2004; Pavlenko & Norton, 2007) as still embodying a sense of Ukrainian-ness. Because of this, she says that she plans to speak to them in the Ukrainian and English languages but to exclude the Russian language. Since Lana explains elsewhere in her interview that she plans to live in New Zealand at least in the anticipated future, it makes sense that she says she will use English with her children, as this is the dominant language in New Zealand. In then choosing a second language, however, she (like Gleb) discusses choosing Ukrainian over Russian. Even though Russian is Lana's native language, she says that she will choose her less dominant language (Ukrainian), which further supports her earlier statement that she is working on changing her mother tongue.

Lana also goes one step further in her narrative than Gleb did by saying that she will also purposefully exclude the Russian language. Lana's reason for this is that 'they should really know who they are,' which for Lana means the use of Ukrainian and not the use of Russian. Therefore, according to Lana's explanation, it is the knowledge and use of the Ukrainian language that allows one to embody what it means to be Ukrainian. In this part of her excerpt, Lana also anticipates negative reactions towards her decision, double-voicing those opposing views by saying 'it maybe sounds a bit mean'. However, she also uses this as an opportunity to answer this critique, reasserting her positive identity practice that being Ukrainian means speaking the Ukrainian language. This view carries with it a dialogic echoing of Discourses in the home country, but in framing her position as a decision for the imagined identity of her future children, Lana is also drawing upon diaspora Discourses of heritage language use and maintenance.

When I then asked Lana to explain more about the motivation for her decision to use Ukrainian and exclude Russian in the future (a very purposeful negative identity practice), she says, 'as I mentioned before I think it's because, um, when you speak language, that language, er, make up your consciousness? So, i- it makes your minds- your mind.' Once again, Lana is drawing intertextually upon ideologies held by some Ukrainians in Ukraine, dialogically echoing these home Discourses. Like Olesya in Chapter 2, Lana also subscribes to a Sapir-Whorfian type belief that language is related to consciousness and therefore affects the way you think (see Casasanto, 2012). Similarly, as noted by Braha (2011), people who are more conscious of their own sociolinguistic ideologies are also more conscious of specific language usage. Therefore, Lana's purposeful move towards Ukrainian and away from Russian speaks to her high level of conscious sociolinguistic identity negotiation. To further exemplify Lana's belief of the connection between language and culture, she begins naming a variety of cultural backgrounds from which New Zealanders come, but she then loses focus as the conversation becomes more abstract.

After indirectly requesting that I repeat the focus of the question, Lana answers by returning to her idea of speaking the Ukrainian language as embodying Ukrainian culture. As she explains, 'I just want to feel, er that I'm more Ukrainian. And, er, because I missed a lot, of that culture, I want to catch up, and, I want to, become, Ukrainian. ((laughs)) Like, proper Ukrainian.' In Lana's explanation, it is interesting to note that she references not currently feeling as Ukrainian as she would like to feel. This is particularly striking, as Lana is from Ukraine and grew up in Ukraine. However, she states that she 'missed a lot', presumably by growing up in a more Russian-dominant area of Ukraine. Therefore, even though Lana grew up in Ukraine, it is not the particular positive identity association with Ukraine that she would like to have.

To feel 'more Ukrainian', for Lana, means associating more with the Ukrainian language and with traditional Ukrainian (i.e. non-Russian) culture. In order to achieve this, Lana is focusing on the Ukrainian language as a means through which to access and embody the particular type of Ukrainian culture that she desires to have, that is, her idea of 'proper Ukrainian'. Thus, while Lana's ideas about language use being an embodiment of Ukrainian culture dialogically echo Discourses of being Ukrainian found in Ukraine, these ideologies have also impacted upon Lana's sense of self, marking her identify as not a 'proper Ukrainian' because she did not grow up with traditional Ukrainian (i.e. non-Russian) culture and language. This is important to note because it displays both what is to be gained and what is potentially to be lost by such Discourses of a particular language embodying a particular culture. Even though Lana is from Ukraine, by not meeting the current preferred Ukrainian identity model, she feels less a welcome member of her home country, less than a 'proper Ukrainian'. Therefore, there is a tale of caution in a narrative such as hers – that in the process of establishing a unifying national identity, people must also be careful to not unintentionally ostracize those who do not meet the preferred definition of belonging.

Further Remarks

This idea of being able to 'change one's mother tongue' to which many of the participants ascribed, challenges previously existing conceptions of how language is embodied. For example, most sociolinguists have argued that language allows the speaker to index particular sociocultural aspects with which they choose to affiliate in an interaction (Blommaert, 2005; Bucholtz & Hall, 2005; Mendoza-Denton & Hall, 2010), and this also matches the current data for this project. However, still others have argued that language is completely inseparable from identity because this is how we 'construct, tell and retell our life stories' (Prescher, 2007: 193). However, it is this latter conceptualization of the embodiment of language that the present data challenge. Rather than being inseparable from one's sociocultural identity, many of the participants in the current study view language as something that is embodied in such a way that it reflects one's identities *and* ideologies, such that a change in reflexive positioning can also mean a change of language embodiment.

Understanding this view of language embodiment also has implications for how we understand communities of practice. For some of these speakers, what you *do* in the context of the war is not in itself enough to grant you membership to this community of practice. Rather, it is the incorporation of *both* positive and negative identity practices that matter the most – that is, practices that align with Ukraine *and* disalign with Russia (cf. Bucholtz, 1999; Seals, 2017b). For speakers who were more invested in changing their mother tongue, they saw it as necessary both to speak Ukrainian and to stop speaking Russian. However, not all participants held this view, as will be discussed further in Chapter 7.

Additionally, those taking part in efforts to change their mother tongue linearly positioned these practices differently. Some participants discursively constructed this practice as something that is tied to prior historical events, while some participants constructed it as a more recent occurrence tied directly to the events of the Ukrainian war. For the former group, they situated their discourses of changing their mother tongue in historical movements, therein drawing more upon institutional symbolic capital. This group also did not view language as a stable variable. Rather, they viewed language as intrinsically tied to motivation, such that efforts to change the mother tongue were a way to actively attempt to resolve the inner conflict that some self-identifying Ukrainians currently felt as speakers of Russian.

For the speakers who connected the 'change your mother tongue' efforts directly to the recent events of the EuroMaidan protests and the Ukrainian war, speaking the Ukrainian language has become as symbolic for them as is wearing Ukrainian embroidery, such as the vyshyvanka. Many of the young Ukrainians in particular felt that a purposeful effort to change one's mother tongue to Ukrainian was a conscious self-re-positioning that aligned with an increasingly popular singular construction of Ukrainian national identity (Shulga, 2015). Additionally, alignment with this rising national identity also made the implicit erasure of Ukrainian identity no longer acceptable (cf. Tsentr Doslidzhennya Suspil'stva, April 2014). For example, for Ukrainians such as Ruslana, it was no longer a minor offense to be called Russian by those who did not know better; instead, this was now deeply troubling to her sense of self and in need of correction, even if it meant speaking an internationally less commonly used language.

Finally, a view from Ukrainians in the diaspora provides further considerations. Some of the participants from within the diaspora were also taking part in this movement because they too felt that knowing and using the Ukrainian language embodies what it is to be Ukrainian. However, while echoing these Discourses from the home country, members of the diaspora also faced additional challenges regarding language choice and use. Already living in English-dominant host countries, choosing between Russian and Ukrainian also meant choosing which heritage language to pass on to future generations (cf. Seals & Olsen-Reeder, 2017). This was particularly difficult for individuals such as Gleb who are Russian-dominant speakers. Deciding to pass down Ukrainian as a heritage language instead of Russian to his children also means teaching himself the language well enough to then teach it to them. Therefore, members of the diaspora taking part in this movement also face the difficult challenge of helping children acquire and maintain a language that is not the former's own dominant language – a difficult balance to strike in the midst of generational language shift.

Notes

(1) Author's translation.
(2) Some Ukrainians attribute discussions of 'patriotism' to leftist radical views about Ukraine asserting its authority and banning all things Russian.
(3) 'Tutor' is a term commonly found in British, New Zealand and Australian English. In North America, the equivalent term is most often 'Teaching Assistant,' though the term 'tutor' in these former contexts is also at times used to refer to any university teaching staff.
(4) Photo by *Bruin* and accessed via Wikimedia Commons: https://commons.wikimedia.org/wiki/File:Ukrainian_Embroidery_offered_at_Soyuzivka.jpg
(5) Photo by *Serdechny* and accessed via Wikimedia Commons: https://commons.wikimedia.org/wiki/File:Ukrainian_girls_wearing_vyshyvankas_at_the_Independence_Day_celebration.jpg
(6) In saying 'patriotism or whatever', Denys has minimized the effect of the word 'patriotism', which has a negative, leftist radical connotation for some Ukrainians.

6 Investment and Loyalty in the Ukrainian Diaspora

The current chapter specifically focuses on interview data from participants in Ukrainian diaspora communities. Diaspora communities are defined here as self-aware communities from a particular homeland, now clustered in multiple hostlands, with some sort of real or imagined ongoing connection to the homeland. Furthermore, 'membership in a diaspora now implies potential empowerment based on the ability to mobilize international support and influence in both the homeland and hostland' (Butler, 2001: 189). This dual mindfulness of influences of both the homeland and hostland is of crucial importance to the current study. As shown in Chapter 5, the balancing of these simultaneous Discourses is challenging for members of the diaspora, and it is this particular challenge upon which this chapter is focused. Furthermore, because it is also important to consider whether individuals joined the diaspora voluntarily or not, the interviews for this chapter are restricted to those who self-elected to move abroad.

Additionally, this chapter considers how integration into society is managed and policed by micro- and macro-societies and communities. How do people talk about and police who is part of 'us' of a socially constructed collective identity, versus who is part of the 'other' (Fligstein, 2008; Wodak & Boukala, 2015)? While this was part of the focus of Chapters 3 and 4, for diaspora communities this also includes a balanced consideration of the attitudes of the individuals, of the diaspora communities and of the host societies (Safran, 1991). Furthermore, these attitudes are influenced by and influence perceived identities of the immigrants, as well as perceived commonalities or differences with the host societies, with other diaspora communities, and with Ukrainians in the home country – all of which contribute to the creation of a complex network. This complexity then adds further difficulty when immigrants are asked by their various networks – with whom and where do your loyalties lie?

In answering these questions, immigrants in diaspora communities consider their investment in languages and communities (Norton, 2013; Norton Peirce, 1995). This investment is connected both to the current and future goals of the individual, by means of acquiring cultural capital. Choosing where and in what to invest is then an example of identity as a site of struggle (Norton, 2013; Weedon, 1987). It is a struggle because it is multiple and in constant negotiation and renegotiation over time. It occurs within and between competing Discourses, and identities can overlap and even contradict each other depending on positionings taken up and assigned in discourse (Norton, 2013; Weedon, 1987). All of these considerations then lead to two primary questions. First, how do members of the Ukrainian diaspora negotiate integration into their new communities? Second, how does (or does not) the war in Ukraine further complicate this negotiation?

All of these developments affected both those in Ukraine and those in Ukrainian diaspora communities around the world, of which there are many. As mentioned in Chapter 1, the largest Ukrainian diaspora communities live in Russia, Canada and the United States. Since the communities focused on in this chapter include those in North America and New Zealand, the populations of these communities are presented again here. In the United States, over 900,000 residents claim Ukrainian descent, and over 275,000 residents were born in Ukraine (US Census, 2004). In Canada, Ukrainian-identifying residents number 1.25 million (cf. Seals, 2014). Furthermore, in New Zealand, over 1,800 residents claim Ukrainian descent, and over 1,100 residents were born in Ukraine (cf. Seals & Olsen-Reeder, 2017). Thus, while there are long-established large diaspora communities in North America, they are newer and smaller in New Zealand, though still relatively strong in number for New Zealand's small population size of slightly over 4 million people in total.

Diaspora and Transnational Research

As globalization and international incidents have become more frequent in recent years, so too has research involving borders and the crossing of them (Liebscher & Dailey-O'Cain, 2013; McCarty, 2014; Menard-Warwick, 2009; Piller & Takahashi, 2011; Watt & Llamas, 2014). As part of this, research focusing on transnationalism and on diaspora communities has also increased. While both focus on the concept of crossing international spaces, the two still maintain a slightly different focus. As explained by Faist (2010: 9):

> *diaspora* has been often used to denote religious or national groups living outside an (imagined) homeland, whereas *transnationalism* is often used both more narrowly – to refer to migrants' durable ties across countries – and, more widely, to capture not only communities, but all sorts of social formations, such as transnationally active networks, groups and organisations.

Furthermore, Faist (2010) is careful to specify that 'diaspora' has become more frequently used in public circles, therein taking on a more political connotation, while 'transnationalism' is still widely relegated to the academic sphere. Yet, this does not make the latter without political connotations itself. Both concepts (diaspora and transnationalism) connect to ideas of imagined community and imagined nationality (Anderson, 1991 [1983]; De Cillia *et al.*, 1999) as a starting point. Without a shared idea of what makes a nation and who belongs to it, there would be no research of people crossing borders (themselves sociopolitical constructs) between said nations.

Additionally, the notions of diaspora and transnationalism also carry slightly different semantic meanings in regard to perceived movement. While 'diaspora' frequently focuses on a crossing of borders that has led to some degree of settlement in the host country (Bruneau, 2010; Dufoix, 2008), 'transnationalism' focuses on the bidirectional (or more) movements of an individual or group between places, or at the very least on the bidirectionality of their continued relationships between places (Dahinden, 2010; King & Christou, 2010). Therefore, while one focuses primarily on the destination, the other focuses primarily on the continued relationship or movement.

Furthermore, each notion has useful aspects while also having more problematic aspects. For example, while 'transnational' focuses more on the current status of the people in question, as well as possibly their recent history, 'diaspora' carries a more longitudinal focus, also considering sociocultural history. As noted by King and Christou (2010), this distinction is important to consider, especially when we start looking to second-generation members of the diaspora, 'for whom the "destination" is also the "origin"' (King & Christou, 2010: 168). Additionally, while the notion of transnational focuses more on an individual experience, the notion of diaspora assumes somewhat of a collective identity, which can be problematic (Faist, 2010). However, this collective identity of sorts cannot be completely dismissed, as it is this supportive community which is what many people within the diaspora highlight as so important when relocating to a new place. Therefore, in the current book, diaspora does not assume a singular collective identity, but rather a community upon which people in a host society can draw if in need of support from others with a similar sociocultural background.

So why focus on concepts such as diaspora and transnationalism instead of simply focusing on globalization? The reason for the present chapter and entire book is that which is also argued by Faist (2010). Namely, there is an underlying semantic connotation in ideas of globalization that universalizes experiences, focusing more on experiences and/or ideologies that affect at a more (literally) global level. However, the focus of diaspora and transnational research relates more to the exception, therein remaining more focused on the individual experience, whether that individual be a person, a family, or a community. Therefore, that individual focus also reminds us that no person has the same experience as any other. Indeed, these experiences are intersectional (Crenshaw,

1993), with all social and demographic factors tied together as a web, with each pull of a thread affecting the others. Yet, everyone has different threads and therefore has different lived experiences. Furthermore, a focus on diaspora research is also a reminder of the marginalization that diaspora communities and individuals face, in the home, host and larger global societies.

A useful differentiation of types of diaspora communities was developed by Bruneau (2010). In his research, Bruneau delineates four types of diasporas. The first is one in which exact demographics are not as important as the 'entrepreneurial pole' (Bruneau, 2010: 39) – that is, the self-motivation to move abroad. The second type of diaspora is focused on the shared religion of the diaspora. Within this category, Bruneau also includes language, though this conflation of language and religion is highly problematic and should not be merged together. Furthermore, language is now recognized through translanguaging research to be a social construct, wherein any conceptions of a single 'language' are merely sociopolitical constructs in which people find value and therefore invest (Canagarajah, 2013a, 2013b; Cenoz & Gorter, 2013, 2015, 2017; García & Wei, 2014). The third type, which Bruneau calls 'more recent diasporas' (Bruneau, 2010: 40), is focused around the political origin of the diaspora.

The fourth type of diaspora outlined by Bruneau (2010) is that which is focused around a cultural and racial shared origin. However, this is another place where conflation is highly problematic. First, culture is not equivalent to race, and neither is equivalent to or subsumed by or within ethnicity. Second, the concept of 'culture' is treated monolithically in this categorization. However, culture is a multifaceted, socially constructed concept and should be treated as such (just like ethnicity). Furthermore, discussions of racial divides are highly problematic and have as such been problematized in depth in social science research. Rather, what I believe Bruneau means to be focusing on is the sociocultural constructs of 'culture' and 'ethnicity' to which many people subscribe. Therefore, while Bruneau's (2010) four types of diasporas provide a useful departure point, the current chapter and entire book maintain a more intersectional focus, as well as a social constructionist one, treating all of the above categories as socially constructed ideas of reality into which people and communities invest, therein imbuing them with meaning.

Such an intersectional focus is important to maintain, especially when interacting with families in diaspora communities. As such, Hua and Wei (2016) have stressed the importance of understanding the diverse experiences of families in the diaspora and how these experiences play a role in their everyday lives and even directly into their family dynamics, both inside and outside of the home. Furthermore, the way individuals within those families are positioned by those within the host society likewise affects their own self-positioning within said society, as well as their investment (or lack thereof) in the host society. As argued by Hua and Wei

134 Choosing a Mother Tongue

(2016), all of these aspects can both directly and indirectly affect multilingualism and language maintenance efforts. Furthermore, as they argue, and as argued here, all language beliefs and practices, especially for those in diaspora communities, need to be considered within a holistic framework, which includes historical backgrounds and experiences, in order to truly understand them.

A Model for Immigrant Identity, Investment and Integration

One of the most significant findings to come out of the current project is the creation of a new model of negotiation, investment and integration (see Figure 6.1). This model considers immigration trajectories, as well as the recursive nature of identity negotiation and renegotiation, within and between home societies and host societies.

As immigrants continue to go through this cycle, they are made to consider and reconsider their identities, loyalties and belonging in relation to their home and host societies and communities. These struggles and negotiations depend not just on self-positioning, but also on others' positioning of the individual and community, which may or may not match up with self-positioning. Furthermore, individuals experience shifts in this recursive framework differently from each other, depending on intersectional factors such as their and others' home and host geographical regions, genders, ages, occupations, etc. For members of diaspora communities, this cycle can be further complexified, as the diaspora communities within host societies intensify the ongoing negotiation between

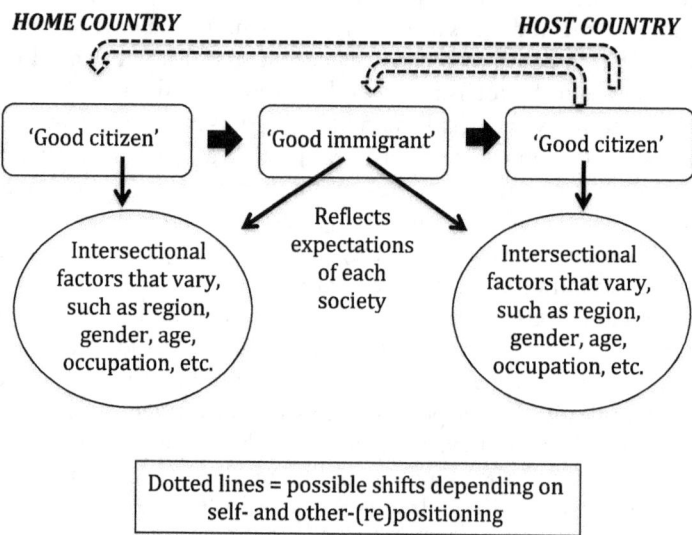

Figure 6.1 Immigrant identity, investment and integration model

home and host societies, since both make up the nature of diaspora communities themselves.

Renegotiating Identity in the Diaspora

To demonstrate how this model can work, illustrative examples are provided below of individuals' struggles with identity, integration and investment. The first comes from Anatoliy (mid-20s, from Central Ukraine, living in New Zealand).

Corinne: How would you say you identify yourself?

Anatoliy: …Well, I think…

Yeah, I'm- I'm actually s- struggling with this… question… uh…

because when I- when I came to Ukraine,

to my city,

it was about two years ago,

I really didn't like what I've seen.

Essentially, nothing changed.

And, I didn't like the way…

how people were thinking,

their attitude…

uh, how they… perceived things. Um…

So, in this sense I'm actually quite different…

Um… I'm not…

that Ukrainian as I was.

I'm not f- fully N- New Zealander… either.

So I'm… kind of in between, uh, probably.

Yeah, well,

Ukrainian New Zealander,

that's probably… uh… best

Anatoliy demonstrates the identity struggle that members of diaspora communities go through living in the host country, especially during a time of war. As he directly states, 'I'm actually s- struggling with this… question.' As he continues to explain, it is not the wording of the question with which he is struggling, but rather with how he feels about his identity. Anatoliy further elaborates by beginning a narrative that places him in time and space two years prior in Ukraine. Partial to his home city in Ukraine, he found upon returning for a visit right before the war began that he no longer felt comfortable there, a place he still identified with as 'my city', showing his alignment with it. It is important to note that during the time he describes, the war had not yet begun. As he says, 'essentially, nothing changed.' However, Anatoliy no longer felt as aligned with the Ukrainian people in his hometown. As he says, he no longer liked, 'how people were thinking, their attitude… uh, how they… perceived things.' Therefore, it was not any particular event that changed his perception. Rather, it was the fact that Anatoliy had re-negotiated his identity and sense of self since living in New Zealand and therefore did not feel that he fit in his hometown in the same way as he had before.

Anatoliy then goes one step further, saying, 'I'm not… that Ukrainian as I was.' In re-negotiating his sense of self, Anatoliy feels that he has lost some of his embodied Ukrainian-ness. Yet at the same time, he is still very much in a state of identity struggle because he states that he also does not feel completely like a New Zealander. Instead, he feels 'kind of in between', representing the complex struggles that take place when negotiating what it means to be a 'good immigrant', a concept which also reflects the ideals of being a 'good citizen' of both the home and host countries, without yet providing a sense of ownership of these identities.

Lana (early 30s, from the Black Sea region of Ukraine, now living in New Zealand) continues the discussion of what it is to be in between places. However, instead of feeling 'not quite either' like Anatoliy, Lana sees her situation as giving her multiple opportunities for who she wants to be in her future self, as discussed in the following excerpt:

Lana: So, I- I'm- I lived in Russia,

I lived in Ukraine,

now I'm living in New Zealand and I can really choose.

((laughs)) Who- whom I want to be in the future and where I want to live,

but it's definitely not Russia?

So it will be either New Zealand or,

I think maybe:,

at some stage if things get better,

and I can be really, useful in the Ukraine,

and there will be really nice place for me when- where I can,

like grew my kids and, er, just find really interesting job to do,

so if, I get my PhD,

and if there will be really need for the lecturers or for people who can do science in Ukraine,

and bring the, you know,

the Ukrainian science on the international level?

So I'm dreaming about something of that as well? ((laughs))
But I also really- really like New Zealand,
and I'm really-
I'm just enjoying being there,
so it's just really, great country?
So at the moment I'm staying in New Zealand,
but, you never know what will ha- what-
what will happen after you finish your PhD. ((laughs))

As evidenced by Lana's multiple mentions of her current PhD studies, she positions herself as 'still in transition', which likely contributes to her perception that she has multiple opportunities to redefine herself, rather than not being sure of who she is. Furthermore, Lana has lived in multiple countries and therefore has had the experience of renegotiating her sense of self more than once. As she says, 'I can really choose. ((laughs)) Who- whom I want to be in the future and where I want to live.' For Lana, her imagined future is available for the taking and molding so that it becomes what she wants it to be. She views her period of transition as an opportunity rather than a struggle.

However, in this opportunity, Lana still dialogically reflects Discourses held by many in her home country – that of allegiance and support for Ukraine during the war. Aligning with this, Lana says, 'but it's definitely not Russia?' using a high-rising terminal, which mitigates this direct statement. Drawing upon Discourses of loyalty to Ukraine, these same Discourses say that a Ukrainian would not then opt to move to Russia. Thus, this is expressed by Lana as 'definitely not Russia'. Instead, Lana says it will either be New Zealand or Ukraine. While Lana is currently living and working in New Zealand and therefore feels some attachment and responsibility towards the country as a resident, she still feels attachment and responsibility towards her home country as well. Therefore, the question of where to live is still in negotiation for her.

It is interesting to note, however, that Lana's mention of moving back to Ukraine is heavily mitigated, with 'maybe:' and 'at some stage' as well as 'if things get better'. Therefore, it is not the current Ukraine at war to which Lana would want to return, but rather an improved future Ukraine to which she could productively contribute. Lana further specifies that this would be in the form of work that would make use of her PhD 'if there will be really need for the lecturers or for people who can do science in Ukraine,' as she has invested much in her PhD studies and future identity as a professional scientist. This discussion of contributing to a need further dialogically echoes Discourses of supporting a country at war, which causes struggle for Lana, as it is to a better Ukraine where she would wish to return. However, even though Lana feels the pull of contributing to the needs of Ukraine as a good citizen of her home country, she also feels the pull of her host country and of remaining in New Zealand. While Lana's investment in both home and host countries provides her with multiple opportunities for her future, this dual investment and associated responsibilities also pull her in two different directions.

While Lana and many in the diaspora experienced identity struggle associated with the negotiation of national loyalty and imagined futures, some participants had already made their decision. This is evidenced in an excerpt from Irina's interview (34 years old, from the Black Sea region of Ukraine, living in New Zealand).

Corinne: So, when you go back home, um,
 do you visit-
 which areas do you visit?
Irina: So [home is here, actually now.]
Corinne: [Oh sorry, sorry X ((laughter))]
Irina: [²Home is where my heart is,
 and I have a] family here,
Corinne: [²((laughs)) Oh is it?
 Yeah.]
Irina: I have a four year old daughter.
 She'll be four in- in a week.
 Uh, and so this is my home,
 actually I believe that [city],
 New Zealand is my home now.

For Irina, her perspective of 'home' and of 'home country' shifted since she had a family in the host country. As she says, 'So home is here, actually now,' referring to New Zealand. She further elaborates that it is her family, especially her daughter, who make her host country also now her home country. She even localizes this further to the particular city that she now lives in, placing emphasis on the city over the country. As she says, 'actually I believe that [city], New Zealand is my home now'. There are likely many reasons why Irina has placed more emphasis on her integration in the host country, but a major reason is clearly the investment in her family's imagined future in New Zealand. As a result of her own self-positioning as a citizen of New Zealand, Irina resisted my positioning of her as an immigrant to New Zealand and instead re-positioned herself once again as a New Zealand citizen, therein showing how individuals can resist and negotiate positionings within the model depending on their individual circumstances and intersectional identitites.

The Host Society's Perception

As shown briefly in the previous example, individuals who immigrate to a new country also must constantly negotiate how others in the host society position them. While they themselves may reflexively position in a particular way, this may have to be renegotiated if someone in the host society positions them differently. Such is the case for Dasha (30 years old, from Eastern Ukraine, living in the United States). As she explains in the excerpt below, one of the most challenging aspects of integration for her into United States society has been how members of the host society perceive and position her.

Corinne: Yeah and um having been in the US now for six years,
and um in the Boston area,
have you found it, ah, easier,
or more difficult to, um-
to live there and integrate…

…

Dasha: Both.
Um, it is of course-
it's a little bit of a challenge,
and it depends a lot on which part you go, ah,
so for say,
if you stay in Boston it's- it's quite-
it's quite easy just because a lot of people are here from different countries, um,
and even though if they are local,
they are usually- are quite worldly,
so they travel different places,
so an accent and being different from them is not-
is not an issue for them.
However if you go to a smaller town somewhere,
New Hampshire which is nearby, um,
or maybe even Connecticut,
ah some people ov-over there,
it's harder just because people-
ah people might not love their area,
and they're uncommon to hear different languages and accents.

Dasha, a resident of Boston for many years, explains in her interview that she felt like she was integrated into the United States now. Upon interviewing her further, she expresses her familiarity with the challenges that immigrants can face, depending on the characteristics and ideals of those in the host society, thus showing the significant role that other-positioning has in negotiating what it means to be a 'good citizen' in the host country. As Dasha says, Boston has many 'worldly' residents who travel frequently, so she feels integration was easier there. However, she also points out specifically that 'an accent' is part of what sets her apart from the host society and could potentially be a problem in the host society by not conforming to their hegemonic expectations, even though this is something she has been fortunate not to experience herself.

Dasha then strengthens this point of the salience of accents for people by comparing Boston to other areas in the United States, even specifically naming states that are known for having many smaller towns and not as many large cities. It is interesting to note that Dasha attributes people 'not lov[ing] their area' to also being those who have a problem with people who come from different countries. It is this hegemonic norm in the host society to which Dasha refers when discussing how these individuals would not be as welcoming to someone who speaks a different language or who has an accent that marks them as different from this hegemonic expectation.

Later in the interview, Dasha returns to these ideas of the host society's perception of those from within the diaspora, as shown in the following excerpt:

Corinne: Yeah and um do-
what's the perception in Boston towards the Russian and Ukrainian languages?

Dasha: Um, I would not-
I would not say that they- um,
I- I don't think that anyone knows that there is two different languages ((laughter)).
If you- if you talk about Ameri- America citizens- ah,
American- American nationalities, yeah yeah,
but ah yeah all-
they don't- they know that they're different countries,
but they don't really go to the language aspect at all,
if they're asking any questions.

Corinne: Yeah and, ah,
does that give you any particular feeling or-
or does it not matter?

Dasha: Um, it is a little bit hard question.
I would say ah maybe three years ago it didn't matter.
I used to-
when people used to ask,
'where you from' and
'are you from Russia',
and I would say yes,
because it didn't really matter to me,
but ah because of the recent- ah recent situation in Ukraine,
and Russia ((laughter)),
I would say it is not really pleasant for me to say that I am from Russia,
so now I try to say that I am from Ukraine,
and if they ask questions,
I would say there is two different countries and go into details about it.
Before I would just say,
if they say 'are you from Ukraine?',
I would say 'yes I'm from Ukraine'.
If they would ask 'are you from Russia?'
Yeah, I would say 'yes I'm from Russia',
because it didn't really matter much ((laughter)).

In this example, Dasha explains that she does not believe her host society even notes her specific language, suggesting that it is just sounding different from the hegemonic expectation that sets her apart. Furthermore, Dasha points out that there is also a seeming lack of interest from her host society in knowing about this aspect of her identity: 'but they don't really go to the language aspect at all, if they're asking any questions.' This perceived lack of interest from many in the host society is notable because Dasha, like Ruslana (see Chapter 5), discusses the increasing importance of a Ukrainian/Russian distinction for her. Since the war in Ukraine began, this has become more of a point of struggle than it was for her previously, as she no longer feels comfortable having her identity as Ukrainian conflated with a Russian identity, illustrated through her voicing of others at the end of the excerpt above.

Distance from the War

For some participants, their geographical distance from the war also became a cognitive distance (cf. Beliaeva & Seals, 2019), though many still talked readily about a continued emotional closeness to the home country. However, participants in the diaspora frequently had difficulty accessing regularly available reliable information about what was happening in Ukraine (cf. Osnach, 2015). For many of the participants, this feeling of being on the outside also impacted upon their cognitive associations with the war in Ukraine.

As an example, Dasha continued talking later in the interview about the identity struggles she has experienced since the Ukrainian war began. For Dasha, the war made the Ukrainian aspects of her identity more salient once again, but she also faced an unexpected confound due to living now in the diaspora, as she explains in the example below.

Dasha: I used to follow [war developments] very closely,
ah looking at the daily updates on the news ah,
but ah recently I have stopped,
just because it's hard to- ah,
it's hard to find the- ah.
There are sources which you can truly trust being over here,
ah not- not-
because so much- so much information,
and all the information is so much different,
so it's- it's really hard to follow from being over here,
so um basically that was the reason why I stopped.
Just because you can see an event,
and you look at the different newspapers,
um English, British ah US, Russian, and Ukrainian,
and they have the event that happened,
but so many different points of view,
like what exactly happened and why,
so they- it's impossible to even find out exactly happened there ((laughter))
…
Um, I feel like it's really strange feeling,
just because I was- ah I was so ah- I was so nervous,
about what's going on,
and I was so worried about it.
I was watching the latest news,
and things trying to ah make some donations,

> to help people with that, ah.
> However when I went ah,
> to Ukraine,
> last year ah-
> in last October,
> I have noticed that ah people just mostly live their daily lives,
> and not involved as much as,
> I would say Ukrainian community over here in Boston is involved,
> in the things going on it.
> But it was really strange to me.
> But I think maybe it's because,
> they're so close,
> and they have to go with the flow,
> and ah still live their daily lives,
> and they really had no choice about that,
> but still that part,
> was a little bit strange to me,
> to see how- how it's over there,
> compared to over here.

As Dasha explains in this excerpt, while she feels that her identity as Ukrainian is particularly salient now during the war, she was surprised that her identity and struggle no longer match up with those living in Ukraine. First, Dasha mentions that in the beginning when the war started, she regularly followed updates. However, the distance in time and space made this more difficult to continue doing: 'because so much- so much information, and all the information is so much different, so it's- it's really hard to follow from being over here.' In this passage, Dasha discursively constructs the divide she cognitively experiences by placing herself 'over here', which is quite a different semantic construction from merely 'here'.

Additionally, being further away from the war makes it more difficult for her to follow the war developments, thus distancing her from the experiences of people in Ukraine – something that was further emphasized when she visited Ukraine and realized that her expectations of Ukrainian residents' current everyday life experiences and war involvement did not match their realities. When having to locate news sources that are not readily available in the host country, many of the participants struggled with sifting through the large amount of it and determining what was accurate or not. As Dasha explains, no matter what country's news sources she turned to or even what language they were presented in, it was (and is) difficult to determine fact from embellishment or even fiction (cf. Masenko & Horobets, 2015; Osnach, 2015).

Dasha then recounts a narrative of an experience she had wherein she volunteered to go to Ukraine to help with the war efforts. She explains that before going to Ukraine, she was anxious due to the media representations of current life in Ukraine. As she depicts, the media coverage of Ukraine was such that she was making donations to war relief efforts because the situation looked so grim for the country. However, her expectations did not match her experience once she arrived in Ukraine. This realization that people's daily lived experiences in her home country did not match with Dasha's perception of what was happening from the host country was unexpected for her. In fact, she was surprised to discover that Ukrainians in Ukraine were less involved in a daily occupation with the war than the 'Ukrainian community over here in Boston is involved.' As a result, she experienced cognitive dissonance and a feeling that it is 'a little bit strange to me, to see how- how it's over there, compared to over here.' According to research done by Liebscher and Dailey-O'Cain (2013), this is because 'time complicates [indexing and positioning] for immigrants, however, because their place of origin changes in the immigrants' absence' (Liebscher & Dailey-O'Cain, 2013: 18). A major event such as a war in the home country can further amplify the cognitive dissonance experienced by those in the diaspora, as the complexification of their pre-existing chronotope becomes more apparent.

Similar to Dasha, Anatoliy (mid-20s, from Central Ukraine, living in New Zealand) also commented on the unexpected differences between life in the home country and life in the diaspora. In the following example, Anatoliy, like Dasha, comments on the difficulties of balancing home country and host country responsibilities and expectations with their realities.

Corinne: Um, so, how much does the- the current… war in Ukraine affect your… daily life?

Anatoliy: Um… when I'm at work…

Er, it doesn't really affect,

because I don't think about it, er…

but when I open Facebook,

and I open it every day…

er, it does affect all the time,

because that's pretty much all I read…

This is how I get, er, news.

Erm… this is where I… see people's, er, experience…

((phone rings))

Er, it's almost time,
but I'll- I'll- I'll- I'll finish, er... that...
Erm, so...
When I start thinking about it,
that does affect me,
because I also have to think, er,
what if it gets worse,
what shall I do.
Shall I bring my parents?
Actually,
I can bring my parents,
but what about my grandparents... right?
Er, it will be very difficult for them to have... er, long flight.
Or- and even if I bring my parents,
what- sh- what will they do in New Zealand?
They don't speak English.
There's very limited, er, community of Russian speaking people,
and they probably don't want to speak to Russian speaking people,
in fact,
I've seen Russian people,
standing in front of the Parliament saying,
stop, er... Nazi... er, in Donbass.
That's- that's an- another horror... stories which... they are... sharing...
Putin is sharing...
that in Ukraine people, er, are Nazis...
yeah, and this is the kind of government that came to power...
er, that, er...
And this is the people who actually know me,
and I know the-
not very closely... er, but close enough...
that... Ukrainian community came... to... honor... er... the leader of Russian community...
I mean, she died, and they just came to pay respect...
So, they actually saw us coming to them,

and... we were actually... getting along... reasonably well...
And after all these things, er, started happening...
they come up with those banners saying,
stop, er... racism... er... and killing in Ukraine,
meaning that that's Ukrainian army who is doing all those atrocious things.
Yeah.
So, er, I would assume that people living here,
they have access to information,
they- they would think differently...
but they're still keep on denying...
Because, you know,
it's uncomfortable to think that your country is actually the, er,
root cause... of so many deaths,
and there's no end yet to that... (sighs)

Anatoliy begins the excerpt by reflecting upon the role that social network websites such as Facebook play in the Ukrainian war's influence in his daily life. While he says that the news on social network websites does not bother him while he is at work (implying he does not access social network websites at work), this news does however have a major impact upon him outside of work. As evidenced by this passage, Anatoliy relies heavily on social network websites for his news. As a result, most of the information that he would see would be that shared by people from similar viewpoints – what communication scientists refer to as 'echo chambers' (Bakshy *et al.*, 2015; Colleoni *et al.*, 2014).

Therefore, it is not entirely surprising that Anatoliy would be shocked by events from differing viewpoints, such as that which he describes later in the excerpt: 'they have access to information, they- they would think differently... but they're still keep on denying.' Of course, the echo chambers echo on all sides and thus influence the opinions and viewpoints for people of all political persuasions, which is why it is also possible to get people believing extremist propaganda, such as in the situation alluded to by Anatoliy when pro-Russian extremists protested against the Ukrainian people in front of New Zealand's parliament building. Furthermore, these echo chambers contribute to the real-life divide between people and factioning between groups, such as what Anatoliy describes for the situation of the Russian and Ukrainian diaspora communities in New Zealand.

In addition to trying to balance news and opinions on social media from the home and host countries, Anatoliy explains how members of the diaspora must also weigh up the news they hear against real-life practical concerns. For example, even though Anatoliy lives and works in New Zealand and is investing in life in his host country, the war in Ukraine has required that he also invest in possible futures for his Ukrainian-based family if the war made it so that they had to leave Ukraine. As Anatoliy narrates a think-aloud of sorts, we get a glimpse into the struggle that he faces if his home country and host country worlds were to more directly collide: 'because I also have to think, er, what if it gets worse, what shall I do. Shall I bring my parents? Actually, I can bring my parents, but what about my grandparents… right? Or-and even if I bring my parents, what- sh- what will they do in New Zealand?' Helping his parents leave Ukraine would not just involve concerns of departure, but also concerns of arrival, as he would be involved in helping his parents establish a new future. Therefore, the war has complicated things such that Anatoliy no longer worries just about his own integration and investment in the host country, but also must worry about imagined futures for his family, including both departure from the home country and arrival and settlement in the host country.

An important aspect of the model above that should be highlighted is its intersectional nature, such that it acknowledges the individual experiences and concerns for each person negotiating what it means to be an immigrant and/or citizen is any given country. As such, Ksusha (36 years old, from Central Ukraine, living in the United States), who is also living in the diaspora, has had a different experience during the war than Anatoliy. However, her different experience is no less disruptive for her identity negotiation, as she explains in the excerpt below.

Corinne: Yeah, um, and do you-
have you- has it felt any different, um
seeing all this,
from the US instead of Ukraine?
Do you think it's made any difference for you?
Like watching it?

Ksusha: Um, I'm um probably easier,
because you know I'm not going through:
any of that stuff,
like I'm not economically affected.
My parents- my parents do but,
I myself, I don't,
except maybe oil prices go down so,

Corinne: Yeah,

Ksusha: Um, actually, uh I-

	it m- might be easier for me,
	than people who are there.
Corinne:	Yeah.
Ksusha:	But on the other hand,
	you really wanted to take part in it, you know,
	you want to help,
	you want to be there,
	but then you realize you're actually more help here,
	because you can make, money and send it there instead of, you know,
	being on the XX end and not helping but,
	during Maidan I really wanted to be there and,
	all I really want to, you know, help uh,
	go to the hospital and help soldiers and wounded,
	people there you know just… be like,
	a pair of hands that can, you know,
	buy food,
	bring something.
Corinne:	[Yeah.]
Ksusha:	[Things like that.]

Ksusha begins by saying that it has been easier living in the United States during the war than living in Ukraine, and she contrasts this with her parents' experience. Ksusha's reference to oil prices going down implies that life in the United States in fact got even easier than it was before because lower oil prices means less expensive gasoline in her host country for cars. This contrasts quite differently with her parents' experience in an economically affected region, the home country.

However, while the practicalities of life may be easier, Ksusha stresses that this does not mean that the war is emotionally easier for her to handle than it is for people in Ukraine. Rather, living in the diaspora brings with it a different set of emotional challenges when thinking about the war in her home country. Ksusha expresses feeling the geographical distance as a difficulty because it prevents her from easily taking part in the war efforts. Even if the geographical distance itself were not an issue, it would also mean pausing her host country trajectory to return to her home country, an option that is not easily accessible for most people in the diaspora. Furthermore, by using 'you' when expressing these emotions, Ksusha also universalizes these feelings, therein including all of those in the diaspora who are having similar experiences to herself. Therefore, she faces the struggles of negotiating loyalties and investments not by herself, but alongside an imagined community of like-positioned individuals.

However, the struggle is strongly evidenced by Ksusha returning once more to her desire to support her home country during the events of Maidan, which she further personalizes through the use this time of 'I' instead of 'you'. Interestingly, while these feelings are expressed individually, the work that she imagines doing is not about the individual, but rather about the collective community, as evidenced by phrases such as 'be like a pair of hands'. Therefore, the overall needs of her home country and those she imagines there lead her to have a dialogue with herself involving identity, investment and the positioning of loyalties.

Language Ideologies and Integration

Another area that was highly salient for participants in the diaspora was that of language ideologies. As discussed in previous chapters, many of the Ukrainians interviewed in this book already contend regularly with ideologies around language choice and use in relation to identity in their home country (Besters-Dilger, 2009; Csernicskó, 2017; Maiboroda *et al.*, 2008; Masenko, 2004). However, members of the diaspora must likewise contend with language ideologies within the host society. The participants in this book who live in diaspora communities all live within English-dominant societies, including Canada, the United States and New Zealand. Therefore, when discussing language ideologies of these host societies, the focus is primarily on the dominance of English and the ways in which non-native English speakers are positioned by members of the host countries. This other-positioning from the host societies is one of the most frequently mentioned ways by which the members of the diaspora felt themselves re-positioned again into the role of immigrant instead of resident or citizen. Such is the experience for Ilona (35 years old, from Western Ukraine, now living in the United States) as outlined in her interview excerpt.

Corinne: How have you found it, um, integrating into the US, um,
in both Seattle and then in, uh,
Southern California as well,
was there a difference?
And was anything easier or harder in one place or the other?

Ilona: Well um, California is definitely more,
accepting of different backgrounds,
than Seattle is, um,
for me:
a big factor was also the age,

> when I came to US I was a teenager.
>
> I didn't speak any English so it was very difficult for me to integrate,
>
> to begin with, um,
>
> and I don't think it had anything,
>
> to do with me speaking Ukrainian or Russian,
>
> it was just because I didn't speak English.
>
> …
>
> I- I learned how to read first and then how to write but,
>
> for a long time I didn't speak,
>
> just because I was,
>
> either embarrassed of the accent or I- I was,
>
> I was very close mouthed,
>
> I- I was reluctant to actually speak,
>
> open my mouth and talk.

Ilona's experiences echo those of Dasha when first living in the United States and struggling with what it means to be a 'good immigrant' and later a 'good citizen' in this society. While Ilona attributes much of her experience to age, what she describes actually has more to do with language ideologies. As she explains, 'and I don't think it had anything, to do with me speaking Ukrainian or Russian, it was just because I didn't speak English.' She too found that speaking specifically English was the crucial host-society expectation to meet, regardless of her home country language. Furthermore, speaking English with her native accent was such a marker for her of not meeting the host-society's expectations that she chose instead to not speak at all for a very long time. Therefore, host country ideologies around what a 'good citizen' of the host country sounds like, as opposed to a 'good immigrant', kept Ilona from speaking in an attempt to keep herself from being othered and marked as an 'outsider'.

Kyrylo (early 20s, from Eastern Ukraine, now living in the United States) likewise experienced the strength of language ideologies in the host country and how these language ideologies actually contradicted the language ideologies of his home country, as he explains in his narrative.

Kyrylo: And then,

after I visited Chicago and there was this Ukrainian community,

I understood like,

((laughter)) if you want to live in,

Corinne: [((laughs))]
Kyrylo: [Chicago you] ((laughs)),
 you should speak Ukrainian,
 and don't speak uh Russian language to Ukrainians,
 because it's like biggest,
 concerns here,
 and uh one of the biggest concerns,
 and uh then I applied to Kyiv Mohyla Academy which is,
 totally Ukrainian,
 and uh there was even legends in Kyiv Mohyla Academy that,
 if someone speak a Russian language uh during,
 not during uh, uh seminars,
 not during, like, class,
 not in classroom even,
 somewhere on uh,
 state like some- some- somewhere in academy,
 if you speak Russian language,
 they can fire you I mean like.
Corinne: [Wow.]
Kyrylo: [((laughs))]
 but it was the legend,
 uh I don't know,
 did it happened or not,
 but it's like,
 okay all freshmans,
 when they're coming to Kyiv Mohyla Academy,
 first, like half year or even a year,
 they speak Ukrainian ((laughing))

Kyrylo, who is originally from Ukraine, had been visiting Chicago in the United States at the beginning of his narrative and therefore takes this as the point of departure for the contrast he sets up in his narrative. However, it is important to keep in mind the background information that Kyrylo lived in several places in Ukraine and is originally from the East, though he and his family speak both Russian and Ukrainian and are themselves taking part in the effort to change one's mother tongue (see Chapter 5). When Kyrylo visits Chicago at the beginning of his story, he encountered a strong pro-Ukrainian, and simultaneous anti-Russian (Csernicskó, 2017), language ideology within the Chicago Ukrainian diaspora. While this ideology is not one shared by all Ukrainian diaspora communities, it is the ideology that was foremost presented to Kyrylo upon his visit to Chicago.

Kyrylo then connects his experience with language ideologies in the Chicago Ukrainian diaspora with his experience at Kyiv Mohyla Academy, which he describes as 'totally Ukrainian', therein positioning the university as aligned with purist ideologies of what it means to be Ukrainian (Braha, 2011; Csernicskó, 2017; Masenko, 2004). Part and parcel with this positioning was the assumption that the university also subscribes to the 'real Ukrainians speak Ukrainian' ideology, which ended up becoming an urban myth of sorts in this context. However, this legend was still believable enough for students beginning to study at the university that 'all freshmans, when they're coming to Kyiv Mohyla Academy, first, like half year or even a year, they speak Ukrainian.' Even though it is a myth that freshmen would be required to speak only in Ukrainian at the university, it diaologically echoes enough pre-existing ideologies in society that the freshmen believe it to be true.

Given the trajectory of Kyrylo's narrative, it is highly possible that he was also one of these freshmen, as he had already experienced the realization of such language ideologies in the Chicago Ukrainian diaspora community. Therefore, once again the diaspora dialogically echoed ideologies found within the home country, but they were once again manifested in a different way such that the 'truth' existing within the diaspora was no longer the same as the 'truth' existing within the home country. Due to experiences with both home and host country ideologies of language use, Kyrylo had to negotiate and renegotiate his own positioning while reflecting upon experiences with both.

Following Kyrylo's description of more extreme language ideologies in the host country than in the home country, Ilona's interview also described such an experience with her own diaspora communities in another part of the United States. Ilona, like Kyrylo, also takes part in the change your mother tongue efforts. However, while Kyrylo is still heavily invested in the home country, Ilona is heavily invested in the host country. Thus, while both align with Ukraine, Ilona positions herself more as a member of the host country now. This then impacts upon her investment in host country diaspora experiences as well, as described in her interview excerpt.

Corinne: Um and when you're with your friends, um, what do you speak then.
Ilona: Um, well:
uh I have distinct groups of friends.

I have my Russian speaking friends,

I have Ukrainian speaking friends and,

obviously I have just uh American, English only speaking friends so,

with Ukrainians most of them speak Russian,

but um, lately,

we've been making a point of, um,

if, people understand Ukrainian I,

only speak Ukrainian.

...

Um it- it's, it's weird, um, over here.

We used to have a like this group,

it was all Russian speaking, uh, picnics,

uh, once a month.

It was a lot of people.

And when,

things started happening over there we:

stopped going to these things, um ((recorder beep)),

you know a lot of Ukrainians stopped going to these things,

and then we kind of branched off and, um,

myself and a friend of mine,

we now organize Ukrainian speaking picnics.

In her interview excerpt, Ilona speaks of having segregated groups of friends, with whom she speaks the dominant language associated with each group. Of particular note is that she says that 'obviously' she has English-only speaking American friends, again showing the hegemonic society norm and expectation of being a monolingual English speaker to be a 'good citizen' of the United States. Furthermore, she also says that now she makes 'a point' of only speaking Ukrainian when people understand it, thus aligning with the Discourse of a 'good citizen' of Ukraine and the ideology that 'real Ukrainians speak Ukrainian'. However, she adds the caveat of only following this rule if the interlocutor understands Ukrainian, thus showing alignment with the practices of friendly non-accommodation (Chapter 5), as well as discursive and ideological negotiation between home and host societies. Ilona also talks of Ukrainians in the United States as 'we', showing her collective identity with them. Part of this identity also involves desisting from participating in Russian-speaking picnics, and establishing separate Ukrainian-speaking picnics within the diaspora, showing further complication of her identity negotiation of what it means to be a member of the Ukrainian diaspora in the United States.

Negotiation Between and Within Diaspora Communities

Some of the participants in the interviews went into further detail about the types of negotiations that they had within and between their local diaspora communities. For these participants in particular, it was important for them that differences *within* the diaspora communities were highlighted just as much as the more often discussed differences *between* diaspora communities. Their narratives of negotiating the differences within diaspora communities again highlight the intersectional nature of the immigrant experience. The first example of this comes from Lana (early 30s, from the Black Sea region of Ukraine, now living in New Zealand), as detailed below.

Corinne: And, have you found,
 in [city], i-
 are the Ukrainian and Russian communities divided?
 Like, um, in other parts of the world,
 or are they more together, or?

Lana: Er, uh yeah, so I'm-
 I think that after what's happened in Ukraine b-
 and between Russia and Ukraine,
 now they're really split?
 A:nd, I think before it was mixture?
 So people think,
 we- people were to-
 those people were tog- together, and,
 because I spoke to the- to those Ukrainians who in the- in our community now?
 And, it was er like, er, community where people were all together,
 like Russians and Ukrainians?
 And after, what happened,
 and Ukrainians said that,
 wha- Russia is, like doing some military aggressive,
 actions towards Ukraine,
 and those people,

>'No, Russia is defending,'
> and blah blah blah,
> and that split-
> actually there are, two communities?
> I'm not sure about like,
> in Ukraine we have, er, in-
> between Ukrainians we have a community,
> we have, erm, like, we have workshops,
> we get together,
> like, er, once- once per two week?
> So and we:- we are communicating,
> together,
> so and, it feels like you have a community of people?
> But, uh I'm not sure that Russian have something,
> becau- er, I have never heard something like that,
> I think, er, I heard that there is a church?
> Er... but I have never, been there and I, couldn't really say.

Corinne: [Yeah.]
Lana: [What's-] What's- wh- what- what- what they are doing there and...
> is it really community for them,
> because I'm, I- I don't really know.

Corinne: Mm-hmm.
> And, when you're at the Ukrainian community events, um,
> did you ever feel like it was a problem to speak Russian,
> or was it fine?

Lana: No, we speak Russian,
> er like a lot of people who especially f- from Kyiv, er,
> and like from Central part, er,
> and from-m-m er Eastern part,
> they mostly speak Russian.
> And, it's be- we speak both languages.
> And sometimes there are some kids,
> they, get used to speak more English ((laughs)).
> They speak English between each other?

But it's- it's okay,
it's normal.
And, er ((clears throat)),
and we speak both and Russian and Ukrainians.
But u:h I'm- I'm- I'm trying to speak more Ukrainian.

When Lana begins answering my question about Ukrainian and Russian diaspora communities, she starts by dialogically echoing what she may have seen as an inferred request in my question. That is, by me asking if the communities were split, she may have been attempting to answer in the affirmative. In doing so, she also draws upon larger societal Discourses of a division between Russia and Ukraine since the war. Lana's use of high rising terminals at the end of 'split' and 'mixture' also indicate that she may be attempting to do positive relational work in the interaction, therein requesting my positive uptake in turn (cf. Warren, 2016; Warren & Fletcher, 2016).

However, in addition to this, Lana is importantly drawing upon intertextual understandings of what is happening in Ukraine. By referring just to 'what's happened in Ukraine', an interlocutor would have to be savvy about the Ukrainian war in order to understand the intertextual link she is making and that this event would lead to an assumed split between Ukrainian and Russian communities.

To further illustrate her statement that the Ukrainian and Russian diaspora communities are now split more than they were before, Lana recounts information told to her by another member of her local Ukrainian diaspora community. In Lana's recounting of the events as told to her, there was once one larger community in New Zealand in which both Russians and Ukrainians took part. This also in fact echoes the stories told to me upon my immigration to New Zealand about the previous membership of the communities.

Lana then says, however, that trouble began after the start of the Ukrainian war. In Lana's story, the Ukrainians first positioned the events as Russian aggression, which made Russians within the community upset. Russians in turn responded that Russia is defending its people. These arguments then led to the communities splitting into two. Notably, both of these recounted sides draw upon some of the most frequent narratives promoted by Ukrainian and Russian media, respectively (see Chapter 3), therein showing the power of the media in influencing people's everyday lives and relationships (Cottle, 2006; MacDuffee Metzger *et al.*, 2016; Masenko & Orel, 2014; Miller & Wert, 2015; Osnach, 2015). Interestingly, after Lana has recounted these reported discourses, she adds to them by saying 'and blah blah blah', therein trivializing these arguments. In Lana's narrative, the split between communities due to these Discourses is more of a shame than something to be happy about.

Lana further discursively illustrates the continuing divide between Ukrainian and Russian diaspora communities in New Zealand by explaining, 'So and we:- we are communicating, together, so and, it feels like you have a community of people? But, uh I'm not sure that Russian have something.' By 'we', Lana means those within the Ukrainian diaspora community, of which she is a member. She describes the community of practice that exists between Ukrainians in New Zealand, therein intertextually drawing upon ideologies of Ukrainians as friendly, community centered people. She further contrasts this against the Russian community, of whose practices she has no knowledge. She says it is 'really community for them', with 'them' meaning the Russian diaspora, therein making clear that in her experience the Russian and Ukrainian diaspora communities do not take part in each other's events since the start of the Ukrainian war.

When I then continued by asking Lana about the language practices within the New Zealand Ukrainian diaspora community, she was quick to confirm that both Russian and Ukrainian languages are welcome, which is also the experience I have had with the New Zealand Ukrainian communities. Lana begins by saying that Russian is spoken in the community, but then interestingly explains this by drawing upon intertextually shared understandings of Ukrainian regional history, as well as Discourses of Ukrainian language ideologies and preferences (cf. Del' Gaudio, 2011; Masenko, 2009). As way of explanation for speaking Russian in the Ukrainian community, Lana explains that there are members from the regions commonly thought to have Russian language dominance and preference. Notably, it is the use of the Russian language that seems to require an explanation, not use of the Ukrainian language because the Ukrainian language is currently unmarked as the language of higher status in Ukraine (Csernicskó, 2017).

As a member of the New Zealand diaspora, Lana also includes English into the language mix when describing language practices in the Ukrainian diaspora. As Lana explains, English is, however, mostly used by the children. In this section of speech, Lana further dialogically reflects echoes of home and host country ideologies regarding language use by children growing up within a diaspora. After pointing out that the children speak English together, she is careful to excuse this practice as normal. This statement dialogically responds to those who would disagree with Ukrainian children speaking English at community events, as many do, especially those from the home country. However, this statement simultaneously reflects experiential discourses found within this diaspora community as well as other diaspora communities in New Zealand that such behavior from children is the norm and bound to happen (cf. Seals & Olsen-Reeder, 2019). Thus, this singular statement reflects Lana's negotiation of both home and host country Discourses and expectations at the same time.

Lana ends by once again reaffirming that both Russian and Ukrainian languages are spoken within the New Zealand Ukrainian diaspora community, therein reflecting the diversity found within. However, she herself is careful to mention that she is 'trying to speak more Ukrainian', again reflecting the prevalence of the 'good Ukrainians speak Ukrainian' Discourse within all Ukrainian communities, home and abroad (Csernicskó, 2017).

Mykola (39 years old, from Eastern Ukraine, living in Canada), a member of Canada's Ukrainian diaspora community, also speaks of the diversity found within diaspora communities. Additionally, Mykola speaks of the choices that members of the diaspora must make when faced with a lack of the linguistic and cultural resources that they had in the home country, as shown in the following excerpt:

Corinne: Um, and, so- so in Canada,
um, ye- are there many, opportunities, um, to-
for- for your kids,
or for anyone who's interested,
to interact more with like um, the Ukrainian community,
or, Russian language speakers,
or Ukrainian language speakers,
or to learn the languages,
is there much opportunity,
for that?

Mykola: There- there are plenty of- of er, Russian schools,
er, Russian weekend schools,
and Russian uh, like community centers,
er the same as Ukrainian actually.
A:nd, I would say Russian and Ukrainians here are way more tolerant to each other,
rather than, they are now,
back in their countries?
And even now,
of course there is a, certain percentage of people, who,
like uh, you know what I mean,
not really tolerant.
But most of people, er, live n- normal lives here,
and they,
okay, they didn't really care.
Since you speak the same language,

most likely you share the same values and shame- same culture,
same background so...
I would say,
may- maybe you may ask someone, like,
after thirty minutes of your, you know, meet-
when you meet someone or,
an hour later you can just, maybe ask,
'Are you from Russia or Ukraine?'
'I'm from Ukraine',
'I'm from Russia',
'Oh, okay, that's fine.'
And that's it,
just keep going. ((laughs))

In response to my question about opportunities to interact with Ukrainian or Russian speakers or to learn these languages, Mykola begins answering by saying that there are Russian and Ukrainian community language schools in his area. However, Mykola then continues explaining that even though the community schools are separated, the Canadian Ukrainian and Russian diaspora communities themselves get along, drawing upon knowledge of the Ukrainian war, as well as the Discourses of fighting between Ukrainians and Russians. Mykola compares the situation in the Canadian diaspora to that of the home country, showing awareness of discourses about what is happening relationally in Ukraine, but also using this as a point of contrast to explain how the Canadian diaspora is different.

Mykola then continues by explaining that 'of course there is a, certain percentage of people, who, like uh, you know what I mean, not really tolerant.' In this statement, he minimizes the influence of this dissenting group by saying 'a certain percentage of people', therein avoiding any substantial or definitive accounting. He also does relational work with me in this statement through 'you know what I mean', which both speaks to a shared understanding of the situation and invites me to support his perspective. He continues by further othering the dissenters, positioning them as the exception to the rule in the Canadian diaspora. In addition to saying that most people don't care, he also says that this majority lives 'normal lives', therein implying that those who disagree with a shared Ukrainian–Russian community are living the non-normal exception to life in Canada.

In the next statement, Mykola then highlights points of similarity between Ukrainians and Russians to further diminish the dissenting view and support the view of Russians and Ukrainians in the Canadian diaspora as a shared group: 'Since you speak the same language, most likely you share the same values and shame- same culture, same background so...' In this statement, Mykola highlights the sameness of Ukrainians and Russians when considered against the backdrop of Canadian society. He then further emphasizes this by voicing imagined Ukrainian and Russian diaspora community members who accept each other and 'just keep going'. In fact, the Discourse of a shared background upon which Mykola draws is the Discourse that was very prominent within Ukrainian diaspora communities in all three locations of this book (United States, New Zealand and Canada) before the war began. However, while many of the Ukrainian diaspora members in the United States and New Zealand have expressed the strong influence of home country Discourses on creating a divide between these countries' Ukrainian and Russian diaspora communities, many within the Canadian diaspora expressed the opposite – that the Canadian diasporas found commonality in their difference.

Another example of this comes from Lilia (27 years old, from Western Ukraine, living in Canada). When she moved from Ukraine to Canada, she planned on using the Ukrainian language due to the large presence of Ukrainians in Canada (see Chapter 1). However, upon arriving, she realized that her expectations did not meet reality, as explained in her excerpt below.

Lilia: Okay, so...
I- I'm just going to show my linguistic, er, observations here.
So, when- when I came to Canada,
and, er I thought it would be-
it would be easy to use Ukrainian language,
because I was-
I was coming to the area where there is a really big Ukrainian community,
and there are still people that can speak Ukrainian.
But I was really surprised that my Ukrainian really differs from- from their Ukrainian.
Because Ukrainian language here was... at a such an in- influence of English A,
and B,
Ukrainian language that first immigrants brought to Canada...
was an old-fashioned nineteenth-century Ukrainian language.
It- it developed in a totally different fashion.
So, ((laughs)) sometimes when people speak here Ukrainian,
I cannot understand them.

Corinne: [Oh, that's interesting.]
Lilia: [I have to- I have to switch to English.
Yep.]

Lilia begins by positioning herself as a linguist (a research field in which she did in fact study), therein aligning with me and drawing upon institutional symbolic capital to support her observations (Bourdieu, 1986; Meadows, 2009). Lilia then continues to explain that before arriving in Canada, she expected that she would be able to easily use the Ukrainian language. This expectation reflects dialogically upon the perception that exists in Ukraine about the Canadian Ukrainian diaspora community – that the Ukrainian language is alive and well. The statement of there 'still [being] people that can speak Ukrainian' further intertextually draws upon the knowledge that once moving to the diaspora, families usually lose the heritage language within three generations (Fishman, 1966; Veltman, 2000). Therefore, to find a diaspora community where the language is flourishing is rare indeed.

In fact, the Ukrainian language *is* spoken by a great many people in the Canadian Ukrainian diaspora, but not in the way Lilia expected. As Lilia explains, the variety she found is 'an old-fashioned nineteenth-century Ukrainian language. It- it developed in a totally different fashion.' Here Lilia is referring to the large emigration from Ukraine that happened during the beginning of the Soviet era. Many people at that time moved abroad to places such as Canada and the United States. There, the varieties of Ukrainian that they spoke took on their own developmental trajectory, different from that occurring in the home country. For example, when the current variety of standardized Ukrainian was created in 1912 (see Chapter 1) and subsequently promoted, this standardized variety was not also used in the diaspora communities, as the beginning of the 20th century is when many of the North American Ukrainian diaspora communities formed (Iarmolenko & Kerstetter, 2016; Seals, 2014). This, as well as the influence of other local languages, resulted in the divergence of North American diaspora and home country varieties of the Ukrainian language (cf. Seals, 2014).

Because of this (at times quite marked) difference between varieties of the Ukrainian language, speakers of the current standardized variety of Ukrainian often have difficulty speaking with those who use the pre-Soviet era varieties of Ukrainian, as expressed by Lilia: 'I cannot understand them. I have to- I have to switch to English.' Thus, while Lilia initially expected to be able to use Ukrainian in Canada, upon arrival, she realized that in many cases this was not a realistic option for her due to major dialect differences. Additionally, her use of a currently more standardized form of the Ukrainian language positions her as an 'outsider' to the Canadian Ukrainian diaspora, a positioning that would be drawn upon in any interactions with her by those using more non-standard forms. This experience in the Canadian Ukrainian diaspora therefore repositioned Lilia as belonging more to the home country than to the host country. The only exception to this is if she instead uses English, which in turn warrants its own considerations, as it would position her in alignment with the majority Canadian society instead of primarily with the Canadian Ukrainian diaspora. As a result, either linguistic choice has implications for Lilia's sociolinguistic identity.

Looking from the Outside In

A further perspective presented from those within the Ukrainian diaspora communities is that of feeling that they are looking from the outside in. That is, they expressed feeling as if living in the diaspora also positioned them outside of Ukraine, thus making their knowledge and opinions of events in Ukraine synonymous with those of an 'outsider'. As a result, they expressed feeling a loss of insider status and associated embodied capital, instead having to validate their views when speaking with friends and family still in Ukraine. However, this 'outside in' position also seemed to benefit them, as these participants explained that they felt as if they gained an additional perspective that they did not have previously. Such is the case as described by Lev (late 30s, from Eastern Ukraine, living in New Zealand).

Lev: Well, situation definitely changed... recently.

Before that...

er... it was absolutely normal...

to say 'I'm Russian speaking Ukrainian patriot.'

And it- it was fine.

Y- you yeah, you just s- speaking... Russian.

But you feel Ukrainian,

and it was absolutely fine.

Now it's s- from- looking from New Zealand,

it's not really... fine, it's... oh...

We- it's weird now.

But I, um ((clears throat))...

er... Skype to my friends there in in Zaporizhia, and they still speak Russian,

In- nothing really changed... to them,

even now.

As Lev's discourse shows, becoming a member of the diaspora can add further struggle to identity by challenging one's beliefs of what is 'normal' in the home country as a 'good citizen'. As he looks now from the outside-in, what he once considered 'absolutely normal' behavior, he no longer considers an acceptable way for a 'good citizen' of Ukraine to behave: 'Now it's s- from- looking from New Zealand, it's not really… fine.' The 'it' that he refers to is living in Ukraine, identifying as a patriot, but speaking Russian (Csernicskó, 2017). However, Lev further explains that his own shifted opinion on this issue does not align with friends of his still in Ukraine. In referring to Zaporizhia, Lev draws intertextually upon the knowledge that this is a Russian-language-dominant area of Ukraine. However, by also referring to 'even now', he intertextually references the Ukrainian war and infers that because of the war, a Ukrainian patriot should speak Ukrainian, therein dialogically echoing the ideology that 'good Ukrainians speak Ukrainian'.

Also speaking from within the diaspora, Vira (mid-30s, from Central Ukraine, living in New Zealand) explains how living abroad has likewise given her a different perspective of life in Ukraine. As she explains in her excerpt, while she has gained a different perspective from the diaspora, this same position of 'outside in' has resulted in some rejection of her perspective from the inside.

Vira: And I, uh, like- I'm losing my friends every time.

My friends from Ukraine.

Not, uh, not through- they are o- ok.

They are alright, he's alive, so all is good, but-

'Oh you- you can't understand us.'

It's- I kno:w- I- I know I can- I could heard this from them.

But actually I got-

They say to me, 'You can't say that.'

I say, 'Oh: I- I can because I- I can see situations from s- from other side.

I can see situation from, uh, like big- big, uh, from big direction.'

Corinne: Yeah, from like a distance.

Vira: Yeah, from- from big distance.

And I- and I- when I- we decided to arrive in New Zealand I think-

Oh, I think, 'Why- Why we live so bad.. in Ukraine?

Why people live so bad?'

I need to understand.

…

> It's good because I can saw how people can live,
> how people can live peaceful...

Vira's experience of looking from the outside in also challenged her idea of what is means to be a 'good citizen' of Ukraine. For her, now that she has achieved a new perspective, it is important to understand 'Why– Why we live so bad... in Ukraine? Why people live so bad?' As she explains, rather than her new perspective being a threat, she could actually help in Ukraine 'because I can saw how people can live, how people can live peaceful.' Her experience was also further intensified, as she reports friends from her home country now rejecting her identity as a 'good Ukrainian' because of her changing perspective and ideologies. Instead, she reports that they tell her, 'you can't say that,' bringing further identity struggle. Therefore, while Vira has gained an outside in perspective due to living in the diaspora, her changing perspectives during the war also challenge dominant ideologies in the home country, resulting in rejection by some, and a new kind of identity struggle for Vira as she negotiates identities both within and between home and host countries.

Redefining Investments in the Diaspora

Finally, it is important to note that living in the diaspora is not all about the struggle between home and host countries all the time. Life in the diaspora also includes a constant revisiting of self, including identification, positioning and investment. For those who have settled into life in the host country, what they once envisioned as being primary areas of investment may shift and change so that new areas of investment take center stage. As an example of this, Denys (mid-30s, from Central Ukraine, living in New Zealand) discusses in the excerpt below his investments after living for two years in the host country.

Corinne: So how invested are you and Vira in the hromada[1]?

Denys: Mm you mean-

Corinne: Like how important is it to you?
Or is it just kinda something that you do?

Denys: Well at the moment it- it is important for my- my family,
because ah first of all we want to keep the language for our children,
and that means that they have to communicate not only with us,
but with someone else,
ah so that's like one of the primary goals,
ah s- um from the other hand,

	ah we've met nice people,
	so why not meet together.
Corinne:	Yeah, yeah.
Denys:	So it's not about ah nationality,
	it's just about ah people we- we met here.
Corinne:	Yeah, community.
Denys:	Yeah, community is really good in my view.

It is first most important to draw attention to the fact that in discussing investment, Denys begins by saying 'at the moment', therein highlighting the moment-to-moment ever-changing nature of identity. Denys explains that currently, his membership in the Ukrainian diaspora community is important for several reasons, the first of which is language maintenance. Denys has realistic expectations when it comes to heritage language maintenance, and that includes knowing that a need for communication in the heritage language must be created (cf. Seals & Olsen-Reeder, 2019). The Ukrainian diaspora community provides a natural environment for this, as the children are often spoken to in Ukrainian and Russian and expected to speak back in these languages.[2]

Furthermore, Denys emphasizes that the second reason why they have invested in the diaspora community is for the people themselves. Crucially, he differentiates this from national identity saying that it is about the people instead: 'So it's not about ah nationality, it's just about ah people we- we met here.' When I prompted if he meant the community, Denys confirmed, saying, 'Yeah, community is really good in my view,' referring to the local diaspora community. The distinction that Denys draws between national group identity and local community identity is important to note because often the focus within diaspora communities is on a shared nationality, which is a sociopolitical construct and reflects what Bruneau (2010) calls 'more recent diasporas', of which New Zealand's Ukrainian community is one. However, Denys's mention of the individual people within the community shows that his investment since arriving in New Zealand and joining the Ukrainian community is in the people themselves. While language maintenance may have been the original reason and may indeed continue to be an important area of investment, local interpersonal connections have also taken on a major investment role.

Further Remarks

The above excerpts provide discursive examples of how individuals in diaspora communities recursively negotiate and renegotiate their identities in relation to home and host societies. Upon arriving in the diaspora communities in the host societies, they must negotiate the expectations of what it means to be a 'good immigrant' and eventually a 'good citizen' in order to successfully integrate into the host society. However, regardless of their own efforts, others' positioning of them can force them to return to this negotiation again and again.

Therefore, integration into the host country is fraught with difficulties that need to be negotiated and re-negotiated. It is especially challenging for members of the diaspora who wish to retain identification with both home and host countries. Pavlo Poliansky, Ukraine's Deputy Minister of Education and Science, also supported this view from a political and educational perspective (as cited in Mykoliuk, 2009, n.p.):

> This may be viewed from the viewpoint of globalism… If Ukrainians (and not only Ukrainians) live in America, Europe, or Canada for many years, preserving their language, traditions, and religion, while remaining at the same time good citizens of their states, we are speaking about integration. But if Ukrainians are afraid of positioning themselves as Ukrainians, communicating among themselves in their native language, and do not dare demand Ukrainian-language schools for their children, these are, I think, the results of assimilation.

Furthermore, these examples show the complicating effect a major political event (such as the Ukrainian War) has on this complex, dynamic system of identity negotiation. Such an upheaval in the home country puts diaspora communities in flux, asking them to revisit what it means to be a 'good citizen' of their original home country, and whether they still align with those ideals. This then has repercussions for even daily interactions in their host society lives and their alignment with home and/or host society ideals.

Finally, the intersectional factors involved in this identity negotiation and renegotiation further come into play in determining how participants view these major political events. Members of the diaspora communities find when returning to the home country that their expectations of current life and experiences in the home country no longer match the realities of those who still live there due to the separation of real and imagined life trajectories (cf. Liebscher & Dailey-O'Cain, 2013). Often, the Discourses that are passed through diaspora communities are echoes of the home country Discourses (cf. Colleoni *et al.*, 2014), but then each also takes on a voice of its own. This further complicates the identity negotiation and struggle of diaspora members, as they must again revisit what it means to now be on the outside looking in.

Notes

(1) Ukrainian word for 'community'.
(2) In fact, the local Ukrainian diaspora community of which Denys and I have both been a part often has prize-giving word games where the correct answers must be given in Ukrainian in order to count, therein encouraging children's use of the language.

7 'It Doesn't Matter What You Speak': Challenges to Dominant Language Ideologies by Ukrainian Young Adults

Before beginning a reflection of the book as a whole, it is important to look at one final topic that arose from an analysis of the data. This last topic dialogically draws upon Discourses presented thus far in the book, especially those concerning the connections between language and identity. Yet, the interviews presented in this chapter introduce a new perspective found among many of the participants – that it does not in fact matter what language you speak.

The position that a specific language does not map onto a specific identity is not a new one. For some cultures, such as many in New Zealand who identify as Māori, abilities in te reo Māori (the Māori language) are not a requirement for identifying as Māori (cf. Ngaha, 2004). This position stems from a long history of linguistic oppression, therein making it impossible for the majority of those who identify as Māori to also be fluent in the language.

Similarly, many Ukrainians, especially young Ukrainians, have reflected upon Ukraine's linguistic history of enforced Russification followed by recent Ukrainisation and decided that proficiency in one particular language (i.e. Ukrainian) is not a requirement for identifying as Ukrainian. This counter-discourse (Foucault, 1977b, 1980) against the ideological meta-discourse of 'good Ukrainians speak Ukrainian' was most prominent among the younger Ukrainians interviewed, especially those in their 20s and early 30s (though not exclusively so). Therefore, it is possible that a new master narrative for Ukrainians is arising – one that takes its cues from diversity and globalization. Excerpts from some of these interviews are presented below.

Underlying Acceptance Amid Complexity of Ideologies

The first set of excerpts come from participants who positioned themselves on the periphery of any particular ideology relating to language and identity. In this sense, they are the more conservative narratives. These participants relied much on reporting facts and opinions of others, therein distancing themselves from direct ownership of the ideologies being presented (Clark & Gerrig, 1990; Sclafani, 2008; Seals, 2012; Thetela, 2001). The first example of this comes from Larysa (early 30s, from Central Ukraine, currently living in Ukraine). Larysa begins in a way that suggests she may be aligning with Discourses of language use equating identity. However, her narrative takes a number of twists and turns before settling on the idea that in the end, it does not really matter what language you speak.

Larysa: Er, but now… er, taking into account all the… ((smacks lips)) events that happened,

of course, er, people er, need to make a choice,

er, just for themselves,

so Ukrainian, er, er,

b- by statistics it was even er,

two years ago named by sixty five per cent of their native language.

Er, and around thirty per cent said that Russian is their native language,

if you'd be pushed to choose.

Er, but now ((laughs)) up to eighty per cent it went up,

seen from the recent research, er,

they name Ukrainian their… native language.

And of course it shows, erm,

the closeness,

and the… identification with the language,

with the history, er…

with all the literature er,

that was written in Ukrainian.

It's- it's a complete association ourselves with the past of- of the country.

So Ukrainian matters a lot,

and I know cases where… people who spoke Russian for the ((laughing)) whole life,

because they were also probably from the East, er,

XXX they switched to Ukrainian consciously.
Er... and they need to make still some efforts, er...
Because they keep thinking maybe in Russian,
but they speak Ukrainian,
in XX,
and there are lots of, er,
cases like this.
And maybe after one- two years it would be of course, er,
absolutely easily ((laughing)) for them ((laughs))...
Er, as for Russian, er,
well, if somebody speaks to me Russian,
or I do speak Russian,
it's okay, er,
but mostly people switch immediately to Ukrainian.
So we have this, er, approach,
speak the language to the person that he speaks to you,
because maybe it's more comfortable for him.
So, e- er, it's never... a problem.
Erm, maybe only from-
in the West it could be a problem,
because they are not, er, fluent, in, er, conversational Russian.
I think all country is bilingual,
but in the Western part which is, actually...
pretty the center of the country in terms of the territory,
they would understand Russian of course,
so then when Russian tourists are coming to L'viv, er,
the larges- the biggest city in the West,
they speak Russian,
((laughs)) nobody ((laughing)) is beating or... er,
giving any strange looks, er,
but they would be answered in Ukrainian.
And if you understand,
people would put efforts to explain,
but just because their conversational Russian, er...
in most cases really not fluent.

In the beginning of Larysa's narrative, she starts to make intertextual references to the war ('taking into account all the... events that happened') and to seemingly draw dialogically upon ideological references to language choice and use in Ukraine. She then segues into stating factual census data. This reporting of data serves two purposes. First, it allows her to draw upon institutional symbolic capital, therein allowing her to position herself as speaking with more authority. Secondly, it distances Larysa from any particular opinions tied to this information, leaving it up to the listener to infer what they will. Furthermore, by adding 'if you'd be pushed to choose' at the end, Larysa shows her knowledge of the fact that most people in Ukraine in fact speak both languages, therein complicating this apparent division.

Larysa then continues to draw upon statistical information, showing the rise in the number of people who said they speak Ukrainian as their native language since the beginning of the war. In addition to showing the rise of the ideological Discourse of 'being a good Ukrainian means speaking Ukrainian', this information that Larysa reports also in turn shows the rise in perceived importance of a shared national identity (Shulga, 2015). Larysa then connects this information to further ideologies about language and identity, which she reports as fact. She then continues by relating information about the 'changing your mother tongue' efforts in Ukraine, apparently further aligning herself with this position.

However, it is interesting what happens next. After reporting so much information to do with speaking Ukrainian instead of Russian in Ukraine, Larysa moves into introducing herself into the narrative and explaining what she would do if someone spoke to her in Russian. Larysa reports in a factual manner that people will mostly accommodate, switching to using the Ukrainian language, but she first states that it is ok if someone speaks Russian to her instead or if she speaks Russian to them, therein aligning with friendly non-accommodation. Therefore, from her own perspective from introducing herself into the narrative, the use of both languages (Ukrainian and Russian) is fine. Therefore, the general population of Ukraine with whom she identifies ('we') take the linguistic approach (accommodation or friendly non-accommodation) that works for them. Thus, according to Larysa, the relationship is more important than the language being used.

Larysa ends her narrative, however, by providing a caveat. As she explains, linguistic accommodation is what she sees happening in most of the country due to widespread bilingualism. However, she says that if a Russian-speaking tourist were to travel to Western Ukraine, they could use Russian, but they would be answered in Ukrainian. Larysa's comment about people not being beaten or receiving strange looks strongly dialogically echoes Klara's joke from Chapter 2. In fact, it is highly likely due to Larysa's laughter while talking about this, that Larysa was purposefully intertextually drawing upon this joke, as it is a well-known joke in

Ukraine, and it is meant to show the ridiculousness of believing that Western Ukrainians would beat a Russian speaker. Instead, as Larysa explains, the reason Western Ukrainians would answer in Ukrainian is not due to purposeful non-accommodation. Rather, she says, 'just because their conversational Russian, er… in most cases really not fluent.' For Larysa, it does not matter in the end what language a person speaks, nor does she believe it to matter for most Ukrainians.

A second example of the perception that it does not matter what language you speak in Ukraine comes from Artem (28 years old, from Western Ukraine, living in Ukraine). However, like Larysa, Artem discusses the complexities of this view under the surface and the effect that ideologies can have on Ukrainians' heretofore more common patterns of behavior regarding language use.

Corinne: Um, so, then I also wanted to ask you, um,
do you think there's been any shift,
in opinion,
recently, um,
about- about the Ukrainian language itself,
and how much it should be used and,
who uses it,
and all of that?

Artem: I think, er, if we take, er,
the same, date,
year from now, er like, er,
back- back year from now.
Er, it shifted a lot.
Like, from both languages,
from Ukrainian and Russian.
Erm, just, because, er,
when, like, during the time of Maidan?
Er, do you know that?

Corinne: Yeah.
[Yeah?]

Artem: [That's when?]

Corinne: [²Yeah.]

Artem: [²Okay.]

Corinne: Yeah.
Ruslana[1] is one of my favorites. [³((laughter))]

Artem: [³((laughs)) Ah, okay. ((laughs))]
Erm, so, eh, during that time, er,
a lot of er,
people in, Western Ukraine, er,
were making like a flash mobs,
they were, er speaking, er Russian,
and I was speaking Russian,
in, er, like social, networks,
and everything,
to support, Eastern part and, eh
people in the East,
were speaking, er Ukrainian?
Er, so it was more of a sign of er, er, sign that-
that we understand each other and support each other?
Erm, s- I- I think it- it er,
this question got way more, awareness but I'm afraid that it may,
er, lose a lot of it- it is-
result, er because XXX.
Because people er, associate Russian, language with Russian,
aggression.

In answer to my question about any shifts in Ukrainian language preference and use, Artem answers by first discursively shifting the timeframe to one year before the interview (before the Maidan protests) and comparing perceptions of language use between the two times. In addition to saying that opinions about language use in Ukraine changed following the EuroMaidan protests and the start of the Ukrainian war, Artem adds a clarifying turn to say that this change has happened for both the Russian and Ukrainian languages, not just Ukrainian. He then directly draws attention to the events of the EuroMaidan protests as a key time that sparked the change in opinions.

Artem then continues by relating a very interesting movement that took place in Ukraine around the time of the EuroMaidan protests. He explains that linguistic flash mobs[2] were occurring in both Western and Eastern Ukraine. As he explains, in these flash mobs, people in dominant Ukrainian-speaking areas such as the West spoke Russian, and people in dominant Russian-speaking areas such as the East spoke Ukrainian (cf. Csernicskó, 2017). Artem even indicates that he himself took part in these linguistic flash mobs ('and I was speaking Russian'). Furthermore, the flash mobs became multimodal, as they continued onto social networking websites. As Artem explains, this was done as a show of support for each other. Therefore, translanguaging and multilingualism were performed as a way to show solidarity across the country.

However, as Artem continues to reflect on this linguistic crossing through the flash mobs, he says that this issue has in fact become much more complex since the start of the war. As he states, while a counter-discursive movement was happening before the war to encourage the position that the language you speak is not tied directly to national identity, 'I'm afraid that it may, er, lose a lot of it- it is- result, er because XXX. Because people er, associate Russian, language with Russian, aggression.' Due to the renewed rise in political association with language since the war began, Artem expresses worry that the counter-discourse of the flash mobs may have been lost. Therefore, it is apparent that while an ideology had started to grow in Ukraine that it does not matter which language you dominantly speak (a movement in which Artem also took part), people's positions on this issue have become much more complex since the start of the war.

Furthermore, the issue of who speaks what is made more complicated by the fact that many of the volunteers in Ukrainian war relief efforts are themselves Russian language speakers. This is the point made below by Ksusha (mid-30s, from Central Ukraine, living in the United States).

Corinne: Do you think that um, that,
there's been any change in the perception of um,
of Russian speakers or Ukrainian speakers in Ukraine?
Since Maidan?
Ksusha: I, don't think so
Corinne: Mhmm.
Ksusha: I don't think so because,
We- uh, they- Ukraine is- uh:
I don't really know percent wise,
but Russian,
speakers,
I know a lot of Russian speakers and-
and they are-
they can be as patriotic as Ukrainian speakers so,
it's no different, you know,
they still consider themselves Ukrainians,
Corinne: [Yeah.]

Ksusha: [You know] most of the- most of the, x,
uh you know volunteers,
they're Russian speakers,
Corinne: Yeah, yeah.
Ksusha: So I don't XXX,
there is not,
I don't think there was any negativity to either group.

It is important to first acknowledge that Ksusha does not believe there to be any difference in language ideologies or stances regarding the use of language in Ukraine since the Maidan protests of 2013. This may therefore indicate that she has not been exposed as much to the ideological Discourses about language within her Ukrainian social networks. Yet, Ksusha is clearly aware of the Discourses regarding the acceptance or not of Russian language in Ukraine because even though I asked her about the perception of Russian speakers *and* Ukrainian speakers in Ukraine, her answer is one of defense for Russian speakers. Ksusha also brings patriotism into the discussion, reflecting on how Russian speakers 'can be as patriotic' as speakers of Ukrainian, therein dialogically responding to ideological Discourses that call into question Russian speakers' patriotism to Ukraine (Csernicskó, 2017; Masenko & Orel, 2014; Osnach, 2015). Interestingly, Ksusha also self-corrects from saying Russian speakers in Ukraine 'are' as patriotic to say they 'can be' as patriotic, therein showing her reflection upon a variety of Discourses to do with language and identity, cognitively negotiating her position.

Furthermore, in discussing Russian speakers in Ukraine, Ksusha states, 'it's no different, you know, they still consider themselves Ukrainians.' While focusing on commonalities between Russian and Ukrainian speakers and minimizing differences, she simultaneously positions herself as different from Russian speakers in Ukraine by categorizing these speakers as 'they' and 'themselves'. Therefore, even though Ksusha is focusing on commonalities in *what* she says, there is a degree of difference created in *how* she says it.

Finally, Ksusha makes her point by intertextually referencing the Ukrainian war relief efforts. 'Volunteers' refers specifically to those volunteers aiding in war relief efforts. In discussing the war, Ksusha draws upon meta-discourses of war relief volunteers being very patriotic and working selflessly in service of their country. Simultaneously, Ksusha is already drawing upon the Discourse of 'real Ukrainians speak Ukrainian' to create a counter-narrative, arguing that in fact language spoken is not equivalent to sociopolitical alignment. As she sums up once again, in Ksusha's view, it does not actually matter what language a person speaks in Ukraine.

Speak What You Know

As previously mentioned, most of the younger participants in the current study were well aware of the Discourses around 'being a real Ukrainian means speaking Ukrainian', but that does not mean that they themselves subscribe to this view. In fact, it was much more common to find the participants, especially in their 20s, discursively display acceptance of all languages, no matter what region they were from or where they currently live. This is important because it challenges the idea that there are set regional language ideologies in Ukraine (cf. Besters-Dilger, 2009; Maiboroda *et al.*, 2008; Masenko, 2004). As most of the participants in this chapter show, it is not this simple.

As a first example of taking the position that it does not matter what language you speak, below is an excerpt from Kyrylo (early 20s, from Eastern Ukraine, living in the United States). Since Kyrylo is from Eastern Ukraine, it may be expected that he would privilege the use of Russian. Furthermore, as he has opted to use more Ukrainian language, it may instead be expected that he would privilege the use of Ukrainian. However, as he discusses below, he considers the use of either to be fine.

Kyrylo: So, um, in that time maybe,
three or four years ago I just decided for myself that,
I need to start to speak Ukrainian uh at least with my friends,
uh and I started with uh,
social network?

Corinne: [Mhmm.]

Kyrylo: [So I] started to XX and uh um,
dial messages in Ukrainian language?

Corinne: Mhmm.

Kyrylo: And uh, start to: speak with them,
some of them,
just ignoring or like or like making bully and uh,
making fun of it if you're starting,
to speak them Ukrainian language.

Corinne: Mmm.

Kyrylo: But uh, sometimes,
when- when we were in university,
it was totally okay if someone speak Ukrainian language and have um,
your like,

	friend talk to you in Russian language?
	And then you continue in Ukrainian ((laughing))
Corinne:	[(((laughs)))]
Kyrylo:	[And so it like ((laughing))] two languages,
	and we understand both of them so why not.
Corinne:	[²Yeah.]
Kyrylo:	[²Yeah] uh so mostly:
	it's the same right now,
	so if people just know,
	Russian language and Ukrainian language and just,
	talk- talking to them on Ukrainian language,
	and they're answering me Russian language,
	or they're answering me Ukrainian language,
	sometimes they even answering me English as you.

In the beginning of this excerpt, Kyrylo explains that he decided around 2010 that 'I need to start to speak Ukrainian uh at least with my friends, uh and I started with uh, social network?' Interestingly Kyrylo expresses his investment in the Ukrainian language as fulfilling a 'need', which would also lead to the expectation that since he is connecting language with identity, he might also feel that other Ukrainians should learn and use Ukrainian. However, Kyrylo's experience was not an entirely positive one. Instead of positively positioning Kyrylo and helping him to feel accepted for learning to speak the Ukrainian language, dominant Ukrainian language speakers 'some of them, just ignoring or like or like making bully and uh, making fun of it if you're starting, to speak them Ukrainian language.'

However, this negativity that Kyrylo experienced on social network websites was not replicated in person at university. As Kyrylo explained in Chapter 6, he attended university classes in Kyiv, where 'it was totally okay if someone speak Ukrainian language and have um, your like, friend talk to you in Russian language? And then you continue in Ukrainian.' In this particular environment where people come together from all over for the self-elected shared purpose of learning, Kyrylo found more acceptance for the use of learner Ukrainian. While at first it seems that Kyrylo may be referencing friendly non-accommodation, it quickly becomes apparent that he is describing translingual practices: 'we understand both of them so why not.' Kyrylo's laissez-faire attitude towards language use in Ukraine is reflective of a more multilingual, multicultural stance that was presented by most of the other younger participants as well.

Furthermore, Kyrylo says that in his observations, the overall position of many Ukrainians towards language use in Ukraine is mostly the same since the war began as it was before the war. While it may at first be tempting to attribute this to the fact the Kyrylo is in the United States and not currently in Ukraine, Kyrylo in fact had not been in the United States for that long at the time of the interview and was still actively contributing to Ukraine through political and volunteer roles. Rather, it is more likely that given Kyrylo's mixed exposure to Ukrainians from all walks of life, he had developed a more universally accepting view of language use, as had many in his social network. This is especially likely to be the case, as Kyrylo even includes an acceptance of English interaction in his description of Ukrainian interactions.

With increasing globalization and transnational communication in the workplace and at home, it makes sense that younger generations would receive more exposure to multilingualism and multiculturalism as the norm. Artem (28 years old, from Western Ukraine, living in Ukraine), likewise draws upon the ideas of increasing travel and overall mobilization when talking about language use, as shown in the following excerpt:

Corinne: Mm-hmm.
Um, and so, what- what are people's perceptions about the use of, different languages in the part of Ukraine where you are right now? Like, the use of Ukrainian, Russian or English if they hear them?
Artem: ((smacks lips)) Um, simple people don't care.
Like they don't, really, care about,
Ukrainians understand er, like, in- in Western part of Ukraine, er, most people er, ((smacks lips)) under,
shhh forty I guess, er,
understand, er, English?
Erm, everyone, that's er,
well basically everyone is- i- understands er, Russian,
pretty well, erm.
We don't, er, for example if er,
like that L- L'viv is er, erm, the city er,
that has history,
that has beautiful architecture, er
people from Eastern part go to visit here.
Er, and er when tourist is asking me,
er some question directions and everything in Russian, er,
I wouldn't er ask him or her, er, to- to ask it in Ukrainian.
It's- it's, like- it's not, normal.

> Er, and, I think,
>
> most of people here are like that,
>
> so like, we- we don't really care.

Artem begins by explaining that 'simple people don't care' which language someone uses in Ukraine when offered the choice of Ukrainian, Russian or English. By 'simple people', Artem does not mean the derogatory sense of the term. Rather, as is clear in the context of the rest of his interview data, Artem means the majority of people in Ukraine – your everyday, non-politician. Therefore, he is expressing the view that most people in Ukraine do not particularly care what language someone chooses to use in communication.

He then elaborates upon his discussion of language use in Ukraine by drawing upon examples to show the normalcy of multilingualism in Ukraine. Even though Ukrainian is the official state language of Ukraine, Artem explains that most people also have access to the Russian language in some form (even if only receptively), and most people under the age of 40 also understand English, thus speaking to the increasing internationalization of Ukrainian education and the influence of globalization. As previously discussed, it is also highly probable that this increasing globalization for younger people in Ukraine has simultaneously led to an increasing acceptance of a multilingual, multicultural Ukraine.

To illustrate his point, Artem then draws upon an example of tourists from the East (which is historically dominant in the Russian language) visiting historical sites in the West (which is historically dominant in the Ukrainian language). Artem also then places himself into the story through the use of 'I' as one of the characters, therein discursively displaying his own views on this language issue as well: 'Er, and er when tourist is asking me, er some question directions and everything in Russian, er, I wouldn't er ask him or her, er, to- to ask it in Ukrainian. It's- it's, like- it's not, normal.' In addition to showing the acceptance of the language most comfortable for the speaker, Artem's hypothetical story also does the work of discursively othering anyone who has a problem with the use of Russian by a Russian speaker in Ukraine by saying this would not be 'normal', therein further supporting his position. Finally, Artem discursively positions himself as being aligned with the majority of Ukrainians, saying, 'and, I think, most of people here are like that, so like, we- we don't really care.' Therefore, for Artem, the majority of Ukrainians with whom he interacts do not mind which language people speak during interaction in Ukraine.

Dispelling Myths – Western Ukraine

A discussion about participants' counter-narratives of language ideologies would not be complete without returning to the region of Ukraine that has appeared again and again in narratives of strong language preference: Western Ukraine. While throughout the chapters, participants have seriously or jokingly pointed to Western Ukraine as a place of strong language ideologies, the West was also an example in the counter-narratives of divisive language ideologies *not* existing in Ukraine. The first example of this comes from Lesya (28 years old, from Western Ukraine, living in the United States), as shown in the excerpt below.

Lesya: Ah back in the West however,
there is still a lot of people who speak Russian,
like myself for example,
like I'm kind of a minority you know,
because I spoke Russian,
my parents spoke Russian,
my friends spoke Russian,
however contrary to what president Putin says,
like the Russians in Ukraine were never like, you know,
persecuted or anything like that, you know.
I did not feel any difference speaking Russian to my friends or speaking Ukrainian, you know,
it was just a matter of being polite and, ah,
addressing a person with the language that he speaks in,
but ah- in the-
so ah that's in the West however.

In this excerpt, Lesya first establishes the normalcy of Russian speakers in the West as a counter-narrative to popular belief about there only being Ukrainian speakers in this region. Further adding embodied symbolic capital to her statement, Lesya then points to herself as an example. Next, however, she states that while there are 'still a lot of people who speak Russian' in the West, she was part of a minority in this region because of the degree to which her life was Russified. Even though Lesya uses the past tense here, this is likely due to the fact that she is recounting events from her childhood as well as from some years past. This retelling of her past by recounting the experiences of herself and those she was closest to serves to show the normalized use of Russian in her everyday encounters growing up.

Then, drawing upon metonymous Discourses of responsibility (see Chapters 3 and 4), Lesya dialogically references media Discourses coming from Russia and from the Russian government (including from Putin) that promote the idea of Russians being unwelcome in dominant

Ukrainian-speaking regions of Ukraine (cf. Osnach, 2015). Not only does Lesya say she has not seen this persecution, she goes as far as saying it has never happened, therein negating any rumors to the contrary. Lesya then draws upon the embodied symbolic capital of personal experience, saying, 'I did not feel any difference speaking Russian to my friends or speaking Ukrainian, you know.' By including 'you know' at the end, Lesya is also doing interactional relational work, inviting me as her interlocutor to align with her position.

Lesya then ends this excerpt by summarizing her position through saying, 'it was just a matter of being polite and, ah, addressing a person with the language that he speaks in.' By referring to politeness, Lesya is also commenting upon the social expectations into which she was socialized (Brown & Levinson, 1978, 1987; Burdelski, 2011; Fukushima, 2002; Kasper, 1990). Therefore, within the society she grew up in, the expectation was of linguistic accommodation.

A second example of multilingual acceptance in Western Ukraine comes from Fedir (Early 30s, from Western Ukraine, living in New Zealand). Like Lesya, Fedir comes from Western Ukraine and is fluent in both Russian and Ukrainian. As shown in this excerpt, Fedir also positions this as normal among Western Ukrainians.

Fedir: Eh, ((sighs)) I know that in-
So, obviously I'm from the Western part, you know,
in- in the Western part it doesn't seem to be,
like, is- people have switched slowly to Ukrainian themselves.
But on saying that,
it's not frowned upon if you speak Russian.
In fact,
if you do speak Russian,
a lot of people will,
assume straight away that Russian is more comfortable for you,
and will try to switch to Russian.

First, it is important to acknowledge that when Fedir begins this excerpt, he comments that 'obviously' he is from the Western part in Ukraine. However, in this instance, this comment is not so clearly reflective of any metadiscourses; rather, this comment was made to me because I know Fedir and his family and already knew that they were from Western Ukraine, so he is commenting upon the redundancy of this information for me as the listener. However, there is some ambiguity in the next phrase when he says, 'in- in the Western part it doesn't seem to be, like, is- people have switched slowly to Ukrainian themselves.' Here it is not entirely clear (even upon re-listening to the interview) if Fedir is saying that people in the West have also slowly switched to Ukrainian or that it is not the case that people in the West have slowly switched to Ukrainian. Yet, given the fact that he includes the word 'themselves' at the end of this statement, which usually serves the function of further agreement during a comparison, it is most likely that Fedir is saying that people in the West have also been slow in switching to the Ukrainian language. This is further made likely to be the case when including the background knowledge that Fedir, who is from the West, also spent his childhood in a dominant Russian-speaking environment. Understanding then that Fedir is saying that people in the West have also been slow to (re)adopt the Ukrainian language is important because this is quite different from the metadiscourse of the Ukrainian language being ever present in the West.

Fedir then continues to discuss this position, saying that even though people in the West have been using more Ukrainian language, 'it's not frowned upon if you speak Russian'. This also dispels a common myth about the West, and one which has been used to inform the discourses and even jokes told by participants throughout the rest of the chapters, providing further evidence that the reality of a situation often does not match up with the more fantastical narratives spread about it. Fedir then further makes his point by saying, 'In fact, if you do speak Russian, a lot of people will, assume straight away that Russian is more comfortable for you, and will try to switch to Russian.' By beginning with 'in fact', Fedir produces a counter-narrative, thereby showing his familiarity with the dominant Discourse about linguistic ideologies in the West. The example he then provides describes linguistic accommodation, similar to Lesya's example above. While other participants in this chapter have described translingual practices across Ukraine as a whole, it is interesting to note that the descriptions specific to the West describe linguistic accommodation instead. This is further evidence of the importance of collecting narratives from people of all areas of a nation and not just from those of certain regions reporting on the others.

The Language I Speak Doesn't Change Who I Am

Finally, while most of the younger participants focused on describing the linguistic practices in Ukraine, a few participants also focused specifically on the connection between language and identity when explaining why the specific language a person speaks should not matter. An example of this comes from Anatoliy (mid-20s, from Central Ukraine, living in New Zealand) who has appeared throughout the chapters in this book. At the end of his interview, I asked him specifically about any connections he perceived existing between language and identity. As shown in the excerpt below, this was a particularly powerful question for him to which he gave an answer showing how embodied translingual practices are for him.

Corinne: Um, and would you say that... your-
the languages you speak are connected with your identity?

Anatoliy: ... ((sighs)) Yes, that is correct.
Because, even, erm...
despite the fact that we have this conf- conflict with Russia...
I do emphasize many times that my dominant l- language is Russian.
Er... Language does... influence a person,
how we think.
Er... but it doesn't really... changes us... in a way...
that... I mean...
Yes, language is part of us,
makes who we are, right?
But... me, Uk- krainian speaking,
or me Russian speaking...
we are not that different,
it's not black and white, you know,
like, t- it's- it's not- er, not- not, er... opposing.
Erm... and, unfortunately.... er,
people are speculating based on the language.
You know, it's like you have... brown eyes,
and you have green eyes...
It's clearly different, right?
But... is this different- is this... difference... that important,
that you can make a judgment about person's personality?
[Right?]

Corinne: [Yeah], I know what you mean, yeah.

Anatoliy: So, er... Th- the same with language.
It does affect how I think, er... in- in many ways,
but it doesn't change...
what I am... right?
So...
Yes, I speak Russian...
and I'm... way more fluent than... Russian...
er, i- in Russian,

> than I am, er, in Ukrainian.
> But it doesn't make me... pro-Russian.
> You know, and the same... er,
> if persons speaks Ukrainian...
> right, it doesn't mean that, er...
> he is saint, you know.
> Erm... he will...
> yeah, I mean,
> people are different...
> So...

Anatoliy begins answering my question by sighing deeply, indicating the internal complexity of this question for him, and then succinctly confirms his view of a connection between language and identity: 'Yes, that is correct.' He then elaborates upon his answer, beginning by drawing connections between ideological discourses of language use in Ukraine during the war and his own feelings about language use. He then draws upon Sapir-Whorfian ideas (cf. Casasanto, 2012) such as those found in the Chapter 5 narratives of changing one's mother tongue, but he then presents a counter-discourse saying, 'but it doesn't really... changes us... in a way,' drawing upon more embodied discourses.

Seemingly unhappy with this initial attempt at explaining, however, he tries again: 'Yes, language is part of us, makes who we are, right? But... me, Uk- krainian speaking, or me Russian speaking... we are not that different, it's not black and white, you know.' In this statement, Anatoliy again draws upon discourses of embodiment, as well as Discourses of language use equating identity to argue that the situation is not as simple as these popular Discourses often make it out to be. He provides himself as an example, explaining that even if he uses a different language, he is still the same person. This presents a different view from some of the participants, particularly from most of the participants in their mid to later 30s. However, Anatoliy is not arguing that language is not connected to identity. Rather, he is arguing that all of his languages are part of his identity and that he should not have to choose.

Anatoliy then continues drawing upon ideas of embodiment, metaphorically comparing language use to eye color. He then asks, 'But... is this different- is this... difference... that important, that you can make a judgment about person's personality?' therein questioning the validity of Discourses such as 'real Ukrainians speak Ukrainian' that draw direct connections between the use of a single language and the speaker's identity or even intentions. He directly follows this by again drawing upon his own embodied symbolic capital, arguing that from personal experience he can say that language use is not directly connected with sociopolitical identity, therein dialogically drawing upon and rejecting the ideological Discourse of 'real Ukrainians speak Ukrainian.' He then follows this with another counter-discourse to this ideological Discourse by saying, 'if persons speaks Ukrainian... right, it doesn't mean that, er... he is saint, you know.' Anatoliy then ends by emphasizing his point that 'people are different' and therefore should not all be expected to speak certain languages in order to claim certain identities.

As Anatoliy emphasizes throughout this excerpt, then, language and identity do not have a one-to-one connection; it is much more complex than this. Therefore, he concludes by aligning with the argument of the speakers in the rest of this chapter that in the end, it does not and should not matter what language you speak.

Further Remarks

Similar to Friedman's (2016) study of two fifth-grade classrooms in Ukraine, the participants from the current study have also discursively positioned themselves in ways that align more closely with the idea of a multilingual, multicultural Ukraine. In Friedman's (2016) study, she found that the students acknowledged the imagined community of Ukrainian-speaking Ukrainians and even dialogically echoed the associated ideologies. However, the children positioned themselves as being only on the periphery of this imagined community, and instead as members of a multilingual, multicultural Ukraine. Such is the primary finding of this chapter – that many of the Ukrainian participants in this project voiced an understanding of, and at times dialogic echoing of, the 'real Ukrainians speak Ukrainian' ideology (cf. Csernicskó, 2017).

However, regardless of this (and in fact in spite of it), they still positioned themselves as part of a multilingual, multicultural Ukraine (cf. Lozyns'kyi, 2008). Furthermore, it is this multilingual, multicultural Ukraine that they positioned as the norm in Ukrainian society – that a person can speak whatever language with which they are most comfortable, and others will accept this.

At the same time, this multilingual, multicultural Ukraine in which participants position themselves is still different from what has previously been spoken of. The linguistic practices associated with participants' ideas of a multilingual, multicultural Ukraine in the rest of the book are instead better described as friendly non-accommodation (see Chapter 5). That is, individuals' non-accommodating linguistic practices are still friendly intentioned, but are also now described as consciously determined, such that interlocutors will accept each other's language preference but also consciously not change their own language choice either. This then allows these individuals to reflexively position themselves as part of multilingual, multicultural Ukraine, while also allowing them to maintain alignment with their own ideas of what it means to be Ukrainian.

Yet, this is different from the practices of participants in this final chapter. They instead describe returning to the use of translingual practices in Ukraine. What exactly this looks like in form is not as important to them as its function – to highlight shared commonality through the acceptance of difference (cf. Vyshniak, 2009). Therefore, for these individuals, accepting linguistic diversity was in itself a positive linguistic practice, highlighting a shared multilingual, multicultural Ukraine with which they align.

Notes

(1) Ruslana (not the person interviewed in this book) is a Ukrainian singer who has been very active in Ukrainian war relief efforts and famously performed on a piano painted the colors of the Ukrainian flag atop barricades during the clashes that broke out at EuroMaidan.
(2) Flash mobs are seemingly sudden (yet in reality pre-planned) events in which many people take part, all doing the same or similar things, and of which the general public had no advance knowledge. These are usually positively intentioned and are often a source of surprise and fun for those who observe them.

8 Conclusion

Throughout this book, narratives have been drawn upon that originally came from interviews with 38 Ukrainians. At times, their experiences crossed over in commonality, and at other times differences came to the forefront, both of which are equally important to acknowledge when working in the language and identity space. Due to the large scale of the data collected (over 50 hours/over 600,000 words), it was not possible to represent everything important that every participant said. However, I have made every attempt to provide a fair representation of key findings from across the data. An overview of the key findings from this book is presented again below, followed by themes that have emerged from across the book.

Chapter 1 began the book with an introduction to the context of language in the participants' home country, Ukraine. An abbreviated recent linguistic history was presented, along with recent events of note, such as the brawl in the Ukrainian Rada over the Russian Language Bill. Historical patterns of sociopolitical alignment and language dominance were also presented in an effort to show the connections that exist between the two. The theoretical concepts of dialogism and discursive positioning were then presented within this context.

Chapter 2 began by presenting the overall framework of the book through a discussion of post-structuralism and social constructionism, including their treatment of identity in sociolinguistic and applied linguistic research. Furthermore, the theoretical constructs of imagined communities, imagined identities and investment were also introduced into the identity research context. To begin exploring these ideas, the pilot research conducted in 2009 with Olesya, Yana and Alyona was introduced. Findings from this chapter included the prevalence of ideological Discourses within the narratives that are intertextually referenced, as well as the importance of a defined national identity for some Ukrainians since the Orange Revolution, which has led to investment in an imagined community at the national level. Finally, it was found that participants' reflexive positioning and alignment or disalignment with Discourses are influenced by their individual social networks and individual lived experiences.

The next chapter (Chapter 3) began with an introduction to the current study, in which 38 interviews were conducted with Ukrainians during 2014 and 2015. The war-related events that took place near and during the interviews were presented, as well as a discussion of the criteria for participant selection and the research methods used. The use of interactional sociolinguistics with a critical lens for the method of analysis was also discussed. The first findings from the present study were then presented, including the discursive implications of choosing how to name a particular event (war, conflict, etc.). Namely, it was argued that participants' reflexive positioning and stance regarding the war could be uncovered through the examination of underlying semantic meaning in the terminology they used in the narratives. Additionally, it was found that participants connected discursively through the chronotope of the Ukrainian War to access an imagined collective experience. Part of this experience also included what it means to be Ukrainian, which was found to focus on the investment in and upholding of shared ideals. Finally, participants were found to discursively achieve commonality by in part highlighting the differences of the 'others'.

Chapter 4 continued looking at Discourses of the war, this time focusing on how participants discursively construct who is responsible for the war. The findings for this chapter focused on the types of linguistic strategies that participants drew upon in making their arguments, including metonymy, repetition, personification, intertextual references, dialogic echoing and discursive positioning. Metonymy in particular was found to be a way that participants constructed responsibility without (for the most part) pointing to individuals. Finally, the juxtaposition of stories of valor and villainy (Marples, 2009) served as a way to accentuate positions of offense and defense in the war.

Stories of 'changing your mother tongue' were the focus of Chapter 5. These unexpected stories from the narratives were introduced and explored, particularly through ideas of embodiment. Participants' constructions of this ideology as historically embedded or as a result of recent events were also investigated. It was found that institutional symbolic capital was, in particular, associated with the former, while embodied symbolic capital was particularly drawn upon in the latter. Finally, diaspora Discourses were discussed, especially focusing on how they echo home country Discourses, but each (home country and diaspora Discourses) still maintain a focus of their own.

Continuing to focus on diaspora communities, Chapter 6 introduced the Model of Immigrant Identity, Investment & Integration. This model was used to explore how participants living in the diaspora recursively negotiate and renegotiate their identities in relation to both the home and host societies. Furthermore, the trajectories of home discourses were discussed. It was argued that the real trajectories were in fact different from the imagined trajectories found within the diaspora communities, therefore resulting in a mismatch between participants' expectations and experiences when returning to the home country.

Finally, Chapter 7 began by looking at counter-discourses to the dominant ideological Discourses discussed in the chapters thus far. In particular, it was found that some of the participants, especially the younger participants, aligned with the counter-discourse that it does not in fact matter what language you speak, nor should it. This was found to be part of these participants' alignment with an ideal multilingual, multicultural Ukraine. Furthermore, returning to translingual practices (as opposed to friendly non-accommodation) was found to be a way that these participants highlighted the acceptance of diversity. The implications for research and theory are further discussed below.

Discursive Themes

The current study has been grounded in a post-structuralist approach to language and identity research, which allowed for the recognition of the moment-to-moment shifting and ever-changing nature of identity (Bucholtz & Hall, 2005; Norton, 2013; Pavlenko & Norton, 2007). The wide-ranging narratives found across this study confirm the validity of this approach. No matter who the participants were, what they were discussing, or the position they were taking, a discourse analysis of their narratives provided evidence of each and every participant's negotiation and renegotiation of identities throughout their interviews. Positioning Theory (Davies & Harré, 1990; van Langenhove & Harré, 1991) and dialogism (Bakhtin, 1992 [1981]) further provided tools with which to track the identity work that participants were doing (Butler, 1999) throughout the interviews.

Throughout the chapters, the participants showed time and again how they discursively used linguistic devices to position and reposition themselves and others in their narratives. In particular, when having difficult discussions, such as those to do with responsibility and/or critiquing other people and nations, participants found metonymy, repetition, personification and voicing of absent others particularly useful. For example, Lev found useful the discursive force in personifying Ukraine as a helpless country being literally beaten by a larger, more powerful Russia. Likewise, Raisa, Lev and Anatoliy found repetition to be a way to indirectly critique other countries' lack of sincere assistance in Ukrainian war relief efforts.

Furthermore, double-voicing through dialogism (Bakhtin, 1991 [1982]) and intertextual references to past events and texts were also linguistic devices of which all of the participants made use. However, to be able to both notice and interpret these references and echoes, the researcher must look beyond just the discourse itself and instead analyze the discourse in light of their background knowledge of the context and of the participants. Interactional sociolinguistics therefore brings an advantage not found within more traditional conversation analysis because IS looks *beyond* the discourse to also include any relevant information from both within and outside of the discourse itself. This need for background information points to the necessity of the researchers themselves investing in the communities and contexts of which the participants are a part. While researchers do not need to have originally come from within the communities with whom they are researching, they do need to invest significantly in them and spend time getting to know them. Without researchers' own familiarity with the communities and contexts, they will undoubtedly miss intertextual references and dialogic voicing that are crucial to the messages being conveyed.

Reconsidering the Local and the Global

As the participants in this book showed (especially in Chapter 6), both the local and global contexts *must* be considered (cf. Heller, 2001) when analyzing discursive events. For example, for participants within the diaspora communities, their identity negotiation and renegotiation were further complexified by the war in Ukraine, which made them revisit to whom and to where they are loyal, and how they show this. Therefore, when doing research with diaspora communities, it is crucial to consider current events in the home country alongside current events in the host country (Liebscher & Dailey-O'Cain, 2013). Both home and host country events affect participants' daily lived experiences; therefore, a full analysis is not complete without considering both. Furthermore, the changing events that take place in home and host countries must also be tracked, as they affect participants' imagined identities and the imagined communities of which they see themselves a part.

Additionally, throughout the interviews, there were a multitude of dialogic echoes of previous discourses. These discourses came from across time and space; while some were recent, others were historical; while some were from the host country, others were from the home country. When specifically looking at dialogism in the diaspora communities, it is crucial to also consider dialogic echoes with the home country and what the other trajectories have been of these original source discourses. This is because while diaspora Discourses reflected home country Discourses, each still had a trajectory and focus of its own. Additionally, this different focus within the diaspora communities reflected different investments and the motivation for those investments. For example, Chapter 5 explored how the 'change your mother tongue' Discourse existed in both the home and host countries. The members of the diaspora host countries also had to consider which heritage language(s) they would pass on to their children and the practicalities involved in their decisions. Therefore, when analyzing dialogism in discourse, researchers also need to pay heed to individuals' differing motivations and investments in order to truly understand what is happening in those communities and for those individuals.

Finally, as explained in Chapter 1, it has long been thought that a sociopolitical and ideological regional divide in Ukraine is the key to understanding connections between language and identity. However, while this may still be true in some cases, Chapter 7 also shows the growing importance of generational experiences. A new focus on a multilingual, multicultural Ukraine, including an expressed non-importance of specific language spoken, seems to have arisen among many of the younger participants. These participants, regardless of the region from which they originally come or where they currently live, positioned themselves as aligning with a counter-discourse to 'real Ukrainians speak Ukrainian' – that of 'it does not matter what language you speak'. This apparent generational move, regardless of region or current location, thus shows the importance of a widely varying sample of participant backgrounds.

Changing Your Mother Tongue

Finally, this entire book, but especially Chapter 5, has major implications for research on embodiment and for mother tongue research. First, much research on the embodiment of language has talked about languages as being a fixed part of the individual, such that languages with which a person feels an identity connection are therein always connected to that person's identity, becoming a part of that person (e.g. Krumm, 2001, 2004, 2010; Prescher, 2007). However, as shown by the participants taking part in the 'change your mother tongue' efforts, not all people feel that language is a fixed part of themselves. Therefore, it is more appropriate to think of embodied language as something that can be negotiated and renegotiated, such as how we think of identity. This then ties ideas of embodiment closer to ideas of indexicality, such that both are manifested discursively and can be drawn upon as needed and desired in various sociocultural interactions (Blommaert, 2005; Bucholtz & Hall, 2005, 2016; Mendoza-Denton & Hall, 2010).

A similar challenge is thus posed to mother tongue research. In general, a 'mother tongue' is discussed as something fixed and dependent upon the language (or languages) used by a person as they grow up. However, the participants in this study directly challenge that, as they conceptualize what they are doing as changing their mother tongue. This then brings up the question – then what *is* a mother tongue? If we continue to ascribe to the former definition, then we are affectively invalidating the views of the participants in this study and many more like them. So, who is best served by the definitions being used? Who do these definitions focus on? Hopefully those reading this book will find themselves aligned with the critical turn in social science research and answer that the participants and associated individuals should be the ones to benefit from the definitions we use. Therefore, we must reconceptualize what a mother tongue is and perhaps look to a more fluid conceptualization of a mother tongue that better captures the lived experiences and complex identities of those to whom this term applies.

Concluding Thoughts

In concluding this book, I would like to present a final excerpt. This excerpt comes from Ruslana who is from the Eastern Ukrainian war zone but was studying abroad on an internship at the time of the interview. Ruslana's excerpt reflects the ideas presented in this book, such as post-structuralist views of negotiated and renegotiated identity, self- and other-positioning, intertextual connections to prior and future texts, investment and imagined identities, among others. At the time of the interview, Ruslana had also just lost all of her PhD research, as it had been at her university when her university was attacked by rebel forces. She explains:

> I was working at the International Department, for s- so... s- so long time, and I always... er... I was always dreaming of winning a scholarship and going abroad. ((sighs)) And... ((laughing)) when I did that, when... now I'm in [city], I'm... here for three months, but I'm... I- I can't say that I'm... er, completely happy. Because I'm thinking about my future... I know that I don't have job, I don't have a place where I could return back home, and I can be...um... safe, so... I- I need just to change all my dreams, I... need just to change all my perspectives, for my future career, because... er... if earlier, if... several months ago I thought that I should... defense my PhD the- thes- thesis, and... I could be... er... ((laughing)) the vice-rector, or the rector, and everything will be ok in my... life. So, now I- I understand that it is impossible, because our university... it is closed. Er... and... it is under the control of Lugansk rebels, er... pro-Russian... rebels, and... it... i- ((short sigh)) i- it is impossible to continue working at the International Department in such... circumstances. So I need just to- to think about my new... career, about my new job, I'm looking for another opportunities.

Ruslana's story is heartbreaking, but it is also an excellent example of Ukrainian perseverance and a willingness to invest in a new future, whatever that may be. Identity is thus something that shifts and changes with the context and circumstances. Just like Ukrainians themselves, what these ideas and associated practices of 'being Ukrainian' look like take on many different characteristics. However, it is this diversity which makes Ukraine such a complex, beautiful place, connecting at individual levels with people from all walks of life and from all different beliefs. Is not this also simply the nature of identity?

Appendices

Appendix A: Transcription Conventions

Name:	pseudonym of an identified participant
[¹text]	
[¹text]	simultaneous, overlapping talk by two speakers
XXX	syllables of indecipherable speech
=	latching, no gap between two turns
(…)	short pause in speech
?	rising final intonation
!	strong emphasis, with falling intonation
.	falling, final intonation
,	low-rising intonation suggesting continuation
te:xt	lengthening of the preceding sound
tex-	an abrupt cut-off, with level pitch
TEXT	loud volume, shouting
((laughing))	laughter during discourse
((text))	non-verbal actions or researcher notes

Appendix B: Participants in New Zealand (in chronological order of interviews)

Pseudonym	Origin in Ukraine	Identifies as	Gender & Age	Date of Interview
Fedir	West	Ukrainian	M30s	September 2014
Gleb	East	Russian-Ukrainian	M30s	September 2014
Anatoliy	Central	Ukrainian-NZer	M20s	September 2014
Zoya	East	Ukrainian	W20s	October 2014
Vira	Central	Ukrainian	W30s	October 2014
Lyuba	East	Kiwi (NZer)	W20s	October 2014
Irina	Black Sea	Russian	W30s	October 2014
Lev	East	Ukrainian	M30s	November 2014
Raisa	East	Ukrainian	W30s	November 2014
Denys	Central	Ukrainian	M30s	February 2015

Pseudonym	Origin in Ukraine	Identifies as	Gender & Age	Date of Interview
Tanya	Black Sea	Ukrainian	W30s	April 2015
Sofia	West	Ukrainian	W20s	May 2015
Lana	Black Sea	Ukrainian	W30s	May 2015
Valentina	West	Ukrainian	W20s	September 2015

Appendix C: Participants in Canada and the United States (in chronological order of interviews)

Pseudonym	Origin in Ukraine	Identifies as	Gender & Age	Date of Interview
Yana	Black Sea	Ukrainian-American	W20s	September 2014
Lilia	West	Ukrainian	W20s	September 2014
Kyrylo	East	Ukrainian	M20s	October 2014
Lesya	West	Ukrainian	W20s	February 2015
Ilona	West	Ukrainian	W30s	April 2015
Mykola	East	Ukrainian-Canadian	M30s	April 2015
Ksusha	Central	Ukrainian-American	W30s	May 2015
Alla	Central	Ukrainian-American	W30s	August 2015
Viktoriya	Central	Ukrainian	W30s	August 2015
Dasha	East	Ukrainian	W30s	September 2015
Dmitri	Black Sea	Ukrainian	M30s	September 2015
Katya	Black Sea	Ukrainian-American	W20s	September 2015

Appendix D: Participants in Ukraine (in chronological order of interviews)

Pseudonym	Origin in Ukraine	Identifies as	Gender & Age	Date of Interview
Kalyna	West	Ukrainian	W30s	September 2014
Artem	West	Ukrainian	M20s	September 2014
Olena	West	Ukrainian	W20s	September 2014
Ruslana	East	Ukrainian	W20s	September 2014
Polina	Black Sea	Ukrainian	W20s	October 2014
Roman	Central	Ukrainian	M20s	October 2014
Milena	East	Ukrainian	W20s	October 2014
Maxim	Central	Ukrainian	M30s	October 2014
Larysa	East	Ukrainian	W30s	February 2015
Klara	Central	Ukrainian	W30s	February 2015
Marina	Black Sea	Ukrainian	W20s	February 2015
Ilya	Black Sea	Ukrainian	M30s	April 2015

Appendix E: Klara's Joke as Told Originally in Ukrainian and Russian[1]

Дівчина Христя з Прикарп- з Карпат[2]
поїхала до Москви, влаштувалася на роботу, зустріла коханого хлопця. Зустріла Миколу...
Была дуже рада, вони закохалися, вони здружилися, у них з'явилася донька, але Оксана...[3]
дуже просила коханого: 'Ну давай поїдемо до батьків, ну я так скучила за батьками, давай поїдемо на село, я тобі покажу, тебе ніхто не ображати б-, тебе всі полюблять, ти ж такі к- х- гарны хлопец,
ти всім дуже сподобаєшся. Я дуже скучила за батьками, давай з'їздимо'.
Він довго казав що 'Ні, ну, тут, знаєш, я боюся, там, е, там українці...
Вони мене будут бити'. - 'Та хто тебе буде бити! Та- та ты приїдеш на село, все у тебе буде добре.'
Нарешті на п'ятий рік вмовила Оксана Миколу,
поїхали вони в- до батьків.
Вони приїхали,
Приїхали на Прикарпаття, вона така рада всіх бачити, вона зі всіма спілкується,
але вона не може навіть с дівчатами поспілкуватися, бо вона куди ні піде, усюди він за нею.
Вон- і вона думає, ну, треба кудысь його вже до хлопців відправити, щоб він, по-перше, не боявся,
по-друге, я могла можливо з дівчатами поговорити.
Вона каже: 'Ну, ось тобі пляшка горілки,
ось тобі шмат сала,
йди в село, заходь в хату, кажи 'Христос народився!'
Тому що це було на Різдво.
'Ну і там вже вы подружитися'
Тільки дівчата всі зібралися,
Тільки вони почали говорити про своє про жіноче, не проходіт і десяти хвилин,
прибігає той Микола:
весь розтріпани...
у нього... його... куртка розірвана, шапка загублена...
Прибігає, очі витріщені, кричить:
*'Я как нормальный человек, всё, как ты сказала,
пришёл, положил им бутылку водки на стол, сало развернул, говорю:*
'Христос народився!' - *как ты учила. А они мне*: 'Славимо його!'
Фиг вы меня словите![4]

Notes

(1) My many thanks to Natalia Beliaeva for this excerpt.
(2) Western Ukraine.
(3) She changes the name of the girl here.
(4) The play on words here is based on homophony: the traditional Ukrainian response to the phrase 'Христос народився!' ('Christ is born!') is 'Славимо Його!' ('Let us glorify Him!'), where the verb **славимо** is homophonous to a colloquial Russian verb **словим** ('we will catch/let us catch').

References

Anderson, B. (1991 [1983]) *Imagined Communities: Reflections on the Origin and Spread of Nationalism*. New York, NY: Verso.
Bakhtin, M.M. (1984) *The Problem of Dostoevsky's Poetics*. Minneapolis, MN: University of Minnesota Press.
Bakhtin, M.M. (1986) *Speech Genres and Other Late Essays*. Austin, TX: University of Texas Press.
Bakhtin, M.M. (1992 [1981]) *The Dialogic Imagination: Four Essays*. Austin, TX: University of Texas Press.
Bakshy, E., Messing, S. and Adamic, L.A. (2015) Exposure to ideologically diverse news and opinion on Facebook. *Science* 348 (6239), 1130–1132.
Barr, S. and Seals, C.A. (2018) *He reo* for our future: Te reo Māori and teacher identities, attitudes, and micro-policies in mainstream New Zealand schools. *Journal of Language, Identity & Education* 17 (6), 434–447.
Beliaeva, N. and Seals, C.A. (2019) Who are 'they' for Ukrainians in Ukraine and in the diaspora. Othering in political discourse. In N. Knoblock (ed.) *Discourses of the Ukrainian Crisis: Linguistic Reflections of Trauma, Aggression and Hope*. New York: Bloomsbury.
Benhabib, S. (1996) The democratic movement and the problem of difference. In S. Benhabib (ed.) *Democracy and Difference: Contesting the Boundaries of the Political* (pp. 3–18). Princeton, NJ: Princeton University Press.
Benwell, B. and Stokoe, E. (2006) *Discourse and Identity*. Edinburgh: Edinburgh University Press.
Besters-Dilger, Y. (ed.) (2009) *Language Policy and Language Situation in Ukraine: Analysis and Recommendations*. Frankfurt: Peter Lang.
Besters-Dilger, Y. (2011) Нація та мова після 1991 р. – українська та російська в мовному конфлікті. In A. Каппелер (ed.) *Україна. Процеси націотворення* (pp. 352–364). Kyiv: Vydavnytstvo K.I.C.
Bilaniuk, L. (2003) Gender, language attitudes, and language status in Ukraine. *Language in Society* 32 (1), 47–78.
Bilaniuk, L. (2005) *Contested Tongues: Language Politics and Cultural Correction in Ukraine*. Ithaca, NY: Cornell University Press.
Bilaniuk, L. (2010) Language in the balance: The politics of non-accommodation on bilingual Ukrainian–Russian television shows. *International Journal of the Sociology of Language* 201, 105–133.
Bilaniuk, L. and Melnyk, S. (2008) A tense and shifting balance: Bilingualism and education in Ukraine. In A. Pavlenko (ed.) *Multilingualism in Post-Soviet Countries* (pp. 66–98). Clevedon: Multilingual Matters.
Block, D. (2015) Researching language and identity. In B. Paltridge and A. Phakiti (eds) *Research Methods in Applied Linguistics: A practical Resource* (pp. 527–540). London: Bloomsbury.
Blommaert, J. (2005) *Discourse: A Critical Introduction*. Cambridge: Cambridge University Press.

Blommaert, J. and Verschueren, J. (1998) The role of language in European nationalist ideologies. In B.B. Schieffelin, K.A. Woolard and P.V. Kroskrity (eds) *Language Ideologies: Practice and Theory* (pp. 189–210). New York, NY: Cambridge University Press.

Bondarenko, O.V. (2008) Українська Ментальність в Розмаїтті Національних Ментальних Формоутворень й Архетипів: Історикокультурний аспект. *Гуманітарний вісник ЗДІА* 32, 66–78.

Bourdieu, P. (1986) The forms of capital. In J.F. Richardson (ed.) *Handbook of Theory and Research for the Sociology of Education* (pp. 241–258). New York, NY: Greenwood Press.

Braha, I. (2011) Українсько-російський суржик в соціокомунікативній ситуації ринку. *Мова і суспільство* 2, 19–126.

Brown, P.L. (1994, 17 March) Ukrainians imbue cloth with life. *The New York Times*. Retrieved from https://www.nytimes.com/1994/03/17/garden/american-translations-ukrainians-imbue-cloth-with-life.html?pagewanted=all

Brown, P. and Levinson, S.C. (1978) Universals in language usage: Politeness phenomena. In E.N. Goody (ed.) *Questions and Politeness* (pp. 56–289). Cambridge: Cambridge University Press.

Brown, P. and Levinson, S.C. (1987) *Politeness: Some Universals in Language Usage*. Cambridge, UK: Cambridge University Press.

Bruneau, M. (2010) Diasporas, transnational spaces and communities. In R. Bauböck and T. Faist (eds) *Diaspora and Transnationalism: Concepts, Theories and Methods* (pp. 35–49). Amsterdam, Netherlands: Amsterdam University Press.

Bucholtz, M. (1999) 'Why be normal?': Language and identity practices in a community of nerd girls. *Language in Society* 28 (2), 202–225.

Bucholtz, M. (2001) The whiteness of nerds: Superstandard English and racial markedness. *Journal of Linguistic Anthropology* 11 (1), 84–100.

Bucholtz, M. (2011) *White Kids: Language, Race and Styles of Youth Identity*. Cambridge: Cambridge University Press.

Bucholtz, M. and Hall, K. (2005) Identity and interaction: A sociocultural linguistic approach. *Discourse Studies* 7 (4–5), 585–614.

Bucholtz, M. and Hall, K. (2016) Embodied sociolinguistics. In N. Coupland (ed.) *Sociolinguistics: Theoretical Debates* (pp. 173–198). Cambridge: Cambridge University Press.

Burdelski, M. (2011) Language socialization and politeness routines. In A. Duranti, E. Ochs and B.B. Schieffelin (eds) *The Handbook of Language Socialization* (pp. 275–295). Oxford: Wiley-Blackwell.

Butler, J. (1999) *Gender Trouble: Feminism and The Subversion of Identity* (2nd edn). New York, NY: Routledge.

Butler, K. (2001) Defining diaspora, refining a discourse. *Diaspora* 10 (2), 189–219.

Canagarajah, A.S. (2013a) Negotiating translingual literacy: An enactment. *Research in the Teaching of English* 48 (1), 40–67.

Canagarajah, A.S. (2013b) *Translingual Practice: Global Englishes and Cosmopolitan Relations*. New York, NY: Routledge.

Carr, E.S. (2011) *Scripting Addiction: The Politics of Therapeutic Talk and American Sobriety*. Princeton, NJ: Princeton University Press.

Casasanto, D. (2012) Whorfian hypothesis. In *Oxford Bibliographies in Anthropology*. Retrieved from http://www.oxfordbibliographies.com/view/document/obo-9780199766567/obo-9780199766567-0058.xml

Castillo Ayometzi, C. (2009) Storytelling as becoming: Identity through the telling of conversion. In M. Bamberg, A. De Fina and D. Schiffrin (eds) *Selves and Identities in Narrative and Discourse* (pp. 41–70). Philadelphia, PA: John Benjamins.

Catalano, T. and Waugh, L.R. (2013) The language of money: How verbal and visual metonymy shapes public opinion about financial events. *International Journal of Language Studies* 7 (2), 31–60.

Cenoz, J. and Gorter, D. (2013) Towards a plurilingual approach in English language teaching: Softening the boundaries between languages. *TESOL Quarterly* 47, 591–599.

Cenoz, J. and Gorter, D. (eds) (2015) *Multilingual Education: Between Language Learning and Translanguaging*. Cambridge: Cambridge University Press.

Cenoz, J. and Gorter, D. (2017) Minority languages and sustainable translanguaging: Threat or opportunity? *Journal of Multilingual and Multicultural Development*, Early view on-line. Retrieved from http://www.tandfonline.com/doi/full/10.1080/01434632.2017.1284855

Chalupa, A. (2014, April 4) Putin's fabricated claim of a Fascist threat. *Forbes*. Retrieved from https://www.forbes.com/sites/realspin/2014/04/04/putins-fabricated-claim-of-a-fascist-threat-in-ukraine/#68259ef1bfa5

Charmaz, K. (2014) *Constructing Grounded Theory* (2nd edn). London: SAGE Publications.

Chen, H.-I. (2013) Identity practices of multilingual writers in social networking spaces. *Language Learning & Technology* 17 (2), 143–170.

Chernychko, S. (2018) Державна мова для угорців Закарпаття: чинник інтеграції, сегрегації або асиміляції? *Stratehicni Prioryeti* 1 (46), 97–105.

Christie, E.H. (2015) Sanctions after Crimea: Have they worked? *NATO Review Magazine*. Retrieved from http://www.nato.int/docu/review/2015/Russia/sanctions-after-crimea-have-they-worked/EN/index.htm

Clark, H.H. and Gerrig, R.J. (1990) Quotations as demonstrations. *Language* 66 (4), 764–805.

Colleoni, E., Rozza, A. and Arvidsson, A. (2014) Echo chamber or public sphere? Predicting political orientation and measuring political homophily in Twitter using big data. *Journal of Communication* 64 (2), 317–332.

Copsey, N. (2005) Popular politics and the Ukrainian presidential election of 2004. *Politics* 25 (2), 99–106.

Cottle, S. (2006) *Mediatized Conflict: Understanding Media and Conflicts in the Contemporary World*. Maidenhead: Open University Press.

Crenshaw, K. (1993) Mapping the margins: Intersectionality, identity politics, and violence against women of color. *Stanford Law Review* 43, 1241–1299.

Csernicskó, I. (2015) A (nyelvi) béke esélyei Ukrajnában. *Magyar Tudomány* 10, 1253–1260.

Csernicskó, I. (2016) *Nyelvpolitika a háborús Ukrajnában*. Ungvár: Autdor-Shark.

Csernicskó, I. (2017) Language policy in Ukraine: The burdens of the past and the possibilities of the future. In S.E. Pfenninger and J. Navracsics (eds) *Future Research Directions for Applied Linguistics* (pp. 120–148). Bristol: Multilingual Matters.

D'Anieri, P. (2005) The last hurrah: The 2004 Ukrainian presidential elections and the limits of machine politics. *Communist and Post-Community Studies* 38 (2), 231–249.

Dahinden, J. (2010) The dynamics of migrants' transnational formations: Between mobility and locality. In R. Bauböck and T. Faist (eds) *Diaspora and Transnationalism: Concepts, Theories and Methods* (pp. 51–71). Amsterdam, Netherlands: Amsterdam University Press.

Danylenko, A. (2015) How many varieties of Standard Ukrainian does one need? Revising the social typology of Standard Ukrainian. *Die Welt der Slave* 60 (2), 223–247.

Darvin, R. and Norton, B. (2016) Investment and language learning in the 21st century. *Langage et Société* 157 (3), 19–38.

Davies, B. and Harré, R. (1990) Positioning: The discursive production of selves. *Journal for the Theory of Social Behavior* 20 (1), 43–63.

Day, E.M. (2002) *Identity and the Young English Language Learner*. Clevedon: Multilingual Matters.

De Cillia, R., Reisigl, M. and Wodak, R. (1999) The discursive construction of national identities. *Discourse & Society* 10 (2), 149–173.

De Fina, A. and Georgakopoulou, A. (eds) (2015) *The Handbook of Narrative Analysis*. London: Wiley-Blackwell.

Del' Gaudio, S. (2010) Об украинском варианте русского языка: спорные вопросы. In A.N. Rudyakov (ed.) *Георусистика* (pp. 69–74). *Первое Приближение*.

Del' Gaudio, S. (2011) О вариативности русского языка на Украине. *Известия Российской академии наук: Серия литературы и языка* 2, 28–36.

Del' Gaudio, S. (2012) Чи має суржик систематичний характер і чи можна говорити про «граматику»? *Мовознавство. Збірник наукових статей. VII Міжнародний конгрес україністів* 41–50.

Del' Gaudio, S. (2015) Украинско-русская смешанная речь 'суржик' в системе взаимодействия украинского и русского языков. *Slovene* 2, 214–246.

Del' Gaudio, S. (2018) *An Introduction to Ukrainian Dialectology*. Frankfurt: Peter Lang.

Demchenko, V. (2012) Про значення терміна койне в соціолінгвістиці. *Мова і суспільство* 3, 54–58.

Derrida, J. (2001) *Writing and Difference*. London: Routledge.

Dervin, F. (2012) Cultural identity, representation and othering. In J. Jackson (ed.) *The Routledge Handbook of Language and Intercultural Communication* (pp. 181–194). New York, NY: Routledge.

Dingley, J. (1990) Ukrainian and Belorussian – A testing ground. In M. Kirkwood (ed.) *Language Planning in the Soviet Union* (pp. 174–188). New York, NY: St. Martin's Press.

Dolgova Jacobsen, N. (2008) 'Identity [iz] a [djifikelt] question': A variationist analysis of the relationship between L1 features and ethnic identity in the speech of Russian learners of English. *EVox: Georgetown Working Papers in Language, Discourse and Society* 2, 1–28.

DuBois, J. (1993) Outline of discourse transcription. In J.A. Edwards and M.D. Lampert (eds) *Talking Data: Transcription and Coding in Discourse Research* (pp. 45–87). Hillsdale, NJ: Lawrence Erlbaum Associates.

DuBois, J. (2005) *Transcription Conventions*. Linguistics 170: Language and Social Interaction. Department of Linguistics, University of California, Santa Barbara.

Dufoix, S. (2008) *Diasporas*. Berkeley, CA: University of California Press.

Eakin, P.J. (1999) *How our Lives become Stories: Making Selves*. Ithaca, NY: Cornell University Press.

Elder, M. (2012, July 4) Ukrainians protest against Russian language law. *The Guardian*. Retrieved from https://www.theguardian.com/world/2012/jul/04/ukrainians-protest-russian-language-law

Ellis, D. (2006) *Transforming Conflict: Communication and Ethnopolitical Conflict*. Lanham, MD: Rowman & Littlefield.

Fairclough, N. and Wodak, R. (1997) Critical discourse analysis. In T. van Dijk (ed.) *Discourse as Social Interaction* (pp. 258–284). London: Sage.

Faist, T. (2010) Diaspora and transnationalism: What kind of dance partners? In R. Bauböck and T. Faist (eds) *Diaspora and Transnationalism: Concepts, Theories and Methods* (pp. 9–34). Amsterdam: Amsterdam University Press.

Fialkova, L. and Yelenevskaia, M. (2016) The crisis in Ukraine and the split of identity in the Russian-speaking world. *Folklorica* 19, n.p. Retrieved from https://doi.org/10.17161/folklorica.v19i1.5721

Fine, M. (1994) Working the hyphens: Reinventing self and other in qualitative research. In N.K. Denzin and Y.S. Lincoln (eds) *Handbook of Qualitative Research* (pp. 70–82). London: Sage.

Fishman, J. (1966) *Language Loyalty in the United States*. The Hague: Mouton.

Fishman, J. (2006 [1972]) The impact of nationalism on language planning. In R. Harris and B. Rampton (eds) *The Language, Ethnicity, and Race Reader* (pp. 117–126). London: Routledge.

Fligstein, N. (2008) *Euroclash: The EU, European Identity, and The Future of Europe.* Oxford: Oxford University Press.
Foucault, M. (1977a) *Discipline and Punish: The Birth of the Prison.* New York, NY: Vintage Books.
Foucault, M. (1977b) *Language, Counter-memory, Practice: Selected Essays and Interviews.* Oxford: Blackwell.
Foucault, M. (1980) *Power/Knowledge: Selected Interviews and other Writings.* Brighton: Harvester.
Friedman, D.A. (2016) Our language: (Re)imagining communities in Ukrainian language classrooms. *Journal of Language, Identity & Education* 15 (3), 165–179.
Fukushima, S. (2002) *Requests and Culture: Politeness in British English and Japanese.* New York, NY: Peter Lang.
Fursov, A. (2016) Thirty days that changed the world. *Russian Social Science Review* 57 (1), 38–59.
Gal, S. (1998) Cultural bases of language-use among German-speakers in Hungary. In P. Trudgill and J. Cheshire (eds) *The Sociolinguistics Reader: Multilingualism and Variation, Vol. 1* (pp. 113–121). New York, NY: Edward Arnold.
García, O. and Wei, L. (2014) *Translanguaging: Language, Bilingualism and Education.* New York, NY: Palgrave Macmillan.
Gee, J.P. (1996) *Social Linguistics and Literacies: Ideology in Discourses* (2nd edn). London: Taylor & Francis.
Georgakopoulou, A. (1997) *Narrative Performances: A Study of Modern Greek Storytelling.* Amsterdam: John Benjamins.
Georgakopoulou, A. (2007) *Small Stories, Interaction and Identities.* Amsterdam: John Benjamins.
Georgakopoulou, A. and De Fina, A. (2012) *Analyzing Narrative: Discourse and Sociolinguistic Perspectives.* Cambridge: Cambridge University Press.
Giles, H. and Coupland, N. (1991) *Language: Contexts and Consequences.* Milton Keynes: Open University Press.
Giroir, S. (2014) 'Even though I am married, I have a dream': Constructing L2 gendered identities through narratives of departure and arrival. *Journal of Language, Identity & Education* 13 (5), 301–318.
Goffman, E. (1981) *Forms of Talk.* Philadelphia, PA: University of Pennsylvania Press.
Goncharova, O. (2019, 2 April) Ukrainian diaspora overwhelmingly supports Poroshenko. *Kyiv Post.* Retrieved from https://www.kyivpost.com/ukraine-politics/ukrainian-diaspora-overwhelmingly-supports-poroshenko-in-contrast-to-voters-in-ukraine.html
Goodwin, C. (2000) Action and embodiment within situated human interaction. *Journal of Pragmatics* 32, 1489–1522.
Griffin, C.J.G. (2009) The rhetoric of form in conversion narratives. *Quarterly Journal of Speech* 76 (2), 152–163.
Gumperz, J.J. (1982) *Discourse Strategies.* Cambridge: Cambridge University Press.
Gumperz, J.J. (2005) Interethnic communication. In S.F. Kiesling and C.B. Paulston (eds) *Intercultural Discourse and Communication: The Essential Readings* (pp. 33–44). Oxford: Blackwell Publishing.
Hall, S. (1996) Introduction: Who needs 'identity'? In S. Hall and P. Du Gay (eds) *Questions of Cultural Identity* (pp. 1–17). London: Sage.
Harré, R. and van Langenhove, L. (1991) Varieties of positioning. *Journal of the Theory of Social Behaviour* 21 (4), 393–407.
Hatoss, A. (2012) Where are you from? Identity construction and experiences of 'othering' in the narratives of Sudanese refugee-background Australians. *Discourse & Society* 23 (1), 47–68.
Heller, M. (2001) Critique and sociolinguistic analysis of discourse. *Critique of Anthropology* 21 (2), 117–141.

Hersenzhorn, D.M. (2012, July 3) Lawmakers in Ukraine approve bill on language. *The New York Times*. Retrieved from http://www.nytimes.com/2012/07/04/world/europe/ukraine-parliament-adopts-russian-language-bill.html

Hillis, F. (2015) Intimacy and antipathy: Ukrainian-Russian relations in historical perspective. *Kritika: Explorations in Russian and Eurasian History* 16 (1), 121–128.

Himka, J.P. (2015) The History behind the regional conflict in Ukraine. *Kritika: Explorations in Russian and Eurasian History* 16 (1), 129–136.

Hroch, M. (1999) The Slavic world. In J.A. Fishman (ed.) *Handbook of Language & Ethnic Identity* (pp. 319–333). New York, NY: Oxford University Press.

Hua, Z. and Wei, L. (2016) Transnational experience, aspiration and family language policy. *Journal of Multilingual and Multicultural Development* 37 (7), 655–666.

Iarmolenko, S. and Kerstetter, D. (2016) Identity, adjustment, and transnational activity patterns of fourth-wave Ukrainian diaspora in the United States. *Tourism Culture & Communication* 15 (3), 237–247.

Irvine, J.T. (2012) Language ideology. *Oxford Bibliographies in Anthropology*. doi: 10.1093/obo/9780199766567-0012

Jaffe, A. (2007) Discourses of endangerment: Contexts and consequences of essentializing discourses. In A. Duchêne and M. Heller (eds) *Discourses of Endangerment: Ideology and Interest in the Defence of Languages* (pp. 57–75). London: Continuum.

Kang, H.S. (2013) Korean American college students' language practices and identity positioning: 'Not Korean, but not American'. *Journal of Language, Identity & Education* 12 (4), 248–261.

Kanno, Y. and Norton, B. (eds) (2004) Imagined communities and educational possibilities. *Journal of Language, Identity, and Education* 2 (4), 241–249.

Kappeler, A., Kohut, Z., Sysyn, F.E. and von Hagen, M. (eds) (2003) *Culture, Nation, and Identity: The Ukrainian-Russian Encounter, 1600–1945*. Toronto: Canadian Institute of Ukrainian Studies Press.

Karavans'kyiy, S. (1994) *Секрети української мови*. Kyiv: Вид-во БаК.

Kasper, G. (1990) Linguistic politeness: Current research issues. *Journal of Pragmatics* 14, 193–218.

Khmel'ko, V.Y. (2004) *Лінгво-етнічна структура України: регіональні особливості й тенденції змін за роки незалежності*. *Наукові записки Національного університету 'Києво- Могилянська академія* 32, 3–15.

King, R. and Christou, A. (2010) Diaspora, migration and transnationalism: Insights from the study of second-generation 'returnees'. In R. Bauböck and T. Faist (eds) *Diaspora and Transnationalism: Concepts, Theories and Methods* (pp. 167–183). Amsterdam: Amsterdam University Press.

Kinginger, C. (2004) Alice doesn't live here anymore: Foreign language learning and identity reconstruction. In A. Pavlenko and A. Blackledge (eds) *Negotiation of Identities in Multilingual Contexts* (pp. 219–242). Clevedon: Multilingual Matters.

Kirkwood, M. (1990) Language planning: Some methodological preliminaries. In M. Kirkwood (ed.) *Language Planning in the Soviet Union* (pp. 1–22). New York, NY: St. Martin's Press.

Kohut, Z.E. (2004) *Korinnia identychnosty: Studiï z rann'omodernoï ta modernoï istoriï Ukraïny*. Kyiv, Ukraine: Krytyka.

Kohut, Z.E. (2011) *Making Ukraine: Studies on Political Culture, Historical Narrative, and Identity*. Toronto: Canadian Institute of Ukrainian Studies Press.

Kovalçhuk, I. (2009, 23 November) *Мовознавець і соціолінгвіст Лариса Масенко*: «В Україні має бути українська мова». *Друг Читача* https://vsiknygy.net.ua/interview/4713/

Kreindler, I.T. (1990) Society language planning since 1953. In M. Kirkwood (ed.) *Language Planning in the Soviet Union* (pp. 46–63). New York, NY: St. Martin's Press.

Kristeva, J. (1980) *Desire in Language: A Semiotic Approach to Literature and Art.* New York, NY: Columbia University Press.

Kroskrity, P. (1993) *Language, History, and Identity: Ethnolinguistic Studies of the Arizona Tewa.* Tuscon, AZ: University of Arizona Press.

Kroskrity, P.V. (1998) Arizona Tewa kirva speech as a manifestation of linguistic ideology. In B.B. Schieffelin, K.A. Woolard and P.V. Kroskrity (eds) *Language Ideologies: Practice and Theory* (pp. 103–122). New York, NY: Oxford University Press.

Krouglov, A. (1999) Sociolinguistic transformations in rapidly changing societies: Russia and Ukraine. In J.A. Dunn (ed.) *Language and Society in Post-Communist Europe* (pp. 36–46). New York, NY: MacMillan Press.

Krumm, H.J. (2001) *Kinder und ihre Sprachen – lebendige Mehrsprachigkeit.* Vienna, Austria: Eviva.

Krumm, H.J. (2004) Heterogeneity: Multilingualism and democracy. *Utbildning & Demokrati* 13 (3), 61–77.

Krumm, H.J. (2010) Mehrsprachigkeit in Sprachenporträts und Sprachenbiographien von Migrantinnen und Migranten. *Der Arbeitskreis Deutsch als Fremdsprache/ Zweitsprache Rundbrief* 61, 16–24.

Kulyk, V. (2007) Языковые идеологии в украинском политическом и интеллектуальном дискурсах. *Отечественные записки* 1, 296–316.

Kulyk, V. (2011) Beliefs about language status and corpus in focus group discussions on the Ukrainian language policy. *International Journal of the Sociology of Language* 212, 69–89.

Kuzio, T. (2005) From Kuchma to Yushchenko: Ukraine's 2004 presidential elections and the Orange Revolution. *Problems of Post-Communism* 52 (2), 29–44.

Kyiv Post Staff. (2012, August 23) Russian spreads like wildfires in dry Ukrainian forest. *Kyiv Post.* Home: Ukraine. Retrieved from: <http://www.kyivpost.com/content/ukraine/russian-spreads-like-wildfires-in-dry-ukrainian-forest-311949.html>

Labov, W. (1973) Sample questionnaire used by the project on linguistic change and variation. University of Pennsylvania, 1 March 1973.

Labov, W. and Waletzky, J. (1967) Narrative analysis. In J. Helm (ed.) *Essays on the Verbal and Visual Arts* (pp. 12–44). Seattle, WA: University of Washington Press.

Lemekh, H. (2010) *Ukrainian Immigrants in New York: Collision of Two Worlds.* El Paso, TX: LFB Scholarly Publishing.

Liebkind, K. (1999) Social psychology. In J.A. Fishman (ed.) *Handbook of Language & Ethnic Identity* (pp. 140–151). New York, NY: Oxford University Press.

Liebscher, G. and Dailey-O'Cain, J. (2013) *Language, Space, and Identity in Migration.* New York, NY: Palgrave Macmillan.

Lo, A. and Reyes, A. (2009) Introduction: On yellow English and other perilous terms. In A. Reyes and A. Lo (eds) *Beyond Yellow English: Toward a Linguistic Anthropology of Asian Pacific America* (pp. 3–17). New York, NY: Oxford University Press.

Lozyns'kyi, R. (2008) *Мовна ситуація в Україні.* Lviv: Ivan Franko National University of Lviv.

MacDuffee Metzger, M., Bonneau, R., Nagler, J. and Tucker, J.A. (2016) Tweeting identity? Ukrainian, Russian, and #Euromaidan. *Journal of Comparative Economics* 44 (1), 16–40.

Magaloni, B. (2010) The game of electoral fraud and the ousting of authoritarian rule. *American Journal of Political Science* 54 (3), 751–765.

Maheux-Pelletier, G. and Golato, A. (2008) Repair in membership categorization in French. *Language in Society* 37 (5), 689–712.

Maiboroda, O., Shulha, M., Horbatenko, V., Azhniuk, B., Nahorna, L., Shapoval, Y., Kotygorenko, V., Panchuk, M. and Perevezij, V. (eds) (2008) *Мовна ситуація в Україні: між конфліктом і консенсусом* (pp. 205–234). Kyiv: Ivan F. Kuras Institute of Political and Ethnic Studies, National Academy of Sciences of Ukraine.

Makaryan, S. (2006) Trends in the citizenship policies of the 15 former Soviet Union republics: Conforming the world culture or following national identity? *Proceedings of the Graduate Student Conference 'Democracy and Its Development'*. Retrieved from http://www.democracy.uci.edu/files/docs/conferences/grad/makaryanpaper.pdf

Makihara, M. (2007) Linguistic purism in Rapa Nui political discourse. In M. Makihara and B. Schieffelin (eds) *Consequences of Contact: Language Ideologies and Sociocultural Transformations in Pacific Societies* (pp. 46–69). New York, NY: Oxford University Press.

Marples, D. (2009) *Heroes and Villains: Creating National History in Contemporary Ukraine*. Budapest, Hungary: Central European University Press.

Marten, H.F. (2010) Linguistic landscape under strict state language policy: Reversing the Soviet legacy in a regional centre in Latvia. In E. Shohamy, E. Ben-Rafael and M. Barni (eds) *Linguistic Landscape in the City* (pp. 115–132). Bristol: Multilingual Matters.

Martin, D.C. (1995) The choices of identity. *Social Identities* 1 (1), 5–20.

Masenko, L.T. (2004) *Мова і політика*. Київ: Вид. дім КМ Академія.

Masenko, L.T. (2009) Language situation in Ukraine: Sociolinguistic analysis. In J. Besters-Dilger (ed.) *Language Policy and Language Situation in Ukraine: Analysis and Recommendations* (pp. 101–138). Frankfurt: Peter Lang.

Masenko, L.T. and Horobets, O. (2015) Офіційна двомовність не об'єднує країну, а сприяє її розпаду. *Портал мовноїполітики*, 20 June. http://language-policy.info/2015/06/larysa-masenko-ofitsijna-dvomovnist-ne-ob-jednuje-krajinu-a-spryyaje-jiji-rozpadu/

Masenko, L.T. and Orel, M. (2014) Нам потрібеи мовний кордон із Росією. Сучасна мовна політика в Україні очима соціолінгвіста. *Портал мовноїполітики*, 26 December. http://language-policy.info/2014/12/nam-potriben-movnyj-kordon-iz-rosijeyu-suchasna-movna-polityka-ukrajini-ochyma-sotsiolinhvista/

May, S. (2006) Language policy and minority rights. In T. Ricento (ed.) *An Introduction to Language Policy: Theory and Method* (pp. 255–272). Malden, MA: Blackwell.

McCarty, T.L. (2014) Negotiating sociolinguistics borderlands: Native youth language practices in space, time, and place. *Journal of Language, Identity & Education* 13 (4), 254–267.

Meadows, B. (2009) Capital negotiation and identity practices: Investigating symbolic capital from the 'ground up'. *Critical Discourse Studies* 6 (1), 15–30.

Menard-Warwick, J. (2006) 'The thing about work': Gendered narratives of a transnational, trilingual Mexicano. *International Journal of Bilingual Education and Bilingualism* 9 (3), 359–415.

Menard-Warwick, J. (2007) 'Because she made beds. Every day': Social positioning, classroom discourse, and language learning. *Applied Linguistics* 29 (2), 267–289.

Menard-Warwick, J. (2009) *Gendered Identities and Immigrant Language Learning*. Bristol: Multilingual Matters.

Menard-Warwick, J. (2013) *English Language Teachers on the Discursive Faultlines: Identities, Ideologies and Pedagogies*. Bristol: Multilingual Matters.

Mendoza-Denton, N. (2008) *Homegirls: Language and Cultural Practice Among Latina Youth Gangs*. Malden, MA: Blackwell.

Mendoza-Denton, N. and Hall, K. (2010) Two languages, two identities? In C. Llamas and D. Watt (eds) *Language and Identities* (pp. 113–123). Edinburgh: Edinburgh University Press.

Miller, A. and Wert, P.W. (2015) The 'Ukrainian crisis' and its multiple histories. *Kritika: Explorations in Russian and Eurasian History* 16 (1), 145–148.

Milroy, J. and Milroy, L. (1985) Linguistic change, social network and speaker innovation. *Journal of Linguistics* 21, 339–384.

Milroy, L. (2008) Social networks. In J.K. Chambers, P. Trudgill and N. Schilling-Estes (eds) *The Handbook of Language Variation and Change* (pp. 549–572). Oxford: Blackwell Publishing.

Mykoliuk, O. (2009, July 28) Russian in Ukraine vs. Ukrainian in Russia: Comparison of the situation with the right to study in one's native language in Ukraine and Russia. *Dyen' Weekly Digest*.

Narvselius, E. (2012) The 'Bandera debate': The contentious legacy of World War II and liberalization of collective memory in Western Ukraine. *Canadian Slavonic Paper* 54 (3–4), 469–490.

Ngaha, A. (2004) Language and identity in the Māori community: Without the *reo*, who am I? In J. Holmes, M. Maclagan, P. Kerswill and M. Paviour-Smith (eds) *Proceedings of Language and Society Conference* (pp. 29–48). Palmerston North: New Zealand Linguistic Society.

Norton, B. (2000) *Identity and Language Learning: Gender, Ethnicity, and Educational Change.* Harlow: Pearson Education Limited.

Norton, B. (2013) *Identity and Language Learning: Extending the Conversation.* Bristol: Multilingual Matters.

Norton, B. (2016) Identity and language learning: Back to the future. *TESOL Quarterly* 50 (2), 475–479.

Norton, B. and Morgan, B. (2013) Poststructuralism. In C. Chapelle (ed.) *Encyclopedia of Applied Linguistics.* Wiley-Blackwell. doi: 10.1002/9781405198431

Norton Peirce, B. (1995) Social identity, investment, and language learning. *TESOL Quarterly* 29(1), 9–31.

Ochs, E. and Capps, L. (2001) *Living Narrative: Creating Lives in Everyday Storytelling.* Cambridge, MA: Harvard University Press.

Onyshkiv, Y. (2012, May 31) Language law fight breaks out ahead of election. *Kyiv Post*. Retrieved from https://www.kyivpost.com/article/content/ukraine-politics/language-law-fight-breaks-out-ahead-of-election-1-128623.html

Osnach, S. (2015) Мовна складова гібридної війни. *Пормал мовноїполітики*, 13 June. http://language-policy.info/2015/06/serhij-osnach-movna-skladova-hibrydnoji-vijny/

Paniotto, V. and Kharchenko, N. (2015) *Актуальний стан справ в українському суспільстві*. Kyiv, Ukraine: Kyiv International Institute of Sociology. Retrieved from http://kiis.com.ua/?lang=ukr&cat=reports&id=529&page=1&t=10

Pantti, M. (ed.) (2016) *Media and the Ukraine Crisis: Hybrid Media Practices and Narratives of Conflict.* New York, NY: Peter Lang Publishing.

Pavlenko, A. (2001) Language learning memoirs as a gendered genre. *Applied Linguistics* 22 (2), 213–240.

Pavlenko, A. (2002) Emotions and the body in Russian and English. *Pragmatics and Cognition* 10 (1-2), 207–241.

Pavlenko, A. (2006) Russian as a lingua franca. *Annual Review of Applied Linguistics* 26, 78–99.

Pavlenko, A. (2008) Multilingualism in post-Soviet countries: Language revival, language removal, and sociolinguistic theory. In A. Pavlenko (ed.) *Multilingualism in Post-Soviet Countries* (pp. 1–40). Clevedon: Multilingual Matters.

Pavlenko, A. (2010) Linguistic landscape of Kyiv, Ukraine: A diachronic study. In E. Shohamy, E. Ben-Rafael and M. Barni (eds) *Linguistic Landscape in the City*, (pp. 133–150). Bristol: Multilingual Matters.

Pavlenko, A. (2011) Language conflict, erasure, and transgression in linguistic landscapes: Russian in post-Soviet countries. Plenary presented at the *Georgetown University Linguistic Landscapes Symposium*, Washington, DC. April 15, 2011.

Pavlenko, A. and Norton, B. (2007) Imagined communities, identity, and English language learning. In J. Cummins and C. Davison (eds) *International Handbook of English Language Teaching* (pp. 669–680). New York, NY: Springer.

Pavlyuk, L. (2015) Vocabularies of colliding realities: A representation of conflict and war in the Ukrainian media. In V. Stepanenko and Y. Pylynskyi (eds) *Ukraine after the Euromaidan: Challenges and Hopes* (pp. 241–255). Bern, Switzerland: Peter Lang AG.

Peterson, E.E. and Langellier, K.M. (2006) The performance turn in narrative studies. *Narrative Inquiry* 16 (1), 173–180.

Piller, I. and Takahashi, K. (2011) Language, migration, and human rights. In R. Wodak, P. Kerswill and B. Johnstone (eds) *Handbook of Sociolinguistics* (pp. 573–587). London, UK: Sage.

Podesva, R.J. (2007) Phonation type as a stylistic variable: The use of falsetto in constructing a persona. *Journal of Sociolinguistics* 11 (4), 478–504.

Podesva, R.J. (2013) Fender and the social meaning of non-modal phonation types. In C. Cathcart, I.-H. Chen, G. Finley, S. Kang, C.S. Sandy and E. Stickles (eds) *Proceedings of the 37th Meeting of the Berkeley Linguistics Society*, pp. 427–448.

Potowski, K. (2007) *Language and Identity in a Dual Immersion School*. Clevedon: Multilingual Matters.

Prescher, P. (2007) Identity, immigration, and first language attrition. In B. Köpke, M.S. Schmid, M. Keijzer and S. Dostert (eds) *Language Attrition: Theoretical Perspectives* (pp. 189–204). Philadelphia, PA: John Benjamins.

Rampton, B. (2017) Interactional sociolinguistics. *Working papers in urban language & literacies*, 205. Retrieved from https://www.academia.edu/30796363/WP205_Rampton_2017._Interactional_Sociolinguistics?auto=download

Rattcliffe, K. (2005) *Radical Listening: Identification, Gender, Whiteness*. New York, NY: Random House.

Rettman, A. (2016, 13 January) Sanctions to have little impact on Russia in 2016, US says. *EU Observer: Foreign Affairs*. Retrieved from https://euobserver.com/foreign/131812

Ricento, T. (ed.) (2006) *An Introduction to Language Policy: Theory and Method*. Malden, MA: Blackwell.

Risch, W.J. (2015) What the far right does not tell us about the Maidan. *Kritika: Explorations in Russian and Eurasian History* 16 (1), 137–144.

Roberts, S. (2004) The role of style and identity in the development of Hawaiian creole. In G. Escure and A. Schwegler (eds) *Creoles, Contact, and Language Change: Linguistic and Social Implications* (pp. 331–350). Amsterdam: John Benjamins.

Rosa, J. and Burdick, C. (2017) Language ideologies. In O. García, N. Flores and M. Spotti (eds) *The Oxford Handbook of Language and Society* (pp. 103–124). New York, NY: Oxford University Press.

RT Staff. (2012, May 25) *Short for Words: Ukrainian MPs Trade Punches Over Language Bill*. Retrieved from https://www.rt.com/news/ukrainian-language-bill-opposition-180/

RT Staff. (2016, December 16) *EU Extends Russia Sanctions Over Ukraine Crisis*. Retrieved from https://www.rt.com/news/370474-eu-sanctions-summit-ukraine/

Rumsey, A. (1990) Wording, meaning and linguistic ideology. *American Anthropologist* 92 (2), 346–361.

Sacks, H. (1992) *Lectures on Conversation*. Oxford: Blackwell.

Sacks, H., Schegloff, E.A. and Jefferson, G. (1974) A simplest systematics for the organization of turn-taking for conversation. *Language* 50, 696–735.

Safran, W. (1991) Diasporas in modern societies: Myths of homeland and return. *Diaspora: A Journal of Transnational Studies* 1 (1), 83–99.

Schiffrin, D. (1996) Narrative as self-portrait: Sociolinguistic constructions of identity. *Language in Society* 25 (2), 167–203.

Schiffrin, D. (1997) The transformation of experience, identity and context. In J. Baugh, C. Feagin, G. Guy and D. Schiffrin (eds) *Toward a Social Science of Language* (pp. 41–55). Philadelphia, PA: John Benjamins.

Sclafani, J. (2008) The intertextual origins of public opinion: Constructing Ebonics in the New York Times. *Discourse & Society* 19, 507–527.
Seals, C. (2009) From Russification to Ukrainisation: A survey of language politics in Ukraine. *UCLA Journal of Slavic and East/Central European Studies, 2*. Retrieved from http://www.international.ucla.edu/cnes/article/106275
Seals, C.A. (2010) Язык как часть национального самосознания: Палатализация в трехъязычном межличностном взаимодействии Украинцев. *Материалы 1-ой Международной научно-практической конференции «Языковая Личность в Современном Мире»*. Magas, Ingushetia, Russian Federation: Ingush State University Press.
Seals, C.A. (2011) Gender and memory: How symbolic capital and external evaluation affect who receives the credit in discourse. *Proceedings of the 5th Biennial International Gender and Language Association Conference IGALA6* (pp. 346–366). Tokyo, Japan: Tsuda College.
Seals, C.A. (2012) When a 'non-issue' becomes an issue in discourse surrounding LGBT communities. *Journal of Language and Sexuality* 1 (2), 231–256.
Seals, C.A. (2013) Multilingual Identity Development and Negotiation Amongst Heritage Language Learners: A Study of East European-American Schoolchildren in the United States. Unpublished doctoral dissertation. Georgetown University: Washington, DC.
Seals, C.A. (2014) *Heritage Voices: Language: Ukrainian*. Washington, DC: Alliance for the Advancement of Heritage Languages, Center for Applied Linguistics.
Seals, C.A. (2017a) Dynamic family language policy: Heritage language socialization and strategic accommodation in the home. In J. Macalister and S.H. Mirvahedi (eds) *Family Language Policies in a Multilingual World: Opportunities, Challenges, and Consequences* (pp. 175–194). London: Routledge.
Seals, C. (2017b) Positive and negative identity practices in heritage language education. *International Journal of Multilingualism* 15 (4), 329–348.
Seals, C.A. and Olsen-Reeder, V. (2017) Te reo Māori, Samoan, and Ukrainian in New Zealand. In C.A. Seals and S. Shah (eds) *Heritage Language Policies around the World* (pp. 221–236). London: Routledge.
Seals, C.A. and Olsen-Reeder, V.I. (eds) (2019) *Embracing Multilingualism Across Educational Contexts*. Wellington: Victoria University Press.
Shankar, S. (2008) Speaking like a model minority: 'FOB' styles, gender, and racial meanings among Desi teens in Silicon Valley. *Journal of Linguistic Anthropology* 18, 268–289.
Sharma, D. (2005) Dialect stabilization and speaker awareness in non-native varieties of English. *Journal of Sociolinguistics* 9 (1), 194–224.
Shaw, S. (2000) Language, gender and floor apportionment in political debates. *Discourse & Society* 11 (2), 401–418.
Shevelov, G. (1989) *The Ukrainian Language in the First Half of the Twentieth Century (1900–1941): Its State and Status*. Cambridge, MA: Harvard Ukrainian Research Institute.
Shimeki, Y. (2007) Ukrainian interpretations of 'ridna mova': An analysis of survey results of students in Kiev. *Russian and East European Studies* 36, 110–121.
Shulga, O. (2015) Consequences of the Maidan: War of symbols, real war and nation building. In V. Stepanenko and Y. Pylynskyi (eds) *Ukraine after the Euromaidan: Challenges and Hopes* (pp. 231–239). Bern, Switzerland: Peter Lang AG.
Silverstein, M. (1979) Language structure and linguistic ideology. In R. Clyne, W. Hanks and C. Hofbauer (eds) *The Elements: A Parasession on Linguistic Units and Levels* (pp. 193–247). Chicago, IL: Chicago Linguistic Society.
Silverstein, M. (2003) Indexical order and the dialectics of sociolinguistic life. *Language and Communication* 23 (3–4), 193–229.
Silverstein, M. (2005) Axes of evals: Token versus type interdiscursivity. *Journal of Linguistic Anthropology* 15 (1), 6–22.

Simons, G.F. and Fennig, C.D. (eds) (2017) Russian. In *Ethnologue: Languages of the World* (20th edition). Dallas, TX: SIL International.
Smith, M.G. (1998) *Language and Power in the Creation of the USSR, 1917–1953*. New York, NY: Mouton de Gruyter.
Stoegner, K. and Wodak, R. (2015) 'The man who hated Britain' – the discursive construction of 'national unity' in the Daily Mail. *Critical Discourse Studies* 13 (2), 193–209.
Subtelny, O. (2000) *Ukraine: A History*. Toronto: University of Toronto Press.
Swain, M. (2006) Languaging, agency and collaboration in advanced second language proficiency. In H. Byrnes (ed.) *Advanced Language Learning: The Contribution of Halliday and Vygotsky* (pp. 95–108). London: Continuum.
Taranenko, O. (2007) Ukrainian and Russian in contact: Attraction and estrangement. *International Journal of the Sociology of Language* 183, 119–140.
Taranenko, O. (2013) Варіантність vs. стабільність у структурі українсько-російського «суржику» (УРС): сукупність ідіолектів vs. Соціолект. In G. Hentschel (ed.) *Variation und Stabilität in Kontaktvarietäten: Beobachtungen zu gemischten Formen der Rede in Weißrussland, der Ukraine und Schlesien* (pp. 27–60). Oldenburg: Studia Slavica Oldenburgensia.
The Guardian Staff (2012, May 25) *Ukraine Parliament Brawls Over Language Bill – Video*. Retrieved from https://www.theguardian.com/world/video/2012/may/25/ukraine-parliament-brawl-language-bill-video
The Telegraph Staff (2012, May 24) *Brawl Erupts in Ukraine Parliament Over Russian Language Bill*. Retrieved from http://www.telegraph.co.uk/news/worldnews/europe/ukraine/9288953/Brawl-erupts-in-Ukraine-parliament-over-Russian-language-bill.html
Thetela, P. (2001) Critique discourses and ideology in newspaper reports: A discourse analysis of the South African press reports on the 1998 SADC's military intervention in Lesotho. *Discourse & Society* 12, 347–370.
Todorov, T. (1984) *Mikhail Bakhtin: The Dialogical Principle*. Minneapolis, MN: University of Minnesota Press.
Toolan, M. (2001) *Narrative: A Critical Linguistic Introduction*. New York, NY: Routledge.
Tsentr Doslidzhennya Suspil'stva. (April 2014) *Протести, перемоги і репресії в Україні: результати моніторингу 2013 р.* Київ: Центром дослідження суспільства. http://cslr.org.ua/wp-content/uploads/2014/05/CSR_-_Protests_in_2013_-_29_Apr_2014.pdf
Tsentr Doslidzhennya Suspil'stva. (September 2014) *Чи назріває новий Майдан? Результати моніторингу протестів, репресій та поступок за серпень 2014 року*. Kyiv: Центром дослідження суспільства. https://cedos.org.ua/system/attachments/files/000/000/056/original/CSR_-_August_-_11_Sep_2014.pdf?1410775900
Ukrainian Independent Information Agency. (2008, July 22). New enhanced agreement between Ukraine and EU called 'Agreement on Association'. *UNIAN Information Agency*. Retrieved from https://www.unian.info/world/131960-new-enhanced-agreement-between-ukraine-and-eu-called-agreement-on-association.html
US Census, 2000 (2004). *Ancestry*. Washington, DC: US Census Bureau.
Van Dijk, T.A. (1998) *Ideology: A Multidisciplinary Approach*. Thousand Oaks, CA: SAGE Publications.
van Langenhove, L. and Harré, R. (1999) Introducing positioning theory. In R. Harré and L. van Langenhove (eds) *Positioning Theory* (pp. 14–31). Malden, MA: Blackwell.
Van Leeuwen, T. and Wodak, R. (1999) Legitimizing immigration control: A discourse-historical analysis. *Discourse Studies* 1 (1), 83–118.
Veltman, C. (2000) The American linguistic mosaic: Understanding language shift in the United States. In S.L. McKay and S.C. Wong (eds) *New Immigrants in the United States* (pp. 58–93). Cambridge: Cambridge University Press.
Voolaid, P. (2013) Click 'like' and post it on your wall! Chain posts on Facebook – Identity construction and values. *Folklore* 53, 73–98.

Vygotsky, L.S. (1987[1934]) Thinking and speech. *The Collected Works of L. S. Vygotsky* (Vol. 1). New York, NY: Plenum.

Vyshniak, O. (2009) Мовна ситуація та статус мов в Україні: Динаміка, проблеми, перспективи (соціологічний аналіз). Kyiv: Institute of Sociology, National Academy of Sciences of Ukraine

Vyshniak, O. (2015) The Maidan and post-Maidan Ukraine: Public attitudes in regional dimensions. In V. Stepanenko and Y. Pylynskyi (eds) *Ukraine after the Euromaidan: Challenges and Hopes* (pp. 171–179). Bern, Switzerland: Peter Lang AG.

Walker, S. (2014, September 8) Donetsk's pro-Russia rebels celebrate expelling 'fascist Ukrainian junta'. *The Guardian*. Retrieved from https://www.theguardian.com/world/2014/sep/08/donetsk-pro-russia-rebels-ukrainian-junta

Warren, P. (2016) *Uptalk: The Phenomenon of Rising Intonation*. Cambridge: Cambridge University Press.

Warren, P. and Fletcher, J. (2016) Leaders and followers: Uptalk and speaker role in map tasks in New Zealand English and Australian English. *New Zealand English Journal* 29 & 30, 77–93.

Watt, D. and Llamas, C. (eds) (2014) *Language, Borders and Identity*. Edinburgh: Edinburgh University Press.

Weedon, C. (1987) *Feminist Practice and Poststructuralist Theory*. Malden, MA: Basil Blackwell.

Wenger, E. (1998) *Communities of Practice: Learning, Meaning, and Identity*. Cambridge: Cambridge University Press.

Wilson, A. (2009) *The Ukrainians: Unexpected Nation*. New Haven, CT: Yale University Press.

Wodak, R. (1996) The genesis of racist discourse in Austria since 1989. In C.R. Caldas-Coulthard and M. Coulthard (eds) *Texts and Practices: Readings in Critical Discourse Analysis* (pp. 107–128). London: Routledge.

Wodak, R. (2001) The discourse-historical approach. In R. Wodak and M. Meyer (eds) *Methods of Critical Discourse Analysis* (pp. 1–13). London: Sage.

Wodak, R. (2009) Critical discourse analysis: History, agenda, theory, and methodology. In R. Wodak and M. Meyer (eds) *Methods for Critical Discourse Analysis* (2nd edn) (pp. 1–33). London: Sage.

Wodak, R. and Boukala, S. (2015) (Supra)national identity and language: Rethinking national and European migration policies and the linguistic integration of migrants. *Annual Review of Applied Linguistics* 35, 253–273.

Wodak, R., Pelikan, J., Nowak, P., Gruber, H., de Cillia, R. and Mitten, R. (1990) *Wir sind alle unschuldige Täter! Diskurshistorische studien zum nachkriegantisemitismus* ['We are all innocent perpetrators!' Discourse-historical studies of postwar antisemitism]. Frankfurt, Germany: Suhrkamp.

Wortham, S. (2001) *Narratives in Action: A strategy for Research and Analysis*. New York, NY: Teachers College Press.

Wright, S. (2007) Children's meaning-making through drawing and 'telling': Analogies to filmic textual features. *Australian Journal of Early Childhood* 32 (4), 37–49.

Yermolenko, Y.S. (ed.) (2000) Культура мови на щодень. Kyiv: Довіра.

Zhang, Q. (2005) A Chinese yuppie in Beijing: Phonological variation and the construction of a new professional identity. *Language in Society* 34 (3), 431–466.

Zimman, L. (2013) Hegemonic masculinity and the variability of gay-sounding speech: The perceived sexuality of transgender men. *Journal of Language and Sexuality* 2 (1), 1–39.

Zimman, L. (2014) The discursive construction of sex: Remaking and reclaiming the gendered body in talk about genitals among trans men. In L. Zimman, J. Davis and J. Raclaw (eds) *Queer Excursions: Retheorizing Binaries in Language, Gender, and Sexuality* (pp. 13–34). New York, NY: Oxford University Press.

Index

Accommodation 5, 116–117, 170, 180–181
American-Ukrainian Community 2, 29, 38, 44, 131, 140, 153, 161, 166
Assimilationism 7, 23, 166

Bakhtin, Mikhail 13–14, 45
Bilingualism 5, 8, 97–98, 169–170
Bruneau, Differentiation of Diaspora Communities 133, 165

Canadian-Ukrainian Community 2, 21, 76, 125, 131, 149, 158–162, 166
Central Ukraine 5, 8, 26, 29–30, 42–46, 62, 70, 79, 89, 100, 115, 118, 135, 144, 147, 155, 163–164, 168, 173, 181
Changing Your Mother Tongue Narrative 17, 97–98, 123, 170, 187–190
Chronotope 48–57, 72, 80, 94, 106, 120, 144, 187
Codified Varieties 5
Cognitive Dissonance 144
Cognitive Distance 141
Collective Identity 76, 95, 130, 132, 153
Communities of Practice/CofP 71, 98, 128, 157
Conflicting Identities 7, 71
Conflicting Ideologies 7, 71, 99
Conscious Identification 69, 118
Constrained Cognitive Function 75
Counter-Discourse 17, 33, 64, 66, 113, 167, 173–174, 178–190
Crimean Peninsula 2, 9, 29, 32–37, 41–42, 46, 65–66
Critical Discourse Analysis/CDA 23, 45
Critical Lens 45, 72, 187
Cultural Capital 7, 130
Cultural Practices 23
Cultural Setting 6
Cyrillic Alphabet 6

Dialect Differences 161
Dialectology 6
Dialogic Echoes 38, 39, 53, 59, 99, 123, 126, 184, 187, 189
Dialogic Narrative 66
Dialogic Voicing 189
Dialogism 1–2, 13–17, 62, 95–96, 186, 188–189
Diaspora Communities 6, 17, 44, 121–123, 130–135, 146, 149, 152, 154–166, 187–189
Diglossia 5
Discourse Analysis 22, 23, 29, 44, 45, 112, 188
Discourse Markers 82
Discursive Construction of Nationhood 23
Discursive Difference 19, 23, 55, 72–73, 130, 144, 147, 149, 174, 182
Discursive Distancing 52, 65
Discursive Negotiation 2, 39, 153
Discursive Othering 50, 51, 53, 58, 59, 66, 72–74, 93, 130
Discursive Positioning 16, 91, 95, 100, 186–187
Discursive Sameness 23, 53, 160
Dominant Language Use 7, 10, 29, 33, 44, 65, 97, 110, 122, 126, 129, 153
Double-Voicing 17, 79, 126, 188

Eastern Ukraine 2–5, 9, 13, 24–25, 30, 33, 41–44, 47, 49, 51, 56–58, 61, 65–67, 72, 77, 85, 103–104, 107, 111–112, 118, 121, 139, 150–151, 155, 158, 162, 168, 172, 175, 177, 178, 191
Echo Chambers 146
Education 1, 2, 4, 21, 29, 32, 88, 107, 108, 110, 166, 178
Embodied Language 98–99, 190
Embodied Multilingualism 98

Embodied Symbolic Capital 64, 69, 73, 78, 89, 93, 94, 96, 179–180, 183, 187
Emergent Discursive Topics 44–45
Entrepreneurial Pole 133
Ethnicity 20, 23, 30, 33, 68, 103, 121, 133
EuroMaidan 12, 16, 41, 43, 88, 102, 104, 111, 128, 172
Evaluative Orientation 55
Expanded Network Approach 44

Friendly Non-Accommodation 4–5, 116–117, 170–171, 176, 184, 188

Globalisation 37, 39, 65, 131–132, 167, 177–178
Grammaticalization 8, 9
Grounded Theory 45
Gumperz, John J. 45

Halician 6
Heritage Language 98–99, 122, 126, 129, 161, 165, 189
Heritage Ukrainian/Heritage Language 6, 98–99, 110, 122–129, 161–165, 189
Heteroglossia 13–14
High Rising Terminal 156
Historically Situated Narrative 104
Home and Host Societies/Countries 2, 100, 122–123, 134–138, 146, 152–153, 157, 164–166, 187, 189
Homophonous Phrase 28, 40

Iconization 98
Identity Alignment 8, 35, 39, 118, 128, 136, 153, 162, 166, 174, 185, 186, 188
Identity as a Site of Struggle 21, 131
Identity Categories 19–21
Identity Constructs 19–23, 50–55, 96, 128, 130, 133, 187
Identity Constraints 20–21
Identity Formation 15
Identity Marker 9, 94
Identity Negotiation 15, 20, 22, 38–39, 72, 103, 126, 134, 147, 154, 166, 189
Identity Performance 20, 38, 96, 173
Identity Responses 14, 17, 22, 73
Identity Struggle 17, 55, 57, 110, 135–138, 142, 164
Ideological Negotiation 153

Imagined Communities 23, 38–39, 132, 149, 184, 186, 189
Imagined Future 22, 25, 57, 137–138, 147
Imagined Identities 1, 22–25, 38–39, 57, 74, 126, 130–138, 147, 149, 160, 166, 184, 186–191
Imagined Nationality 74, 132
Immigrant Experience 154
Implied Timelines 48
Indexing/Indexicality 15–16, 23, 47–48, 98–99, 102, 127, 144, 190
Institute of Sociology at the National Academy of Sciences in Ukraine 43
Institutional Discourses 96
Institutional Symbolic Capital 63, 66, 73, 78, 94, 96, 128, 161, 170, 187
INTAS Project 30, 40
Interactional Purpose Marking 8
Interactional Sociolinguistic Discourse Analysis 45, 72, 103, 187–188
Interactive Positioning 20
Internalised Ideologies 7, 9, 16, 67, 82–85, 97–99, 107, 110, 183
Interpersonal Identity 71
Intersectionality 20, 38, 48, 132–138, 147, 154, 166
Intertextual Links 14, 22, 28, 34, 102, 156
Intertextual References 25–26, 38–39, 45–48, 73, 84, 100–103, 116, 170, 187–189
Intertextuality 13–14, 16–17, 22, 25–26, 28, 32–34, 38–39, 45–55, 61, 64, 69, 73, 76, 81–96, 99–103, 107, 113–117, 121–126, 156–157, 161–163, 170, 174, 186–191
Investment 1, 9, 17, 21, 25, 38, 62, 72, 130–165, 186–187, 189, 191

Khrushchev, Nikita 4
Kravchuk, Leonid 10
Kuchma, Leonid 10
Kyiv 26, 29, 43

Labov, William 29, 50
Labovian Interview Structure 29
Language as a Singular Construct 37–38, 128, 132
Language Embodiment 127–129
Language Indexing Ethnicity 23
Language Indexing National Identity 23
Language Maintenance 134, 165

Language Network 14
Language of Status 30
Language Perceptions 53, 77, 113, 136–140, 144, 161, 171–177
Language Preference 5, 30–33, 37–38, 46, 62–67, 116–118, 157, 172, 179, 184
Language Shift 65, 98, 104, 107, 119–121, 129
Language Standardisation 3, 5–6, 9, 32, 161
Language Status 3–4, 7, 30, 62, 67, 73, 132, 157, 162
Language Stigmatisation 8, 85
Language War 32–33
Language/Linguistic Ideologies 3, 6–10, 13–15, 26–37, 66, 111–112, 123–126, 149–152, 157, 174–175, 178–181
Language/Linguistic Policies 3–4, 7, 10, 30–31, 43, 47, 62, 74, 103
Lenin, Vladimir 4
Lexical Variation 6
Linguistic Appropriateness 28, 37
Linguistic Consciousness 8, 9, 25, 47, 60, 67–70, 81, 98, 104, 116–118, 123–128, 169, 184
Linguistic Flash Mobs 172–173
Linguistic Identity Portraits 99
Linguistic Inferiority 7
Linguistic Oppression 65, 167
Linguistic Purism 6, 7, 8, 9
Linguistic Repression 9, 13
Linguistic Strategies – Metonymy, Personification, Repetition, Dialogism, Positioning 16, 95, 187
Local Identity 60

Maidan 2, 9, 16, 24, 41–44, 69, 72, 88, 97, 102, 104, 111–112, 115, 128, 148–149, 171–174
Master Narratives 51, 53, 61, 70, 89, 93, 94, 100, 106, 110, 167
Mediation (Lev Vygotsky) 16
Membership Categorisation 15–16, 28, 98, 128, 130, 156, 165
Metacognitive Comment 92
Metadiscourse 2, 180–181
Metonymy 16, 74–76, 84–86, 95, 179, 187–188
Minority Language 4, 8, 14, 120
Mixed Language 7–8, 32

Model of Immigrant Identity, Investment and Integration 17, 134–138, 147, 187
Monolithic Conceptualisation of Identity 37–38, 53, 71, 91, 133
Morphological Differences 6
Morphological Tense 6
Morphology 6
Multilingual Identities 99
Multilingual, Multicultural Ukraine 178–190
Multimodal 173

Naming Events 46, 54, 72
Narrative Analysis 21
National Consciousness 30, 33–34, 39, 43, 102
National Identification 2, 42, 104, 112, 114, 118
National Identity 2, 10, 23, 26, 30, 33–34, 39, 40–41, 60–67, 71, 74, 94, 97, 102–104, 107, 113–129, 165, 170, 173, 186
National Loyalty 2, 138
Native Bilingualism 5
Nativization 4
New Zealand Ukrainian Community 2, 44, 49, 51, 67–71, 77, 79, 86, 100, 115, 121–129, 131, 135–138, 144–149, 154–165, 167, 180–181
Non-Accommodating Bilingualism 4
Non-Standard Varieties 162
Northern Ukraine 8, 37
Norton, Bonny 20–21

Older Ukrainian Language Use 7, 44, 111
Orange Revolution 10, 16, 24–40, 43, 102–104, 186
Orthodox 4
Othering 53, 55, 56, 58, 65, 72, 159, 178

Palatalization 6, 29
Participation Framework 15
Patriotism 111–118
Performativity 20, 38
Personal Narratives 48
Personification 16, 77–79, 94–96, 187–188
Phonology 6, 29, 44
Poliansky, Pavlo 166
Polish 6, 54

212 Choosing a Mother Tongue

Political Identity 60, 100
Polyphony 13–14
Poroshenko, Petro 12, 13
Positioning 1, 2, 15–16, 20, 22,25, 32, 35, 38–39, 41–73, 91–111,118, 121, 128, 131, 133–134, 140, 144, 149, 159, 161, 166, 176
Positioning – Theory of 15–16, 188
Post-Structuralism 19–21, 38, 71, 186–188
Power Relations 19–21
Presidential Election, 2004 10, 24
Presidential Election, 2010 10–11
Presidential Election, 2014 12
Presidential Election, 2019 12, 13
Pronunciation 4, 14
Purist Language Ideologies 8–9, 31, 152

Reflexive Positioning 15, 17, 20, 22, 128, 139, 184, 186–187
Regional Language 3
Regional Language Ideology 175
Regional Language Status 3
Regional Variation 6
Renegotiating Identities 57, 69, 131, 134, 135–139, 152, 165–166, 187–191
Repetition 16–17, 44, 77, 79, 83, 95–96, 187–188
Russian Language 4–7, 10, 25, 30, 33, 37–38, 53, 66, 105–110, 112–120, 121–126, 151, 176–178, 157–158, 173–174, 186
Russian Language Bill 3, 186
Russification 4, 7, 30, 43, 65, 167,

Sapir-Whorf 126, 183
Self-Identification 15, 38, 67–71, 102, 104, 113, 164–168
Self-Positioning 15, 39, 53, 93, 110, 133–134
Semantic Meaning 55, 61, 132, 187
Semiotics 14
Shared Ideals 72, 187
Shared Language Identity 23, 120
Shared National Identity 23, 60–65, 170
Shared Religious Identity 133
Shifting Identities 3, 4, 15, 17, 20, 29–30, 41, 53, 55, 65, 82, 97–109, 113–129, 134, 138, 163, 164, 171–172, 188, 191
Silverstein, Michael 6
Slavic Language Family 6

Social Constructionism 19–22, 38, 120, 133, 186
Social Network 20, 24, 39, 44, 130–131, 146, 172–177, 186
Sociolinguistic Identity Negotiation 2, 15–17, 20–23, 38–39, 46, 57, 69, 72, 96, 103, 117, 126, 131–140, 147–149, 152–166, 174, 187–191
Sociopolitical Identity 120, 122, 184
Southern Ukraine 5, 13, 24, 29, 30, 36–37, 97
Soviet Union 3–5, 7, 30, 92, 101, 103–104, 110
Sovietization 4
Stalin, Joseph 4
Standardised Varieties 3, 5–6, 9, 32, 161
Subjectivity 20, 38
Surzhyk 8–9, 32
SUSTA 28
Symbolic Domination 8, 9

Transcultural Identity 55
Translingual Identity 37, 55, 117, 176, 181, 185
Translingual Interaction 117
Translingual Practices 176, 181, 185, 188
Transnational Identity 37–38, 48, 55, 67–73, 131–132, 177
Tymoshenko, Yulia 10, 12

Ukrainian Communist Party 5, 54–56
Ukrainian Culture 9, 69, 113, 121–122, 127
Ukrainian Diaspora 13, 99, 121, 130–131, 146, 152, 154, 156–158, 160–162
Ukrainian Independence 3, 7, 28, 30, 107
Ukrainian Language 1, 4–9, 25, 30, 33–38, 61–67, 70, 73, 97, 99–100, 103–107, 110–111, 115–118, 122–129, 141, 157–161, 170, 172, 175–178, 181
Ukrainian Language Politics 9–12, 30–31, 77
Ukrainian National Identity 9–10, 30, 35, 62–63, 94–98, 102, 114–118, 128
Ukrainian Rada 2–3, 13–14, 186
Ukrainian War 2, 10, 12, 16, 25, 28, 33, 39, 46, 48–57, 61, 63, 69, 72–74, 75–89, 94–95, 97–98, 111–112, 115, 119, 128, 142, 146, 156–159, 163–166, 172–174, 187–191
Ukrainisation 4, 10, 30, 43, 167

Voice Indexing 98
Vowel Reduction 6
Vowels 6

Western Ukraine 4–6, 12, 24, 26–33, 35–37, 43, 54, 64–65, 74–76, 83, 88, 97, 99, 149, 160, 169–172, 177, 178–181
Women's Narratives 21

Yanukovych, Viktor 10, 12, 24, 41–43
Younger/Young Adult Ukrainian Language Use 7–9, 28, 30, 34, 39, 43, 60, 62, 69, 94, 99, 107, 113, 118, 128, 167, 175–178, 181, 188, 190

Zelensky, Volodymyr 12, 13

For Product Safety Concerns and Information please contact our EU Authorised Representative:

Easy Access System Europe

Mustamäe tee 50

10621 Tallinn

Estonia

gpsr.requests@easproject.com

www.ingramcontent.com/pod-product-compliance
Lightning Source LLC
Chambersburg PA
CBHW052041300426
44117CB00012B/1915